ZERO TO ONE MILLION

How to Build a Company to One Million Dollars in Sales

RYAN P. ALLIS

Published by Virante, Inc.

Allis, Ryan P.
Zero to One Million: How to Build a Company to One Million Dollars in Sales /
Ryan P. M. Allis. – 4th ed.
p. cm.
Includes bibliographical references
ISBN: 0-9740411-2-2
1. Entrepreneurship   2. Marketing

PRINTED IN THE UNITED STATES OF AMERICA

What Others Are Saying About Zero to One Million

Forgive Ryan Allis for being so young. Forgive him for imparting timeless wisdom based upon his own real-life experience as a entrepreneurial superstar. The kid just can't help it. He has made a million-dollar dream come true and he shares how he did it this roller-coaster-of-a-read book. Your banker will love you for reading it.

Jay Conrad Levinson
The Father of Guerrilla Marketing
Author, "Guerrilla Marketing" series of books

Ryan Allis shares and intriguing story of business success that has few parallels. I know of no other person so young who has demonstrated this level of achievement in business. Young people need individuals like Ryan to look up to and emulate as they work to accomplish their own personal and business goals.

David S. Chernow
President and CEO
Junior Achievement Worldwide

Zero to One Million is going to inspire a new generation of aspiring entrepreneurs. If you are thinking about starting a company or own one now, this is the book for you. – *Jeff Reid, Executive Director, Center for Entrepreneurship, UNC-Chapel Hill*

Ryan writes this book as he is creating his multi-million dollar company. His viewpoints are those of someone in the midst of the struggles and triumphs that every successful "entrepreneur in the making" goes through. Ryan has written one of the best business startup and growth books that I have ever read. This book is written in a way that seems like your best friend has just found his success and wants to help you achieve that same success. For me, this book was one I just could not put down. It is a very easy and enjoyable read. I recommend "Zero to One Million" as an inspirational read to any young person with a dream of one day starting his or her own company. – *Joshua A. Mitchell, CEO of Riakt Studios*

Zero to One Million gives a lot of insight into the world of business. I enjoined the recap of history. Ryan is right in his assertion that not all are given equal standing in the world. This is a sad fact of life but also a great factor in why humanity strives to succeed. His understanding of entrepreneurship and economics is amazing. Through his book, he has drastically moved my mind set, from isolationism to that of open markets. Freedom and wealth will flow best through open gates. – *Tiana Laurence, Aspen, CO*

Zero To One Million provides good instruction how to lay a foundation for a successful company. Ryan explains how he got his foundation of being an entrepreneur and gives pointers on how to become a successful entrepreneur. He does all of this while giving a background on how entrepreneurship affects each of us individually and why it is important for our country to continue to think entrepreneurially. This book is a gem for young inspiring entrepreneurs like myself and to others who feel they may need help with advancing the sales of their business. – *Jason Robertson, North Carolina*

Ryan Allis has written a book that acts as an inspiration for business people all over the world. At an age where most people are developing a sense of business savvy, he has mastered it and shares his knowledge with the masses. I read this book with a highlighter in hand to ensure that I would not miss out on the underlying points of importance. He proves that the dream of entrepreneurship can be a reality for anyone, and I look forward to his insight in books to come. – *Nicholas Lombardi, Wallingford, CT*

Ryan Allis gives a captivating account of his experience as an entrepreneur. Most books on entrepreneurship are either too exciting or too focused on the hard work. This one presents entrepreneurship as a field of endeavor that I liken to gardening: you have to plant correctly, water correctly, fertilize correctly, and the business will grow. Entrepreneurship is the business of patience, not enthusiasm, not money, not motivation, not hope, not determination nor courage. While all these play their part, patience seems to be the critical ingredient that most people don't have to succeed. If you keep doing the right things, your business will grow to one million dollars in sales. – *Martin Messier, Brazil*

For those who are ready, this book can be your launching pad. I found it enlightening and incredibly empowering. Ryan allows his passion to fully shine through and after reading *Zero to One Million* I have been inspired to find mine in life. I've always wanted to make a difference in our world, and Ryan beautifully articulates how that time is now. He truly grasps how our world is rapidly changing and reveals that is an emerging minority of young entrepreneurs that will make this change in the coming years. Don't wait... have a bias toward action and take control of your life now! – *Greg Mueller, Durham, NC*

This book is not a get rich quick guide, it is a handbook that you will continue to use as a reference and it is a book that will instill important business concepts. One of the most important aspects of being an entrepreneur is confidence. As I read this book, I found myself more and more confident in the goals that I had set for myself, and the business that my partners and I were in the process of starting. Ryan clearly outlines the steps to starting a business, and provides a very informative section devoted to search engine optimization. This book should be read by anyone who has a desire to start a business, and has a pro-active attitude towards life. It is great to know that someone of Ryan's age could be so business-savvy, self-disciplined, and biased towards action... that is empowering. – *Jacob Bohall, Hilton Head, SC*

I love *Zero to One Million* --not like—LOVE! You've inspired me! My goals, mission and creed are framed and on the wall. I love the MAR Model for evaluating business ideas. You manage to get all this stuff that I've known about for years and somehow get me to act on it, be excited about it, and get results! I just keep raving about it to people. I most often say, "One of the references on the book says 'Ryan in the next Robert

Kiyosaki,' and they're absolutely right." Ryan's writing gets me into action. It took me a few weeks (instead of a day) to read the book because I kept DOING what he was talking about. I came away from each chapter not only having my thoughts cleared, but with an action plan and an elevated spirit, fire in my heart, wind at my heels, ready to get on with it. – *Jade Barclay, Queensland, Australia*

Zero to One Million was awesome. I spent the better part of the first night I received it (when I was supposed to be sleeping) reading it. I was doing the old flashlight under the covers trick since I had to be up at 6:00 the next morning for school, and mom would have sent me to bed had she known. No matter - I felt it was good preparation for me becoming an entrepreneur. The book has made a difference in one life. All books I had read previously (Robert Kiyosaki, Robert Allen), while containing good information, had left me still a little confused as to where I was going. After reading this book, there was no doubt in my mind. I am going to be an entrepreneur—and a successful one. I really liked the book's down-to-earth style with practical examples. Thanks a million (pun intended). – *Greg, British Columbia, Canada*

After reading *Zero to One Million* and implementing the strategies and techniques in Mr. Allis's book, my business revenue has almost tripled in a short 4-months time. I am the CEO of a nutraceutical corporation and interact with CEO'S from companies in the USA and Internationally. I can honestly say I have tried multiple methods and hired multiple marketing and management teams in the past, spending hundreds of thousands of dollars with little to no results. I have also read multiple books on subjects of personal and business development including Stephen Covey, Richard Gerber, Anthony Robbins, Louise Hay, Dale Carnegie and more. *Zero to One Million* covers the beginner to advanced stages it takes to become successful and financially secure. I would recommend this book to all entrepreneurs and successful business men and women. – *Dr. Edward F. Group, Houston, TX*

This book contains a wealth of information and inspiration. Ryan is the next Robert Kiyosaki. – *Michael Simmons, author, The Student Success Manifesto*

I like *Zero to One Million* a lot. I like the style. It is easy to read - even for me. You have done a great job of picking up on the copy writing nuances that make a piece impossible to put down. - *Robert Ryan, Petagonia*

I think one of the best ways to learn is by example and that is what is so beautiful about *Zero to One Million*. I believe that the way to becoming successful in life is to study those who are. In this book not only does Ryan teach you so much about the history of economics and business, but he shares every step of how he got to where he is today. – *Jenna Horshaver*

I wish to thank the following family members, friends, colleagues, and institutions who have made this book possible.

Andrew Allis, Sr.	Jeff Reid
Pauline Middleton Allis	Monica Doss
Andrew Allis, Jr.	Evelyn Williams
Erin Mulfinger	Carter Griffin
Marti Kiely	Conor Mullett
Steve Kiely	John Burton
Aaron Houghton	Michael McNyne
David Roth	Robert Fletcher
David Rasch	Kristina Hager
Brandon Milford	Alex Hardy
Tim Oakley	Merrill Mason
Chuck Hester	Buck Goldstein
Robert Plumley	Barry Roberts
Amber Neill	Colin Wahl
Cindy Hays	Christy Shaffer
Matt Allen	Dave Rizzo
Michelle Tabares	Merrette Moore
Alan Cox	Randy Myer
Geoff Caitlin	Alston Gardner
Alan Underwood	Jud Bowman
Erik Severinghaus	Scot Wingo
Wes Garrison	Kevin Fitzgerald
Malcolm Young	Michael Doernberg
Russ Jones	Carolina Entrepreneurship Club
Jeff Staub	Collegiate Entrepreneurs' Organization
Jean Walsh	The Kauffman Foundation
Joanna Wolek	The State of North Carolina
Gerry Hills	UNC Center for Entrepreneurship
Michael Simmons	UNC Kenan-Flagler Business School
Sheena Lindahl	The Entire iContact Family

TABLE OF CONTENTS

Foreword from Michael Simmons

Zero to One Million was written to provide a guide for anyone to build a company from nothing to over one million dollars in sales. It is about expanding access to entrepreneurial opportunity. It's about spreading the knowledge of how to build a successful venture.

Zero to One Million is a guide for aspiring and current entrepreneurs that explains, step-by-step, how to build a company to one million dollars in sales. The book provides an unprecedented level of access and insight into an actual multi-million dollar company. Ryan's experience building iContact to over $8 million in annual sales and over 75 employees gives the book great depth and excitement.

Ryan shares how and why every element worked and examines every process, every system, every technique, and every strategy in a manner that can be applied to any business, whether you have just a fledging idea, a mature local company, or a high potential start-up. This book shows how anyone can build a million dollar company, or if already there, expand sales even further.

This book is organized into three parts. In part one Ryan tells his captivating story. It narrates how he went from being an eleven year old providing computer consulting services for $5 per hour on Anna Maria Island, Florida to a marketing consultant for a company in the health products industry at age 17 that went from zero to one million dollars in sales in just over a year, to being the co-founder of an investor-backed software start-up at age 18, to being CEO of a company with over $8 million in annual sales by age 23.

The second part on the book provides a ten step process for building a company to one million in sales. This section covers how the system of entrepreneurship works and how to find your core motivation, determine what to sell, evaluate opportunities, write a business plan, obtain funding, develop a product, build your marketing and sales strategies, build your team, become a manager, and build systems. These chapters will take you from the point of not being sure what to sell up to the point where you are ready to launch and expand. The essential due diligence, planning, and infrastructure building processes are detailed with a step-by-step guide that can be applied to any type of start-up or small business.

Step seven covers marketing and sales strategy. Many aspiring entrepreneurs create an innovative product, do their market research, raise the money, incorporate their company, build the infrastructure, and bring on great people, but fail to ever get sales going. This section details how to complete market research, gain competitive intelligence, execute marketing campaigns, build customer relationships, and grow online sales. The web marketing section provides a guide to creating your web site, getting to the top of the major search engines, building links, leveraging email marketing, and launching a partner program.

Once you have succeeded in executing your marketing plan, your company will be entering a period of growth. How you manage that growth and how you adapt to these changes will determine whether you can sustain that growth and cross the proverbial chasm or run into problems such as cash flow shortages, high employee turnover, or competitive price wars.

Steps eight through ten explain how to create the new infrastructure that is needed to take your company to cash flow positive and to an acquisition or IPO ready state and build the systems and processes needed to grow your organization, develop new products, and branch out into international markets. Part three ends with a helpful review that provides one hundred steps to building a company to one million dollars in sales in the chapter on how to scale your business.

Part three is an important section, especially for the younger entrepreneur. Covering the topic of personal development, it presents the strategies used by successful entrepreneurs. It covers the important skills of planning, goal setting, networking, having a bias toward action, and dealing with failure. The author explains his experience and what he has learned along his journey, and profiles the strategies for success used by many other successful entrepreneurs.

Zero to One Million is a book unlike any other on business or entrepreneurship. There have been books about entrepreneurship, books about economics, books about personal development, and case studies about successful companies, but never have these topics been combined in such a step-by-step, detailed guide.

Whether you are sixteen with wide eyes and big dreams, twenty-eight with an MBA and a vision, a thirty-two year old mother of two, or fifty-five and venturing out on your own after a lifetime in corporate America, this book will be an invaluable resource and inspiration.

Though nothing can ever be guaranteed without your action and perseverance, you will find steps within these pages that have been used time and time again to build companies to one million dollars in sales and beyond. I wish you the best of luck as you begin your journey of building your own company toward its first million.

Sincerely Yours,
Michael Simmons, Author
The Student Success Manifesto
Brooklyn, New York
October 2007

From the Author

I wrote *Zero to One Million* so I could share what I have learned over the past six years helping building three companies to more than $1 million in sales in the hope of expanding access to entrepreneurial opportunity. Whether you are considering starting a company, buying a company, being an entrepreneur within a company, or growing an existing business, my hope is that this book can serve as a guide to helping you take action toward setting your vision, reaching your biggest, hairiest, and most audacious goals, and turning your dreams into meaningful realities.

I am glad to be able to share with you the iContact story. iContact began in 2002 after my business partner Aaron Houghton and I met at a meeting of the Carolina Entrepreneurship Club. We set up shop in a two room office in downtown Chapel Hill, NC. We lived in the office, slept on a futon, cooked on a George Foreman Grill, ate Ramen Noodles, and jumped in dumpsters to get proof of purchase tags off of chair boxes for the $50 rebates at Staples. We did whatever we had to keep expenses low and get the company to the point where we had real revenue and people were willing to take us seriously.

Today, we've been fortunate to build a great team which has enabled us to build an organization with over 75 employees and more than $8 million in annual sales—and growing quickly. While we have a long way to go, I feel like I've seen a glimpse of the view from the fiftieth floor of the business skyscraper. And I'm here to tell the story and share the steps. Why? Because I want you to get there. I want you to be the person who creates further prosperity and opportunity in your community. No matter where you're from, no matter who you are, no matter your access to opportunity or past—you have the ability to get there—with the right guide.

I know of the desire in your mind, the passion in your heart, and the motivation in your soul. I am here to share what I know with the hope it can provide a guide on the path toward achieving success, however you define success for yourself. Exhaustion—drop dead exhaustion—and tireless passion caused by dedication to a dream, to people, to building something Great, something that is worth building. I understand it. I know it. I live it. I want you to have the tools needed to follow your passion.

It can be extremely difficult to get started and get over the difficulty of people writing you off, turning you down, and telling you your dream will never come true. The keys I have found are to associate yourself with people who build you up and encourage your dreams, to write down your goals and frame them, and to every day take a positive action forward. One key message of this book is to get started today, as there is no other day than today that you can take an action.

To share one of my favorite metaphors from *Good to Great*, building a business is like pushing a big wooden wheel. The first push does next to nothing. Subsequent pushes barely move the wheel. Only continued effort in a single direction sustained over multiple months get the wheel to a noticeable clip. During this time of prolonged strain and few noticeable results, many people drop out of the game. You must have persistence in this game.

While very slow at first, eventually the big wheel starts to move. Soon the momentum of the energy and inertia of the movement start to take over and the wheel begins to move by itself. The motion snowballs and it begins spinning at a thousand revolutions per minute—faster and faster. It takes people, it takes systems, it takes commitment, it takes continued effort over multiple years. The 'how' behind finding the motivation, behind finding the right direction to push in, and behind building the systems that create sustainable momentum is what this book attempts to share.

It took us thirty-five months at iContact to build the company to $1 million in sales. I met my partner Aaron Houghton on October 2, 2002. On September 1, 2005 we made it to the $1 million in sales milestone. It takes time, focus, sacrifice, dedication, energy, and passion to make it there. But first, it starts by taking action—one action each day that can compound into creating something tangible and meaningful over time.

In my opinion, the purpose of business is not to make revenue nor profits but rather to create a positive impact, to innovate, to create great products, to create jobs. Cash and profits should be seen as the lifeblood that allows you to strive after your true mission. To be a truly successful entrepreneur, your core motivation cannot be the money alone. Financial success can be part of it, but there must be more that drives you, more that pushes you to get out of bed each and every day for the five, six, eight, ten years it will take to build a lasting, growing, thriving organization. Once we reach a level of success, we must give back as enlightened entrepreneurs.

Today, we as humans have a tremendous opportunity to use our entrepreneurial talents and money to work toward solving the biggest remaining issues in our world. I hope to spend my life working through entrepreneurship, social entrepreneurship, investing, philanthropy, public policy, and politics to end poverty in developing nations and at home, ensure environmental sustainability, help people understand that we are one humanity and that our commonalities are much greater than our differences, and help expand access to opportunity, healthcare, and education across the world for every human of every nation.

This book is a first step toward this mission that I hope to work toward through entrepreneurship, social entrepreneurship, investing, public policy and politics over the next six decades. I thank you for picking up a copy of *Zero to One Million* and hope you have the opportunity to use it as your guide as you work toward creating something meaningful. I hope I can convey an interesting story while providing a guide that will enable you to reach your dreams. If succeed in this goal all I ask is that you spread the word and take a positive action every day toward your vision.

My Sincere Regards,
Ryan P. Allis
October 2007
Chapel Hill, North Carolina

P.S. – Please do stay in touch. I can be reached via ryan@icontact.com or via Facebook. I am happy to help in any way that I can.

Part One:
My Story

Chapter 1 How I Got Started

> "If you had one shot, one opportunity, to seize everything you ever wanted. One moment. Would you capture it? Or just let it slip?"
>
> - Eminem

Who I Am

I am the son of an Episcopalian priest from Mansfield, Pennsylvania and a social worker from Yorkshire, England. I was born in Pittsburgh, Pennsylvania in Women's Hospital on August 14, 1984. I lived there for two years before my family moved to Woonsocket, Rhode Island for the next eight years of my life.

At age ten, on the day after Christmas in 1994, my parents and I moved to Bradenton, Florida. There I attended King Middle School and Manatee High School, graduating in the class of 2002. I moved to Chapel Hill, North Carolina in the Fall of 2002 to attend the University of North Carolina as an economics major. This story, however, begins in Spring of 1995.

When I was eleven, I received a Macintosh LC computer from my Uncle Steve who lived in Massachusetts at the time. I learned everything I could about that computer and packed as much as I could onto the 34MB hard drive. I traded in my airline frequent flyer miles to subscribe to the computer magazine *PC World*, which I would read it its entirety. I used the computer daily and loved to play great games like SimCity and Cannon Fodder.

The next summer I was thinking about what I could do to earn extra money while school was out. My family and I were now living on Anna Maria Island, just off the coast of Bradenton. I realized I had become pretty good at setting up and troubleshooting computers and that there were a number of senior citizens in our area that were starting to purchase them to get on email and the Internet.

So I placed a free classified ad in the Island newspaper. "Need Computer Help? Call Ryan at 778-6406 for Onsite Help from Responsible 12 year old. Just $5/hour." I also placed flyers at the local post office, City Hall, library, laundromat, and Chamber of Commerce. I put flyers in mailboxes but stopped when I got a call from the Postmaster General telling me I was violating mail statutes.

After a couple days of anxiously waiting my phone began to ring. I scheduled my first appointment that Saturday with Fred from 45th Street. I did one hour of work with Fred and he paid me $10. The first week on the job I learned my first important business lesson when I got a call from Fred's friend Betty from 67th Street—that word of mouth marketing is the best type of marketing you can have.

> "The first week on the job I learned my first important business lesson, that word of mouth marketing is the best type of marketing you can have."

That summer my business did pretty well and I began to learn the power of word of mouth. There weren't too many twelve year olds giving computer help at the time, and my services became a topic of conversation at the retirement homes, country clubs, and Church services. I printed up business cards and made sure to give at least five to every client. By the end of the summer I had earned $413, an amazing amount in my young eyes.

The following summer, now a teenager, I once again placed my ads and contacted my client base. I began installing memory, giving purchasing advice, and teaching clients how to use email and the Internet. Now, however, I could charge $8 per hour because of the higher demand for my services, the word of mouth spreading, and my additional experience. By the end of the summer I felt enormously wealthy having earned $1200. I socked most of these earnings away in a mutual fund.

In November of 1997, my eighth grade year, my family moved off of Anna Maria Island and onto the mainland about five miles to the east. Fortunately I was still able to go to the same school and was still close enough to my client base. In the second semester, I learned HTML, the basic computer language used to create web sites. This knowledge would prove very useful down the road.

My First Clients

The next June, I once again placed my ads, and invested $12 each week for a classified ad in the mainland paper. It was now 1998, and I had gained considerable knowledge about computers. Halfway through the summer, a lady by the name of Lois gave me a call. She had a problem with her laptop and needed it fixed. After I had fixed the problem, she told me that she was interested in setting up a web page and wanted to know if I could do it. I told her that I had not had much experience, but I'd give it a shot and see what I could remember from my HTML class.

It turned out Lois was an airplane stewardess that bought back pearl rings, pendants, and necklaces every month when she flew to China. After a few months of successfully selling the pearls to her friends, she decided she wanted to try selling her pearls through the Internet. To get going, we registered a domain name for her pearl business, obtained a merchant account, and purchased an online shopping cart. She had pictures taken of her products and wrote descriptions for each.

Her sales started slow as I was not too far along the learning curve. Within a month, however, Freshwaterpearls.com had a full ebusiness running with seventy products available online. I optimized the pages for the search engines, started a monthly sweepstakes, and posted articles on pearls to the site. We began monthly newsletter *The Pearl Ezine* and within six months had 5,300 subscribers. We started making three or four sales a day and my design and marketing skills continued to improve.

However, we soon ran into trouble. It was difficult for Lois to keep track of inventory, send out orders on time, and take care of customer service while being a stewardess and out of the country for two weeks at a time. The customer communication, supply-chain, and customer service was not at the level it needed to be.

The company reached a critical point—would Lois hire her first employee and attempt to build a true business with systems and processes or would she continue to try to run everything herself? This dilemma is of course the classic dilemma of the small business entrepreneur. She decided to try to continue to run everything herself.

Unfortunately, after nine months or so, the site and business folded. At the same time, I had learned much more about business, ecommerce, and web design than I ever would in a classroom, and this experience would later serve as a great asset.

From this experience, I learned my second important business lesson: When your business is making enough revenue to be able to hire an employee, make the leap and bring on your first team member. Otherwise, you will be building a job for yourself and not a true business.

During my freshman and sophomore years in high school, I continued learning about web

> "When your business is making enough revenue to be able to hire an employee, make the leap and bring on your first team member. Otherwise, you will be building a job for yourself and not a true business."

design and development. After developing a couple sites of my own, I took over developing the web site for my high school during my sophomore year.

The summer after tenth grade I was lucky enough to be selected as one of six United States ambassadors to La Ruta Quetzal, a fifty-three day expedition to Spain and Mexico conducted entirely in Spanish and sponsored by the Government of Spain that brought together 350 students from 43 countries. I would have to put off my entrepreneurial endeavors for a couple months.

The Birth of Virante

On June 20, 2000 I left for Madrid. I had traveled in Western Europe previously but had not been to Spain. Upon arriving in Spain I met up with the other students and staff. We slept outside in tents each night, and each day we would either hike or take a bus to a different town. Eighteen-hour days and weekly thirty-mile hikes were the norm. By the time we had finished in Mexico City on August 11, 2000, I had made some great friends and had enjoyed some amazing experiences.

I mention this trip because a very important thing occurred while I was in a park in Mexico City on the last night of the trip. I had my first "entrepreneurial brainstorming session". I was about to return home and figured it was time to develop a business plan for the next year. During this session I came up with the name Virante (Vih-rahn-tay). I honestly do not remember how or why, but somehow it ended up on my paper. I said to myself, "I like that. I guess it does sound a bit Spanish." And so it stuck. I planned to start a web design and development firm by the name of Virante when I arrived back in Florida.

A few days later I returned to school. The first day of eleventh grade was my sixteenth birthday and I could finally drive! No longer would I have to beg to be driven around or ride my bike to an appointment. Each day after coming home from cross country practice and on the weekends I would work on Virante. I registered my web site and began designing the site, adding my portfolio and resume, creating a Flash intro, and promoting my new "company" Virante Design & Development.

I didn't know a thing about S-Corporations, LLCs, 83(b) elections, equity, stock options, or tax laws. That knowledge would come later. However, I was skilled at graphic design, web site development, and ecommerce integration. During my junior year I used and improved these skills as I picked up a few new clients. I built web sites for a land development company, an on-site medical care company, a film company, a dating service, a travel agency, and a painting company. I also designed business cards, brochures, and logos, and consulted on marketing web sites.

I knew little about contracts, marketing offline, or what in the world 2/10 net 30 was. I once almost had a multi-thousand dollar contract to revamp the AutoZone web site but lost out simply because I showed my inexperience by asking what they meant by 2/10, net 30, which I soon thereafter learned are time frames for a discounted and full payment on an invoice. However, I was learning. Some of my clients needed database work done that was a bit too advanced for me at the time, so I formed a partnership with a programming firm in Nevada. I outsourced this work to them and they sent some of their design work to me. This partnership ended up working out very well and taught me the value of strategic alliances.

I began bidding on projects through sites such as guru.com and smarterwork.com and picked up one client in Miami and another in Leicester, England. By the middle of the summer of 2001 I had created about ten web sites, and had worked with about twenty companies in one way or another. Everything was going quite well and once again word of mouth was spreading.

I read in a marketing book about the benefit of sending out pressing releases, so in about the middle of July that year I decided to write a press release on what I was doing and send it to the local papers. This turned out to be one of the luckiest decisions I ever made. On July 26, 2001 I was featured on the front page of the *Bradenton Herald*. I had absolutely no idea I'd be on the front page, and was taken aback when I saw my picture right on top in the newspaper rack while walking into Wal-Mart that morning.

Five days later on the 31st, I was in the Business section of the *Sarasota Herald-Tribune*, the newspaper of the bordering city to the south. Both articles featured Virante Design & Development prominently, printing the Virante logo and giving the web site address. I had seventeen messages on my machine by noon on the 26th; every one of them wanting me to develop their web site.

This overload presented a problem. I could not possibly create seventeen web sites at once as the most I had ever previously worked on at the same time was three. I called each prospect back and scheduled appointments with the most promising clients. On August 1, I thought that I would be set for new work for the next few months. By August 3, this reality had changed.

Landing the Job

At the same time as the front page article, the owner of a local company in Holmes Beach, Florida saw my small twenty word ad offering computer help in the Island newspaper and gave me a call. I set up an appointment with him the next day. Upon walking inside his office, I noticed Corey Rudl's marketing course over on the counter. I mentioned to the owner, "Oh yeah, I read through that course a couple years ago. Good stuff." I went on to fix a broken disk drive in his computer and we talked a bit about his business.

It turned out he had just let his web designer go and he needed a new one. I ran to my car to get a copy of the newspaper article from a few days earlier, and he said, "So when do you want to start?"

The business owner had been developing a product for a couple years and was just beginning to promote it. He wanted me to set up a web site for the product and a system where customers could order the product online. I told him I could do it.

On August 14th, 2001, the first day of my senior year of high school and my seventeenth birthday, I began work. I had been able to convince my school to give me an internship class the last two periods each day so I was able to work from noon until about 7pm at the company's office. After I finished the web site, I was to begin promoting the web site and encouraging sales of the product. I would work as an independent contractor for tax purposes; though unofficially have the title of Vice President of Marketing.

When we began the company had not made a single sale through their web site. It was selling only a few hundred dollars of product each month to a handful of retail customers and one health food store to which they sold the product at wholesale. It would take another two weeks before we made our first sale through the web site. Sales came slowly at first. The company did $1500 in September 2001 and $5600 in October 2001.

By April of 2002 the company was doing over $85,000 in sales each month, and in the Fall of 2002 the company passed $1,000,000 in total sales. The company was fortunate to be able to reach one million dollars in sales without any venture capital funding or debt, bank loans, or private investment and with just one product and five employees.

At the age of 17 I had the opportunity to see a company grow from nothing to over $1 million in sales in just over a year. I learned a lot from managing a monthly marketing budget of about $50,000 and seeing the company grow from two to six employees. This experience was essentially my internship. I did not yet realize I was an entrepreneur—I viewed myself as a marketer, but what I was learning about financing, payroll, bank relations, product positioning, and human resources would help me tremendously when I did set out to be an entrepreneur myself.

At the end of the year, I made the decision to go up to Chapel Hill, North Carolina to begin my first year of college at UNC.

"What I was learning about financing, payroll, bank relations, product positioning, and human resources would help me tremendously when I did set out to be an entrepreneur myself."

> "In a certain sense, if things hadn't worked out, I could always go back to school. I was officially on leave."
>
> - William H. Gates, 1974

The Decision to Go to College

At 5:00am on August 14, 2002, my 18th birthday, I got in a white rented PT Cruiser with my dad and drove up to Chapel Hill, North Carolina. I was to begin college at the University of North Carolina in five days. While it was a difficult decision to go to college, especially after the success we had had with the health products company in high school, I felt it was the best choice for me based on my long term goals.

Just a few months before, in April 2002, I was sitting on the floor of my living room in Bradenton, Florida with four acceptance letters laid out in front of me. I wondered which college was for me, and if college was for me. After visiting each college and receiving the financial aid packages, I decided on UNC-Chapel Hill as the cost was considerably less than New York University and was outside the state unlike the University of Florida. However, the success at the health products company gave me a new decision to make. Should I even go to college at all?

I was a good student and had a chance to go to a great university on a near-full ride, so why would I even consider not going? Well, it was April and I saw that the company I was working for was taking off. I knew that if I deferred college for a year I had the chance to make quite a bit of money – perhaps one or two hundred thousand dollars. I was seventeen and had the chance to make a couple hundred thousand dollars in salary and commission if I would just defer college for a year. With this possibility in mind, I was considering not going to college right away after knowing my whole life that I would. I had to make a choice. Should I accept admission from UNC or defer? I had until August to make my final decision.

During that summer, I met two younger persons who had deferred admission to their respective colleges and had built very successful companies. I knew I could do the same. I felt that college would prepare me to work for someone else and I knew that I did not want to work for anyone but myself. I felt that in college my time would be taken up learning things I would never use and I would be in a constant battle to get a good GPA so one day I could get a good job. I knew this was not what I wanted. I thought I had the skills and resources to succeed without college. I would develop some software and informational products, and my career as an in-demand author, consultant, successful entrepreneur, and investor would be launched. I knew I could do it.

However, I wanted something more than this and knew there was much more to life than money. Further, I was not sure that I could survive the psychological stress of being 18 and not having a single friend younger than 27. I knew going to college, at least for a year or two, would probably help me develop my network and would help me learn to live on my own. So I choose to go off to UNC.

Although I often became frustrated at not having enough time to work on my businesses or read what I wanted to read, I know the choice I made was what was best for me. College really made me go through many formative and developmental changes. I learned how to take care of myself, learned that I must put the twisty-tie back on the bread or else it would mold, learned how to hard boil and egg, and learned I shouldn't put whites in with my colors in a hot wash.

Just as important, I developed a network of contacts and built strong relationships that have been a great asset to me. I found other students like myself, made some friends, and found a partner among these friends with whom I would later start iContact.

The Carolina Entrepreneurship Club

My first semester in college I discovered the Carolina Entrepreneurship Club. At the Master Panel of Entrepreneurs event hosted by UNC in mid-September I met a man by the name of Jeff Reid. Jeff was the Executive Director of the Center for Entrepreneurship at UNC and suggested I talked to an undergraduate by the name of Paul Vollman. Jeff said Paul, along with a few others, was in the process of starting an undergraduate entrepreneurship club and that I should get involved.

I emailed Paul and set up a meeting right away. I told him I wanted to help. After talking with him, he made me the Tech Chair for the club, which meant I was responsible for the web site and listserv. The first meeting would be in two weeks, in early October.

The smell of chicken nuggets and honey mustard permeated the room as I walked into the first CEC meeting on October 5, 2002. About twenty-five students showed up to hear local entrepreneur Todd Ballenger and local private equity businessman Hunter Bost talk about their experiences and the differences between entrepreneurship and intrapreneurship. At that first meeting, I was introduced to someone who would prove to play a key role in my life. His name was Aaron Houghton, a senior computer science major at UNC.

When I met Aaron that night he already knew who I was as I had created a popular web discussion forum for the school that was featured in the school newspaper. Being a web developer, he kept close tabs on the other web designers and developers at the school. We met and he invited me up to his office the next weekend.

Aaron's company, Preation, Inc., had been around since 1998. His sophomore year, as his business expanded, he moved his offices to a 700 square foot, four room location right in the heart of downtown Chapel Hill at the intersection of Franklin Street and Columbia Street. At his office that weekend, Aaron showed me a few of the software products he had developed for Preation clients. An email list management software called the Preation Email List Manager, caught my eye.

At the company I worked with my senior year in high school, a desktop-based program by the name of Mailloop was used to send out the company's email newsletter. While Mailloop worked well for us initially, the problem we encountered was that it was simply too slow. Even on the company's broadband connection, it would often take twenty-four hours or more for the newsletter to be sent, completely tying up all the resources of a computer during this time.

The software Aaron had developed, however, was web based, meaning that it could be accessed from any computer with an internet connection anywhere in the world and once you composed your message and hit send, you would be done right away. You could close your browser and go on to other work while the server sent out the emails within a matter of minutes. In addition, Aaron's software had some other features that made it unique in comparison to what else was available in the market at that time. Further, at the entry level it cost only $10 per month instead of the $400 upfront cost of Mailloop. It was simply a better solution and, with my entrepreneurial mind always running, I saw the possibilities immediately.

At that meeting, I agreed to work with Aaron to develop the software from a beta version used by a handful of his customers to a commercial version that would attract and handle thousands of customers. With software with a demonstrated need in the marketplace, my experience in web marketing and business development, and Aaron's programming abilities, we would have a good opportunity to build a profitable product line for Preation.

Virante, Inc.

Since August 2000 when I returned from Mexico City, I had been operating under the name of Virante Design & Development for my sole proprietorship. Now it was time to formalize things a bit. I was about to enter into a contract to market software that had a chance to bring in a significant amount of revenue and wanted to reduce my liability exposure as well as lay the foundation for the company to grow. Over Fall Break, I incorporated Virante, Inc. as a North Carolina corporation and filled out form 2553 from the Internal Revenue Service to elect to be an S-Corporation, providing certain tax advantages as a small business.

Three weeks later, I received the Articles of Incorporation for Virante from Elaine Marshall, Secretary of State for North Carolina. I was finally the Chief Executive Officer of a real incorporated company. My official company headquarters was 610 Ehringhaus Dorm, although I often worked at Aaron's offices.

I formed Virante, Inc., not to do web site design, as I had done before, but rather to do web marketing consulting, search engine optimization, and to joint venture with Preation to sell the email list management software.

I began to go in on the weekends and work with Aaron on building and improving the software. We first had to come up with a better name for it than the Preation Email List Manager. We sat down for a couple hours and brainstormed. We wrote down words related to what the software did and then generated every possibility we could think of. Eventually, we came up with the name IntelliContact (the name was shortened to iContact in June 2007, which I will use to refer to the product going forward). We checked to make sure the domain name was available and then checked with the U.S. Patent and Trademark Office to make sure the name had not already been trademarked.

Once these two things were cleared, we decided to go with the name. We registered the website and transferred the web-based software over to the new site. We had a logo designed, designed the site, added sales copy, feature descriptions, related white papers, and FAQs to the site. We also created a Flash tour, obtained a security certificate, started the process of obtaining a merchant account so we could accept credit cards, and began work on the back-end programming of the shopping cart and affiliate program. Aaron and I also worked out a contract in which Virante would work to market the iContact software in exchange for a percentage of the sales.

MBA Classes at 18

A few things would happen over the next five months that changed our direction in selling the iContact software. As I had built a good relationship with Jeff Reid from the Center for Entrepreneurship at UNC, he agreed in November 2002 to be my faculty advisor for an independent study in entrepreneurship during the second semester.

While I was initially told by the head of the undergraduate business program that there was "No way he would allow a freshman to do an independent study," I eventually was able to convince him. After explaining my prior experience and knowledge to that point he allowed me to do the independent study.

The curriculum for the independent study consisted of writing a case study, reading two textbooks on entrepreneurship, interviewing six experienced entrepreneurs, and sitting in on three MBA classes there at Kenan-Flagler Business School. It was this last part that excited me most. The first half of the semester, or 'first mod' as it is called, I sat in on BUSI 299Q, Venture Capital Deal Structure and Valuation, and BUSI 221L, Legal Issues for High Technology Start-ups.

The second mod, I sat in on BUSI 296S, Managing a Small Business. These classes, except for some of the math in the venture capital valuation class, were right at the level I was at. The class Legal Issues for High Technology Start-ups was especially helpful. The professor for that class, Merrill Mason, was an adjunct professor and practicing attorney with Hutchison & Mason, PLLC, which later became the law firm for iContact.

As part of the independent study, I also started something called the Distinguished Entrepreneur Interview Series. To be interviewed, an entrepreneur had to be the CEO or founder of a company that was doing more than $5 million dollars in annual sales. I teamed up with Jeff Reid and leveraged the network of the Center for Entrepreneurship to identify participants. I found that there was no better way to build my own network, as well as increase my knowledge about what I needed to do to get to this next level, than by talking with these entrepreneurs. Excerpts from some of these interviews have been published in the appendices.

For the course I also studied in detail the texts, *New Venture Creation*, by Jeffrey Timmons as well as *Entrepreneurship* by Donald F. Kuratko and Richard M. Hodgetts. I would especially recommend obtaining and reading *New Venture Creation*.

In addition to the independent study and MBA classes, I had been elected as Vice President of the Carolina Entrepreneurship Club for second semester. We had a speaker series event each month, signed the Club Constitution on February 24, 2003, and began to host other types of events such as Business Roundtables, Legal Help-Desks, and Start-up Clinics. By the end of the second semester we had 53 dues paying members and were having two events per month. In late April, I was elected President of the Club and began working on plans and goals for the upcoming school year.

I came to Chapel Hill in August 2002 as someone who knew web marketing and a bit about business development. At the health products company in high school I handled the web site, the affiliate program, the marketing campaign, and the customer relations. I also gained experience in cashflow management, human resources, income statements, balance sheets, budgeting, and product development. The owner developed the product, handled the financing, and dealt with the bank, payroll, bookkeeping, inventory, and supply-chain management. While I gained more experience than anyone would expect a seventeen year old to gain, I still felt coming in to UNC that I was mainly a marketer and not an entrepreneur. I wanted to become a full-fledged entrepreneur.

By taking accounting first semester, incorporating Virante, being the Vice President for the Carolina Entrepreneurship Club and attending the speaker series meetings, building my business resource site at www.zeromillion.com, reading two entrepreneurship textbooks, interviewing successful entrepreneurs, and sitting in on those three MBA classes, I had made good progress toward becoming a true entrepreneur. While my core competency remained in web marketing, I now had experience in company formation and knowledge of raising capital, product development, managing employees, and bookkeeping.

> "I now had the fundamental business knowledge I needed to become a full-fledged entrepreneur. Now, however, I had to test my ability as an entrepreneur in the real world."

Unlike that day in 2001 when I lost the AutoZone contract, I now had the fundamental business knowledge I needed to become a full-fledged entrepreneur. I now knew about equity, non-compete contracts, non-disclosure agreements, cashflow, income statements, balance sheets, non qualified stock options, 83(b) elections, C and S corporations, venture capital traunches, FICA, angel investors, pro formas, down rounds, term sheets, and internal rates of return. Now, however, I had to test my ability as an entrepreneur in the real world. It was now time to build a company of my own to one million dollars in sales instead of doing it for someone else. And so the 'Journey' began.

Starting iContact

From knowledge gained from the Legal Issues for High Technology Start-ups class, Aaron and I decided to change the way in which we would structure the business foundation behind the iContact software (which was originally called IntelliContact). Instead of selling the software as a product of Preation, we decided, in March 2003, to incorporate a new company that would sell the software. We chose to do this for three reasons.

First, the new entity would make it much easier for us to sort out ownership in the company. It would have been confusing to give out equity in the company when Preation's main business was in web site development and not email marketing software. Second, it would have been more difficult to handle the accounting of expenses and payroll. This would make it more difficult to plan and spend for iContact when we did not have a clear idea of our revenue and expenses and how much we needed to make to break even.

Finally, we wanted the advantage of having a company that could one day be sold or acquired without affecting the business operations of Preation. We knew that the best ways to accomplish our goals of building a great product, creating a lot of jobs, and building shareholder value was to form a separate company, build a great team, attract a few thousand customers, expand our product line, and then sell to another company or go public. We would only be able to do this if everything was clear and properly separated from the start.

We started this process with a visit to our lawyer on April 15, 2003. Knowing that my professor for the Legal Issues and High Technology Start-ups class, Merrill Mason, was a well renowned lawyer for entrepreneurial ventures in the area, we decided to go talk to him. Merrill gave a free initial consultation during which he outlined the process of forming the company. While both Aaron and I had already incorporated a company before, incorporating a company with more than one shareholder (we had five initially) is much more complex. While this method ended up costing us $3000 instead of the $300 it would have cost to do it online, in the end doing it properly turned out to be worth every penny.

Merrill told us that before we came to see him again, we would have to come up with a company name and decide the breakdown of ownership. He also told us about the non-compete, non-disclosure, confidentiality, consulting, employment, and stock restriction agreements we would have to sign in addition to the company bylaws, stock options plan, organizational consent, 83(b) elections, and Certificate of Authority.

Highlight 1: A Day in the Life of a Young Entrepreneur

Reprinted from www.zeromillion.com with permission.

April 15, 2003...

A First Trip to the Lawyer

I woke up at 8:45am, rather early considering I had gone to bed at 4am. I put on my new suit, brushed my teeth, and went down to the ground floor to meet my friend and business partner Aaron. I jumped in his car and we headed to Raleigh. Thirty minutes later we ended up at the entrance to my law firm. We waited in the boardroom for ten minutes before being greeted by Merrill, our attorney.

We told Merrill that we wanted to start a company. Both Aaron and I had incorporated companies before, so we knew the basics. But we had some questions on the proper vesting schedule, profit sharing agreements, and some terms in the shareholders agreement, so Merrill helped us with them. During the meeting we agreed to vest our stock over two years, which means that we would receive the stock gradually over time as it vested to the full amount. We also decided to incorporate the company as a Delaware C corporation due to the advantages in case law, added ease in raising investment funding, and advantage in the case of an exit event (selling the company).

To close the meeting, Merrill told us what we needed to get to him to get the company going. He needed the name of the company, the state of incorporation, the breakdown of ownership, the vesting schedule, salaries, the bonus schedule, the number of shares to create, the address of the company, and what we would define employment as for each person's employment agreement. We agreed to have the 'who gets what and what should we call this company' discussion later on in the week and send everything to him then.

After the meeting, Aaron and I drove back to Chapel Hill. I had already missed my History Recitation on Cardinal Richelieu and was not about to show up to my 12:30 psychology class in a suit. So I had Aaron drop me off at my dorm on south campus and then walked down to the Kenan Center where I work at the Center for Entrepreneurship and Technology Venturing (CETV). I had some prep work to get done for the next big event in my day.

The Start-up Clinic

In five hours the CETV Start-up Clinic would commence. I had been planning this event for a month and was excited that the day was finally here. Before the event, I had a brochure and survey to create and a presentation to prepare. I finished these, and then went to the room to check that the A/V equipment was working properly.

At the clinic, six businesses run by UNC students would be presented to a panel of experienced coaches including two successful entrepreneurs, a venture capitalist, and two business professors. Each business would have five minutes to make a presentation and then ten minutes for feedback and advice from the coaches. At 5:20, I went down to the McColl 2575 where the event was to commence in forty minutes. I met with the presenters and then welcomed the coaches. By 6:00pm about sixty audience members had arrived. We began at 6:05. A team representing MainBrain School, a company selling school administration software, began their presentation at 6:15, followed by Alpha V, Inc., iContact, UNM Solutions, LLC, VenturePresentation, and GMA Entertainment, Inc. I moderated the event and also presented iContact, the email list management software company I am co-founding with Aaron. After the

> clinic, we held a reception at which the presenters, coaches, and attendees were able to network and exchange advice and contacts. Following the reception I cleaned up and then got a ride back to Ehringhaus Dorm.
>
> I had been wearing a suit for thirteen hours. I came in, unbuckled my belt, and let out a sigh of relief. I walked to the balcony and leaned, fending off my drunk suitemate. Finally, the day was over. I had a splitting headache, but it was worth it.

Aaron and I came back from the lawyers and got to work deciding on the equity share and thinking of a name for the company. Often, one of the most difficult early stage decisions for an entrepreneur is what to name the company. The fact that we had to have five people (our initial shareholders) agree on the name complicated the process exponentially.

We began by brainstorming and compiling a list of all the potential names we could think of. We came up with names such as Alatro, Aspensmith, Calprion, Chapelsoft, Dyneap, Mobilardi, Preasio, Reactera, Redsync, and Sentelis. We wanted a name that seemed like a technology company, but stayed away from being so high-tech that it would seem that it was destined to fail like so many dot coms and IT companies did from 2000 through 2002. We took our initial list of 300 possibilities and cross referenced it first against domain name registrations and then against the U.S. Patent and Trademark Office's trademark database. Once this was done, we ended up with about fifty possibilities. We had everyone in the office vote and then discussed them as a group.

Initially, we could not find one we all agreed on so we went through the process a second time. We brainstormed another 300 names and after checking them ended up with fifty more possibilities. We voted once more and then finally decided on a name from the first round, iContact. Calprion was the second place name and Sentelis came in third. In all, we spent about twelve hours over four weeks coming up with the name.

In the mean time, we had finished school and my journey as a full time entrepreneur had begun.

An Entrepreneurial Summer

I returned from England on June 2, 2003 and we finally settled on the company name. Although we had the name finalized, we were still yet to settle on the equity distribution between myself, who would be CEO, Aaron, who would be Chief Technology Officer and Chairman, Erik, who would be the Systems Administrator, Charles, who would be the VP of Marketing, and Wes, who would be the Network Administrator, and Preation, which would transfer ownership of the software to iContact.

The three main parties involved were Aaron, Charles, and myself as Wes and Erik would only be working part time for the company. Aaron and I negotiated between ourselves, and then I negotiated with Charles. Finally, once we had settled on percentages, salaries, accrual formulas, and bonuses, we offered equity to Erik and Wes. Once they were in agreement, we returned to Hutchison & Mason, PLLC on July 1 to formally incorporate iContact as a Delaware C corporation. As things are processed much faster in Delaware than North Carolina, by the next day, we had a company. The formation process was far from complete however.

Highlight 2: My First Week As an Entrepreneur

Reprinted from www.zeromillion.com with permission.

Finishing my airplane meal at 37,000 feet on June 2 I realized that my life was about to change. I had been dropped off at London Victoria station a few hours earlier and been on the London Eye the day before. The week before I had been given an eighteen hour baptism of fire in Dublin—partying from 7pm until 1pm. Two weeks before I had relaxed in the seaside town of Southsea, finished the plan for the next fifteen months of my life, and enjoyed a couple football matches.

Now, however, I was on a plane to Raleigh-Durham, North Carolina. I would arrive in five hours and enter a new world—a world of working one hundred hour weeks, obtaining insurance, paying bills on time, filling out forms, defending lawsuits, hiring employees, signing contracts, fighting fraud, maintaining records, having to deal with rent and taxes, and keeping track of financials. In short, I was beginning the first week of my life as a full time entrepreneur.

I came in around 3:30pm and made it to a taxi by 5pm after passing through very tight security. I took a taxi to Chapel Hill and was dropped off at my office. With no apartment or dorm, I would have to sleep at my office. I walked in and experienced the second greatest moment a serial entrepreneur can have—an empty office—an office devoid of material things in sight, but an office full of vision and imagination of what soon would be.

Since the prior tenant, my friend Wes, had moved out two days before, I walked into an empty new office at 101 N. Columbia St. Suite 400. Seeing the office bare (minus seven boxes containing all my personal belongings in the corner) for the first time struck me. There were so many goals I wanted to accomplish, a company I wanted to build, and so many memories I knew were to come. During that moment I could envision my future and see a well-decorated busy room with four employees. I saw the blank walls and floors that would hold my whiteboard and desks for at least the next six months. It was an experience that will only be superseded when the company born in that room is successfully sold or goes public.

I went to bed that night on the floor after being awake for a full twenty-four hours. I fell asleep at 2:00am and curled up with a few shirts bundled to serve as a pillow. I woke up the next morning with a stiff neck. I washed up in the bathroom, stretched, and began my work. I began scheduling meetings, ordering business cards, and getting my personal and business finances in shape. The next evening I went out to the Rathskeller restaurant with my business partner Aaron, his girlfriend Sarah, Sarah's roommate, and Aaron's business partner Erik. I had such a feeling of accomplishment that night as I downed two hot plates of All-You-Can-Eat Spaghetti in the Chapel Hill landmark.

Over the next week that empty office would go through a transformation. After meeting with a friend from Kenan-Flagler Business School and UNC's Entrepreneurship Club at lunch one afternoon, he decided to come on board and work with me as a partner in building iContact. He allowed me to store my effects in a spare room in his apartment and began to help me furnish the office. I inherited a glass desk from the former tenant and we purchased a classic wood desk at the UNC Surplus Auction.

After we each had desks we ordered a whiteboard, desk pads, pen holders, staplers, staples, and business card holders. My new partner had his parents bring over a mini-fridge that helped reduce our eating-out expenses and he purchased a multi-function printer, scanner, copier, and fax machine. We also purchased a white loveseat from a graduating senior and moved that up to the office and inherited a black futon from my friend Erik that turned out to be a lifesaver. No longer would I have to sleep on the floor!

That second night my new girlfriend Erin came by to see me and the office. Although we had lived on the same dorm floor since August 2002, I only met her in late April. It was such a relief to have someone to go out and have fun with. I was very glad that she lived about a half-hour away, and took the time to come and see me. The office was almost as good as an apartment. We could watch movies on the board room projector and had a television with cable, a George Foreman Grill, a futon, phones, a loveseat, two mini-fridges, broadband internet access, a water cooler, and a bathroom. If we just had a shower there I'd never have to leave.

During those nine days in Chapel Hill I made a point to meet with a least one person each day and was working to ready the iContact software for launch. I got my first lesson as a full-time entrepreneur a few days in as our hosting company filed Chapter 7 bankruptcy forty-eight hours before we planned to launch our flagship product. The lesson was to always backup your data and code and always plan for things to take longer than you expect them to.

On June 12 I took a taxi back to Raleigh-Durham airport. I was off to Baltimore/Washington International for training for the LeadAmerica CSLC Business & Entrepreneurship Conference. I would have the chance to teach entrepreneurship and leadership to high school students for ten days and I was very much looking forward to it. I went from being all alone in my bare office to having a business partner and a fully furnished office, a growing network, and a new company ready to launch. I had made it through the first week of my life as an entrepreneur.

A few weeks later, on August, 4, we returned to Hutchison & Mason to review the formation documents. There were thirty-three documents in all including five non-compete, non-disclosure, and confidentiality agreements, three consulting agreements, two employment agreement, four stock restriction agreements, one promissory note, a board consent for the promissory note, a stock options agreement, the company by-laws, an organizational consent, four 83(b) elections, a non-qualified stock option agreement, an application for a certificate of authority, an assignment of inventions, a stock ledger, a capitalization chart, an organizational checklist, and four stock certificates. It is a much more complex process when forming a company with more than one shareholder.

By mid-August, we finally had the documents signed. We were an official company. We already had quite a bit of momentum, however, as since October 2002 and throughout the process of forming the company, we were working full time on improving the software, building the web sites, writing sales copy, presenting at trade shows, obtaining a merchant account and launching our affiliate and search engine optimization campaigns. By the time the documents were signed, we had twenty paying customers and one hundred affiliates who promoted our software in exchange for a commission on every sale they referred.

During the summer I also went to two ten day Lead America Business & Entrepreneurship Conferences to teach entrepreneurship to high school students. I had the time of my life, first in Washington D.C. for training and then in Chicago and then Boston for the conferences. I wrote about my experience in Chicago in the article, "The Time of My Life: Teaching Entrepreneurship" on July 14, 2003,

> Only by teaching does one really learn. Through teaching entrepreneurship I added quite a bit to my knowledge about entrepreneurship and business. I learned about Porter's Five Forces, additional types of alternative financing, new distribution models, the marketing wheel, and a new type of break-even analysis. Just as important, however, was my learning about people and leadership. I learned how to relate and connect to younger teenagers. I learned how to handle a position of authority. I learned how to write a forty-five minute speech in two hours. I learned different teaching styles. I learned that if you know what you are talking about and can gain someone's trust, he or she will follow you. I learned how to inspire and motivate. I learned how to understand motives and read the body language and tone of

a person. I learned how to build rapport and relationships. And I learned how to go ten days with a total of forty hours of sleep.

It was fun. It was an entrepreneurial experience. I had the time of my life teaching those kids and seeing them take an idea and build it into a full business plan in eight days. It was uplifting knowing that maybe what I did or what I said just might make a difference in a few lives. Maybe I'll hear from Jonathan Dermer or Brandon Washington or Ashley Marchetta or Kris Paascila in a few years with news of a promotion, that they've launched their flagship product, or that they'll be taking their companies through an Initial Public Offering next week. The relationships I built, the people I met, the hard and soft skills I learned, the opportunities I had…it was three of the best weeks of my life. I'm off to Boston Thursday to do the same thing for ten more days. I cannot wait!

The summer of 2003 was one I will never forget. From vacationing in England and Dublin to living at my office and sleeping on the futon to launching iContact to traveling to Chicago and Boston teaching entrepreneurship to high schoolers, I had a great time. I lived the life of the bootstrapping entrepreneur and I loved it.

Finally, at the end of the summer I moved into an apartment two miles from the office. Chapel Hill was again abuzz with twenty-five thousand students and the Carolina Entrepreneurship Club was back in session. It was time to build iContact.

From Zero to One Million

With the marketing campaign launched in early July, we had twenty paying customers for iContact by the end of the summer. Charles and I were working full time on increasing the number of affiliates we had and building links to our informational web site, while Aaron worked on adding new features to the software.

Unfortunately for the company, Charles left in August to pursue a new venture in the health industry. We were in need of someone to take over his marketing role so we could continue the affiliate and search engine optimization campaign. Fortunately for us, our offices were across the street from UNC-Chapel Hill. We put up flyers in the business school and within three days received two resumes. We ended up offering an internship to Josh Carlton, a 2003 University of Richmond Graduate that happened to see our flyer while at the business school with his girlfriend as she began the Masters of Accounting program.

We had now worked for a year determining our business strategy, forming the company, developing the software, and implementing our sales model. Now, it came down to execution and whether I could evolve from being a simply a marketing guru into an experienced entrepreneur and manager.

By October of 2003, iContact had over fifty paying customers for iContact. Josh had done well and became our Director of Marketing. Our web site was in the top of the major search engines for "email marketing" and "email marketing software" and we had recruited over two hundred affiliates who promoted our product online in exchange for a percentage of the sales revenue.

In November of 2003, our Vice President of Business Development David Roth joined the team after seeing an article about the company in the local newspaper. At age 57, David was the first 'gray hair' to join the team, and helped us gain credibility. By the end of 2003, we had booked a grand total of $11,964 in sales and had 78 paying customers. We had gone from non-existent to an operating and growing entity with four full-time employees. Though the initial growth took longer than we thought, we were on our way. We ended 2004 with $296,000 in sales, 12 employees, and 1200 paying customers.

> "By the end of 2003, we had booked a grand total of $11,964 in sales and had 78 paying customers. We had gone from non-existent to an operating and growing entity with four full-time employees. Though the initial growth took longer than we thought, we were on our way."

My goal since age 18 had been to build a company to $1 million in sales before my 21st birthday. After 35 months of building iContact, we hit the $1 million in total sales milestone on September 1, 2005—just 18 days after my 21st birthday. I missed the goal by 18 days but I was still elated. iContact was now a million dollar company.

Venture Funding

We ended 2005 with $1.3 million in sales, 22 employees, and 3600 paying customers. We ended 2006 with $2.9 million in sales, 38 employees, and 7,600 paying customers. We are on track to end 2007 with $6.5 million in sales, 72 employees, and 16,000 paying customers.

In May 2006, after three years of bootstrapping the company, we were able to raise a seed round of $500,000 of funding from a local venture capital firm in Durham called NC IDEA. We ended up raising the funds as convertible debt which converted into equity ownership in May 2007 at an agreed upon formula of 4x trailing twelve month (TTM) revenues. The investor ended up getting a pre-money valuation of $15.8 million of the company and owning 3.36% of the company.

After this first round of financing, our sales grew from $200,000 per month in May 2006 to over $530,000 per month in May 2007. I will discuss both the fundraising process as well as how we were able to rapidly scale our customer acquisition and create the marketing, human resource, and technical systems needed to make the growth possible in part 3 of the book, "Ten Steps to Building a Company to $1 Million in Sales." The sales growth of iContact in the twelve months following the initial investment financing is illustrated in the following graph.

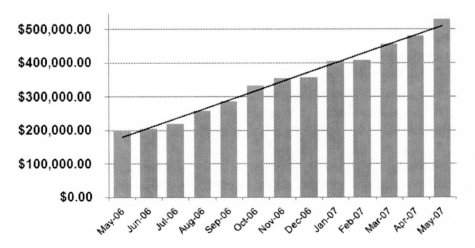

In June 2007, iContact raised its second round of funding, which we called our Series A since the first seed round was small. The company raised $5.35 million from a firm in Reston, Virginia called Updata Partners and our original partner NC IDEA. Since then, our strong growth has continued at a rapid pace. Our annual sales since company inception are shown on the chart below (2007 is estimated):

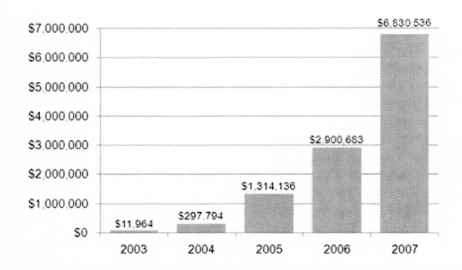

Highlight 3: Updates on iContact

Update on iContact, July 2004 – Now, in July 2004 I am happy to announce that we have 520 clients and are on track to do $300,000 in sales in 2004 and $1.2 million in sales in 2005. We are currently up to ten full time employees, are the fifth largest player in the SMB email marketing field. I've learned a lot about managing people, building systems, and leading a team. We're growing quickly now, have great people, have built outstanding software, and are positioning the iContact software very well in the market.

Update on iContact, September 2005 – iContact passed the $1 million mark this month! I can now say that I have built my own company to $1 million in sales. We are up to 3100 clients for our iContact software and sixteen full-time employees. We're now in a 6,000 sq. foot office space in Durham, North Carolina.

Update on iContact, January 2006 – iContact ended 2005 with $1.3 million in sales, a 438% increase over 2004. We are up to 3800 clients for our iContact software and have twenty three full-time employees. We have recently added on more office space and are up to 9,000 square feet. We have also expanded with the launch of iContact Enterprise and have started to build a telesales force. We are in the process of raising our first round of investment capital that will hopefully help us go from being the third largest player in the SMB segment of the email marketing industry to the first.

Update on iContact, May 2007 – We ended 2006 with 38 employees and $2.9 million in sales. In May 2006 we raised $500,000 of investment from local venture capital firm NC IDEA and since then have grown our monthly sales from $176,000 to over $530,000. We are now up to 57 full-time employees and growing quickly. We moved upstairs to the second floor of our building in February into a 17,000 square foot space. We finally hired a full-time Director of Human Resources Cindy and our first Executive Assistant Michelle that is making my life a bit easier and allowing me to focus on growing the business. We are getting lots of press momentum and have been on the covers of Fortune Small Business and Success Magazine recently and on The Big Idea With Donny Deutsche Show with the help of our great Director of Corporate Communications Chuck Hester. We now have some big name clients like AT&T, Bank of America, Intuit, Vonage, Symantec, Barack Obama 2008, International Paper, ReMax, Super 8 Motels, Centex Homes, Century 21, Ford and Nissan using iContact and we were named the Top Web 2.0 Application in the Marketing Category by SEOMoz. We are on track to raise approximately $5 million of additional financing in June.

Update on iContact, October 2007 – We raised $5.35 million from Updata Partners on June 30. We are utilizing the funds to invest more aggressively in customer acquisition. We are now up to 70 employees and $650,000 in monthly sales and have expanded our office to 25,000 square feet. We have won the Best Places to Work in the Triangle Award from the Triangle Business Journal and the Fast 50 Award from TechJournal South. We are focused on growing the company as quickly as we can while building our capabilities in human resources, recruiting, technology, systems, customer support, sales, business development, and marketing. We have hired a new Director of Sales Matt Allen to grow our Enterprise sales and now have over 40 Enterprise customers including many members of the Fortune 500. We are focused on growing the experience we have in the company and building a company that can either be acquired or go public. We have over 15,000 customers and are adding over 1,300 new customers per month.

It is here where my story ends for now. I hope the story has inspired you and given you motivation to go out and build a venture of your own or grow your company further. But first, you'll need a guide to get there. I will begin in part two by explaining the background knowledge needed to be a successful entrepreneur including the basics of how our global economy works and the changes in business and our world that are shaping how we as entrepreneurs must think and act.

The Story in Photos

The "Original Six" March 2004

Moving into our new 6,000 square foot office space, January 2005

14 Employees, Summer 2005

19 Employees, March 2006

Seed Round Funding Celebration, May 2006

After the second "iContact Day" July 2006

Moving Upstairs to 17,000 Square Feet, February 2007

39 Employees, March 2007

My partner Aaron Houghton on the right, myself on the left in front of the
television in the lobby, March 2007

Part Two: Preparing to Be an Entrepreneur

Chapter 3 The Market System

> "It is not from the benevolence of the butcher, the brewer, or the baker, that we can expect our dinner, but from their regard to their own interest."
> - Adam Smith, *The Wealth of Nations*

The History of the Market System

One of the most important advances needed for the creation of a market system took place sometime between 12000 and 10000 B.C. with the advent of specialization and the start of the Neolithic Age. Instead of each tribe hunting and gathering their food, different persons within each tribe would become experts at a certain task such as hunting, gathering, cooking, tool making, shelter making, or clothes making.

As methods of agriculture improved, the first towns and cities were seen. Dependable food supplies allowed people to build permanent houses and settle in one area. As settlements increased in size, new forms of society such as religious centers, courts, and marketplaces developed. The advent of towns produced further specialization, creating jobs in tool making, pottery making, carpentry, wool making, and masonry, among others. The specialist created items faster and of a better quality than each family making its own, increasing standards of living.

The earliest signs of the market system at work can be seen with the advent of bartering within tribes as far back as 6000 B.C. in Mesopotamia. If Tom had twenty cows and Igor had eighty hens, and Tom and Igor agreed that one cow was worth four hens, then the trade could take place. The problem with the barter system, however, was that in order for a trade to take place, both parties had to want what the other party had. This 'co-incidence of wants' often did not happen.

The demands of growing business and trade caused a money system to be developed. Silver rings or bars are thought to have been used as money in Ancient Iraq before 2000 B.C. Early forms of money would usually be specie, or commodity money. Examples range from seashells, to tobacco leaves, to large round rocks, to beads.[1]

While the money system still had much development to go through (credit and paper money did not yet exist), its invention over four thousand years ago was of crucial importance to the world we live in today. The use of an accepted medium to store value and enable exchange has greatly enhanced our world, our lives, our potential, and our future.

By the year 1100, the prevailing system in the Western World was feudalism. It was a world of kings and lords, vassals and serfs, kingdoms and manors. Long distance trade was expanding and new worlds of foreign spices, oriental treasures, and luxurious silks were discovered. Three hundred and fifty years later, after weathering a Black Death and the Hundred Years War, Europe emerged by expanding trade to new levels and building the foundation for the start of the competitive market economy we know today.

With a population spurt starting around 1470 A.D., cities, markets, and the volume of trade grew. Banking, initially started by Ancient Mesopotamians, grew to new heights and complexities, the guild system expanded, and the idea that a business was an impersonal entity, with a separate identity from its owner, started to take hold.[2] Imports from the new world drove expanded trade and bookkeepers created standardized principles for keeping track of a firm's accounts based on Luca Pacioli's advances. Early entrepreneurs, merchants, and explorers, began to raise capital, take risks, and stimulate economic growth. Capitalism had begun.

> "Early entrepreneurs, merchants, and explorers, began to raise capital, take risks, and stimulate economic growth. Capitalism had begun."

It began with much resistance, however. The idea of gain was shunned and shamed. The practice of usury, charging interest on loans, was banned by the Church. Jobs were assigned by tradition and caste. Innovation was stifled and efficiency was forcefully put down, punishable by death. In sixteenth-century England, when mass production in the weaving industry first came about, the guildsmen protested. An efficient workshop containing two hundred looms and butchers and bakers for the workers was outlawed by the King under the pretense that such efficiency was improper and reduced the number of available jobs. Makers of innovative buttons in France in the late 1600s were fined and searched and the importation of printed Calicos cost the lives of 16,000 people.[3]

The world would soon see, however, that innovation was generally a good thing that made lives better and that efficiency was a path toward a higher standard of a living. As Robert L. Heilbroner says in *The Worldly Philosophers*, "The precapitalist era saw the birth of the printing press, the paper mill, the windmill, the mechanical clock, the map, and a host of other inventions. The idea of invention itself took hold; experimentation and innovation were looked upon for the first time with a friendly eye."

With the advent of a complex marketplace and capitalists, the battle of ideas raged to explain the sources of wealth and to explain the workings of the market. Between approximately 1550 and 1800, a philosophy called mercantilism was at the forefront. The mercantilists had the misguided notions that a country's wealth was solely based on how much treasure and gold it could obtain and how much more it exported than imported. Monopolies and tariffs were promoted and competition and trade were discouraged. They had gotten it all wrong.

Fortunately for Europe, new schools of thought sprung up in the 18th century that promoted commerce, and not the hoarding of gold, as the source of wealth. Adam Smith further backed this idea and was the first to capture and explain the essence of the marketplace. He did so in his famous 1776 work *An Inquiry into the Nature and Causes of the Wealth of Nations*, slaying the mercantilist dragon in the process. Within, Smith outlined certain laws of the market that are worthy of mention.

Smith explained that self-interest acts as a guiding force toward the work society desires. As Smith notes in *Wealth*, "It is not from the benevolence of the butcher, the brewer, or the baker that we expect our dinner, but from their regard to their self-interest." While one would naturally assume that everyone following only his or her self-interest would not create a very good society, there is another force that prevents selfish individuals from exploiting the marketplace in a healthy economy. That regulator is competition.

This principle can be explained best with the following excerpt from *The Worldly Philosophers*.

> A man who permits his self-interest to run away with him will find that competitors have slipped in to take his trade away; if he charges too much for his wares or if he refuses to pay as much as everybody else for his workers, he will find himself without buyers in the one case and without employees in the other.

Those workers will go to the competitor who is willing to pay more and those customers will go to the competitor who charges less. The wonderful paradox of the market, through the interaction of supply and demand and competition, creates a price that properly allocates industry so as to produce the proper quantities of goods and services. No intervention, planning, or forethought is needed to create exactly what society desires, in the exact amount it desires. What a wonderful contraption the market is! As long as society can promote competition and innovation, standards of living will continue to grow and wealth will increase.

While such things as crime, corruption, and market failures do exist and perhaps the world cannot be simplified to quite this degree proposed by Smith, the market system, undoubtedly, has been one of the most significant innovations of mankind in its history.

Following Smith there were many other economists, ideologists, sociologists, and philosophers that pontificated on the workings of the increasingly complex marketplace. Ricardo outlined the all-important principles of trade while Malthus predicted overpopulation and doom. Mill contemplated on liberalism while Bentham promoted utilitarianism. Marx painted a bleak picture of forced labor and surplus value while Keynes later showed there sometimes was a reason for an active government.

By the time of Smith's death in 1790, the nascent Industrial Revolution had already reared its head. The effects of the Renaissance, the humanist movement, and the new focus on science and empiricism would translate into the launch of a movement that would impact the world as none before it had. It was this revolution, often harsh and cruel, that prompted the ideology of communism and created robber barons and industrial titans. It was also this same revolution, however, that led to the development of the innovations, technology, and standards of living we have today.

> "It was this same revolution that led to the development of the innovations, technology, and standards of living we have today."

From the Industrial Revolution, the concept of mass production and economies of scale came about. Bigness, trusts, and vertical integration became the key to riches in the day. It was Andrew Carnegie and J. P. Morgan in steel, John D. Rockefeller and Frank Kenan in oil, and Henry Ford in automotives. While some of these titans had questionable ethics, no one can deny that they were innovators. They forged alliances, developed new ways of doing business, and created efficiency across industries.

Out of necessity, regulatory organizations such as the Environmental Protection Agency, the Antitrust Division of the Department of Justice, the Securities and Exchange Commission, the Food and Drug Administration, the Financial Accounting Standards Board, and the Federal Trade Commission would soon be created in the United States while similar organizations were created across the developed world. Theodore Roosevelt would go on his trust-busting and anti-monopoly campaigns while Franklin D. Roosevelt would create new laws relating to the distribution of wealth. John Maynard Keynes would go on about public spending while Milton Friedman and Frederick A. Hayek would fight large government in the name of freedom. Lyndon Johnson would forge his Great Society while Reagan lowered taxes. The Berlin Wall would fall, and the Internet, as well as increased trade and flow of capital, would create profound change in business. To make a long and fascinating story short, we've gone from hunting, gathering, bartering, and grunting to specialization, miniaturization, internationalization, mass-production, and six sigma—all due to the invisible hand, innovation, and industry. And such is the history of the market system.

How the Market System Works

Let's take a look at how the market system of today works. To do this, let's look at four important concepts—the factors of production, supply and demand, comparative advantage, and the circular flow of money.

The Resources Needed to Create Wealth

Let's start things off with a question. What is needed to create wealth? Within the marketplace, there are many resources that go into the production of goods and services. These resources can be grouped into four categories. These categories are **land**, **labor**, **capital**, and **entrepreneurial ability**.

The resource of entrepreneurial ability is where you come into play. It is the entrepreneur that organizes and arranges the use of land, labor, and capital to create an output demanded by the marketplace. It is the entrepreneur's responsibility to decide on what amounts of each resource to use and then use those resources efficiently to create a product or service that is valued higher by the marketplace than the collective value of the resource inputs. As Campbell R. McConnell and Stanley L. Brue say in *Economics*, "Both a sparkplug and a catalyst, the entrepreneur is at once the driving force behind production and the agent who combines the other resources in what is hoped will be a profitable venture."

The Law All Entrepreneurs Must Understand

The second concept that is essential for all entrepreneurs to grasp is that of supply and demand. While you may have studied supply and demand in high school or college economics class, it's important to review the principle as it can have a very practical impact on business decision making.

In a supply and demand graph, there are two curves and two axes. Demand is represented by a downward sloping curve and supply is represented by an upward sloping curve. On the vertical axis is price and on the horizontal axis is quantity. An equilibrium price and quantity will always be reached at the point the supply and demand curves intersect. Why? Simply because if the price were higher than the equilibrium price suppliers would produce more and buyers would buy less, bringing the price back down in short order, and if the price were lower than the equilibrium price, buyers would buy more and suppliers would produce less, bringing the price back up in short order.

As can be seen in the following graph, the market would **demand** about 13 widgets when the price is $2.

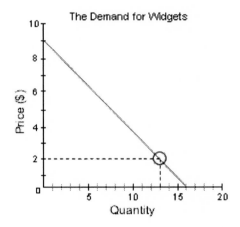

At a price of $2, thirteen widgets will be bought. But would suppliers be willing to sell widgets for $2? Would they even make a profit at this price level? Let's look at the supply curve to see what amounts producers of widgets would be willing to sell at each price level.

From the below graph, one can see that if the market was willing to pay $2, suppliers would be willing to produce 3 widgets.

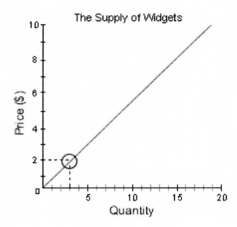

This creates a bit of a problem, however. If at $2 the market demands 13 widgets and only 3 are produced, there will be 10 people without widgets. There is a shortage in the marketplace. Widgets are scarce. Because those ten people know they will not get a widget unless they pay more, they bid up the price. A few of these ten people will not be willing to pay as much as they must to obtain a widget. A few of them will, however. This process eventually leads to an equilibrium price and quantity, where the suppliers produce exactly how many widgets the market demands at a set price.

To determine this equilibrium price and quantity of widgets, let's put the demand and the supply curves together on the same graph.

From this graph one can see that at a price of about $4.80 there will be 8 widgets demanded by the market place and 8 widgets supplied by producers. This is the equilibrium price and level of output, right where the supply and demand curves intersect. Now, if demand increases, the price and quantity supplied will also increase. If supply increases, perhaps due to a new technological innovation, widgets will be less scarce and the price will go down and output will go up. These are the basic laws of supply and demand.

So what does this mean to an entrepreneur? What is important to take out of this? Well, there are three important lessons here.

Lesson One: How to Price Your Products

If you charge too much you may make a large per product profit but not make many sales. Vice versa, if you charge too little you may make many sales but little profit or perhaps a loss. To find the price that will maximize revenue, you will have to experiment. Test different price points and see what the reaction is on sales, total revenue, and net profit. You will not have the resources to hire a team of Ph.D.s to do elasticity and econometric studies to determine the exact point. You can come close through trial and error and by seeing what your competitors are charging.

Lesson Two: Sell What the Market Demands

The law of supply and demand holds true in all situations and can often be cruel to those who do not abide by it. Before you begin your business, make sure you take time to determine the approximate demand for what you will be selling in the marketplace. Ask yourself if there is a need? What problems does your product or service solve? How will you differentiate yourself from all the competitors doing the same thing? Use the MAR Opportunity Evaluation model provided in part three and be sure to do proper due diligence and market research. If you don't you may find yourself out of business and not able to sell your product at the price you must in order to make a profit.

Lesson Three: Supply and Demand Works in Labor Markets as well as Product Markets

While the models above use the example of a good, the widget, the law of supply and demand is equally applicable to factor markets, that is, the market for employees and workers. The difference is that supply is supply of workers and demand is demand for workers. As the business owner, you are no longer the provider, but rather, the consumer of labor. If the supply for labor in your area is low, you will have to pay more to attract the quantity and quality of employees you need to build your business. Similarly, if there are many employers in your area, there will be more choices for workers in the area and thus wages will be driven higher.

Trade & Comparative Advantage

While there is much work to be done to reduce poverty and increase access to opportunity across the world, over the past five hundred years a tremendous increase in prosperity and standards of living has taken place. There are numerous reasons for this improvement including the humanist movement, the scientific revolution, the spread of liberalism, the promotion of innovation and enterprise by governments, the creation of laws that protect private property, the spread of access to credit, and the development of a system which rewards hard work and investment. One of the most important reasons for the great increase in the standards of living across our world over the past five centuries has been the great increase in trade.

Returning to mercantilist times, it was thought that a nation could only increase its wealth if it sold more to other nations (exported) than it bought from other nations (imported). Thinking briefly, this notion might make sense. If a country started with $10 and bought $8 of goods and only sold $5 of goods, its 'wealth' would now be down to $7. Calculating wealth in this way, however, does not take into effect the value of the goods purchased. In fact, there is now more wealth than there was before—for both countries. Trade allowed each country to purchase what it needed at a lower cost than what it would have paid if it would have produced within its own borders.

Until the economist David Ricardo came along, this mercantilist view of trade persisted. It was not until Ricardo's publication of his *Principles of Political Economy* in 1817 that sense began to spread. Within his treatise, he explained and promoted the theory of comparative advantage, the key theory that explains why specialization and free trade can be such beneficial forces.

The theory of comparative advantage essentially states that the country that produces a good most efficiently, in terms of all the other possible production alternatives, should produce that good. In a two good model, the theory would state that if country A produces computers and cheese more efficiently than country B than country A should not produce both goods, but only produce only the good that it produces most efficiently in comparison to country B, and then trade with country B to obtain that second good.

So why does all this theory affect the entrepreneur? There are three reasons. First, we as entrepreneurs must understand the basics of the market on a macro scale before we can impact industry, innovate, and create wealth for our society and profits for our businesses. Secondly, while growing your business to one million dollars in sales and beyond, international sales will likely become a large part of your business. The health products company I worked with in high school, was selling its product in over thirty countries by the time I left to go to college.

Finally, in the world of ideas there is much debate about policies, and especially policies related to free trade, fair trade, overseas competition, tariffs, and subsidies. It is important to know the basis of the arguments for authentic free trade and to understand how and why trade has benefited the world and increased standards of living over the past few centuries, while also keeping in mind that while these benefits are significant and distributed, opening up markets can create short-term pains.

Seeing Both Sides of the Coin: The Flow of Goods and Capital

There is one more model that entrepreneurs-to-be must know. This is the Circular Flow Model. The Circular Flow Model presents a simple method for understanding the relationships in the marketplace between businesses (the producers) and households (the consumers). It shows how producers provide goods and services to consumers who provide labor and entrepreneurial ability to businesses, both in exchange for money. Let's take a look at the model.

The Circular Flow Model

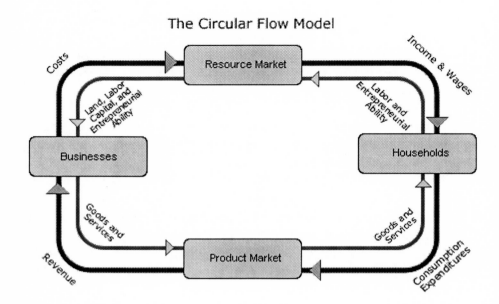

In the model, the outer, clockwise, path represents the flow of money. Businesses pay households for services as workers, and households pay businesses for the products and services provided to the households.

The inner path represents the flow of goods. Households serve as a source of labor and entrepreneurial ability for businesses. These resources are purchased in the Resource Market, where the equilibrium quantity and price is set by supply and demand. Businesses purchase land, labor, capital, and entrepreneurial ability from the resource market, and then combine these inputs into valuable outputs known as goods and services. These goods and services go on sale in the Product Market, in which the desired quantity and equilibrium price for each and every service is simultaneously and automatically set through the dynamic workings of the marketplace. This the cycle continues on ad infinitum.

While this concept is basic, it is useful to have this simple model. Many younger persons, without experience in the workplace and living as a consumer their whole lives, can only envision the right side of this model. By knowing how this capital and goods flow works we can better understand our roles as consumers, employees, and entrepreneurs as well as the dynamic and constant interaction of supply and demand for both our services and the products we purchase.

So what was the purpose of this primer on the market system? You may have wanted to dive right into the information on how to evaluate opportunities, raise funding, launch a product, build a team, market on the web, and build international sales. Understanding the global market economy first creates a very important framework for understanding the concepts presented later on how to build a company to one million dollars in sales. All entrepreneurs must understand the basic laws of the market system, for if they do not they will not be entrepreneurs for long.

The Role of the Entrepreneur in the Market System

The entrepreneur is the catalyst that brings together the resources of land, labor, and capital to create valuable goods and services and in the hopes of building a profitable business. The word entrepreneur is of French origin and derives from *entreprendre*, which means 'to undertake.' The American Heritage Dictionary defines an entrepreneur as "a person who organizes, operates, and assumes the risk for a business venture."

The entrepreneur plays a vital role in society. Without entrepreneurs, there would be no businesses, no inventions, no innovation, no progress, and no wealth. Without the entrepreneur and the system that provides incentives for entrepreneurs, we would have no printing press, no bifocals, no airplane, no air conditioner, no radio, no microwave, no computer, no telephone, no television, and no George Foreman Lean Mean Fat Burning Grilling Machine. In short, the standard of living would not be much better than that of 1450. The world would not be able to support the 6.5 billion persons it does, and the doomsday Malthusian predictions of overpopulation would have been realized many decades, if not centuries ago.

> "Without the entrepreneur and the system that provides incentives for entrepreneurs, we would have no printing press, no bifocals, no airplane, no air conditioner, no radio, no microwave, no computer, no telephone, no television, and no George Foreman Lean Mean Fat Burning Grilling Machine."

If it is your goal to become an entrepreneur, whether by running a small business in your home town or launching a high potential venture with VC funding, you should be commended. While being an entrepreneur is surely not for everybody, if you are the type who has a bias toward action, brings efficiency and innovation into everything you do, creates systems and processes, is not afraid to make mistakes, can build and inspire a quality team, and will persist until pigs fly in a frozen over hell while the cows come home and the Cubs win the pennant, you deserve a pat on the back. You are an entrepreneur. In mind, in body, in spirit, in soul—you are an entrepreneur.

Chapter 4 An Entrepreneur's Philosophy

> "More gold has been mined from the thoughts of men than has been taken from the earth."
>
> - Napoleon Hill, *Think and Grow Rich*

The Philosophy of an Entrepreneur

Values, philosophies, and ideas are immensely important. As John Stuart Mill said in *Representative Government*, "It is what men think, that determines how they act." Ideologies can be the cause of wars, hatred, death, or prosperity. As such, it is very important for each human to analyze their own ideology, to not without question pick up the religious, economic, and political views of his or her parents, and to truly know why they do what they do and for what they would or would not sacrifice. As such, in this chapter I will explain the principles of my philosophy—the philosophy of an entrepreneur.

There are many questions to be answered in determining one's economic philosophy. Personally, I am a believer in competitive market economies and the potential of the human spirit.

I surely do not use the ideal of liberalistic laissez faire—no regulation and no government interference, as a façade to pay less taxes and enrich myself while those without the same opportunity as I languish. On the other hand, I do believe that those who create the foundation for innovation in our economy, the entrepreneurs and business owners, should be given incentives to produce and that their incentive should be taxed or regulated only very carefully. Without such incentives or with too much regulation, the wealth that is needed to have the ability to provide jobs or assistance to the impoverished would be non-existent.

> "I do believe that those who create the foundation for innovation in our economy, the entrepreneurs and business owners, should be given incentives to produce and that their incentive should be taxed or regulated only very carefully."

The competitive market economy has been able to develop largely due to the development of the philosophy of liberalism over the past four hundred years. Without key persons such as Martin Luther, Adam Smith, Thomas Hobbes, John Locke, and John Stuart Mill, capitalism would be very different. To truly become a successful entrepreneur, it is important to understand the ideological basis of the competitive market economy. Let's take a moment to see just how liberalism has shaped the markets and the world of an entrepreneur.

Understanding Liberalism

Today, the main players on the ideological battleground are socialists, social liberals, neoclassical liberals, conservatives, and libertarians. As Francis Fukayama points out in *The End of History and the Last Man* liberalism, in its classical sense, has won the battle and been accepted by nearly everyone. Although dissent still exists, the ideas of Thomas Hobbes, John Locke, Voltaire and J.S. Mill have, for now, won the day.

To illustrate this point, I will point out that both of the major political parties in the United States are parties that have liberalism at their foundation. Republicans are generally neoclassical liberals while Democrats, often the ones referred to as liberals, are generally social liberals. Both forms of liberalism seek the same end, an increase in liberty, but simply go after this goal in different manners.

The key difference is that neoclassical liberals believe that less government can lead to more liberty while social liberals believe that equality of opportunity does not truly exist and the government can take positive actions to rectify this liberty-reducing wrong. In the United States, the belief that Democrats are liberals and Republicans are not is a bit of an historical misnomer that does not speak to the true definition of liberalism.

Liberalism sprang up as a reaction to two of the characteristic features of medieval society in Europe—religious conformity and ascribed status. This reaction took place in different times in different places. By the early 19th century however, 'liberalism' had entered the vocabulary of politics and a distinct 'liberal' viewpoint emerged. Liberals wanted **freedom of religion** and **separation of church and state**. These ideas were diametrically opposed to the thinking of the Middle Ages during which church and state were supposed to work together to defend and spread religion.

The other feature of medieval society which early liberals disagreed with was ascribed status. In medieval times, a person's class standing was fixed (ascribed) at birth and one could not improve his or her lot or have any upward mobility. The liberals instead wanted to create a society based on achieved status in which everyone had an equal opportunity to work his or her way up in society.

Liberalism demanded **equality of opportunity** and an end to aristocratic privilege. This surely was not possible under the system of feudalism that developed after the collapse of Charlemagne's empire in the ninth century. Other characteristics of a liberal society include a **competitive market economy**, a **rule of law**, and a **free exchange of ideas**.

With the wealth controlled by those who had the most incentive to keep the system as it was, it would take a number of events and many centuries for liberalism to emerge. Adding to the chance liberalism would succeed was the Magna Carta, Renaissance, Black Death, expansion in trade and commerce, the discovery of the new world, the Protestant Reformation, the English Bill of Rights of 1688 and the American and French revolutions.

Thomas Hobbes (1588-1679) is recognized as one of the early founders of liberalism. In *Leviathan* (1651), he introduced the ideas of self-interest and that government should only be obeyed as long as the person or persons in power protected its people. Hobbes argued that government was formed by the consent of the people and that all individuals are equal.

John Locke continued on Hobbes' path by stating in his *Letter Concerning Toleration* that it was wrong for governments to force their subjects to conform to a particular religion. He stated that governments should tolerate diverse religious beliefs as long as those beliefs did not directly jeopardize the order of the state.

Locke set forth the natural rights of all humans as life, liberty, and property—rights that no one could take away without cause and explained that the populace had the right to overthrow any government that threatened these natural rights. These beliefs were committed to writing once again thirteen years on with the French Declaration of the Rights of Man.

Liberalism is the core of what I believe. I firmly and wholeheartedly believe in freedom of religion, separation of church and state, and equality of opportunity for all humans. I believe government is created with the consent of the governed and that its main roles are to provide security, protect and promote liberty, and make laws. Finally, I believe that a democratic republic, even with the flaws it has, is the best form of government man has created to date.

Let's take a look at the competitive market economy that has developed within this philosophical framework.

The Case for the Competitive Market Economy

A child born to a wealthy family in Bethesda, Maryland will have a very different life and set of opportunities than a child born to a peasant family in Zimbabwe. Looking at the equality of opportunity between these two persons would be difficult, as the economic and political situations in the United States and Zimbabwe are vastly different. But what about a child born to a wealthy U.S. family versus a child born to an impoverished U.S. family? And what about a white child versus a black or Hispanic child? Are the opportunities the same? Is there truly equality of opportunity?

In many cases, surely there is not. The child born to the wealthy family is likely to grow up in a good neighborhood, go to good primary and secondary schools, likely private ones, be cared for by both parents, be encouraged to go to college, have his college paid for, be provided with a car, house, and a good job upon graduation, and receive a large sum bequeathed to him upon his parents passing.

The poor child is much more likely to have only one parent, to not have that parent around too often, be living in poor conditions, be exposed to drugs and violence at an early age, and have an increased risk of getting in trouble. He may attend poor schools and rarely have the encouragement or additional assistance needed to do well. He may never reach college or finish high school and end up uneducated, an early parent, and with a low-wage job. The cycle of poverty will continue to the next generation.

So how, if I believe that there truly is not equality of opportunity in the United States, can I strongly support its economic system? I hope the following anecdote will help illustrate the answer.

Standing Up for the Competitive Market Economy

The day after the start of the 2003 war in Iraq, my psychology professor decided to postpone the class on developmental psychology in favor of having a 'discussion' on why he was against the war and why it was an immoral and illegal war. While I did not have a problem with him expressing these feelings, I did have a problem when he turned the anti-war speech into a tirade on the American competitive market economy.

Thankfully, Dr. Lawson opened the floor for comments after his twenty minute speech. With three hundred students in the lecture hall looking on, no one raised their hand to speak. I raised my hand, and taking my notes with me, proceeded to the front of the room as the professor handed me the microphone. I began with a comment that in Iraq Professor Lawson would have been stoned, hung, shot, or otherwise killed and one of the things I liked about this country was that one could speak their mind without fear. I continued by saying that personally, I had come that day to learn psychology. This caused the students to cheer. I think they were quite surprised by this point. Who was this kid taking on his professor in front of hundreds of people?

Fortunately, we all knew Dr. Lawson well, or at least knew he was a very easy-going guy. We discerned this through stories of his twelve years living in developing countries and going to the beach and doing yoga every day. I was sure that he would welcome differing opinions, so I continued. I mentioned that I was not going to talk about the war, as we had all heard the pros and cons ad nauseum, but rather, wanted to give a rebuttal to some of his comments about the competitive market system.

Comments like, "Money is the root of all evil" and "the rich are battling the poor in America" made me want to respond. So I stood up and told Dr. Lawson that in my opinion money is the root of much of the prosperity we have and that without money societies would have to resort to barter, greatly reducing the amount of trade and welfare in the world.

I argued that the reason that we had the high level of quality facilities we had in that room was because of the market and that without a competitive market for desks, lights, seats, microphones, projectors, carpet, wood, paint, and construction labor the room we were in could never exist, that the high standards of living we have are directly due to the market economy, and that without this competitive market economy we would have little incentive to produce or to make high quality goods at low costs.

> "The reason that we had the high level of quality facilities we had in that room was because of the market and that without a competitive market for desks, lights, seats, microphones, projectors, carpet, wood, paint, and construction labor the room we were in could never exist."

In response to his comment that there was 'the biggest disparity between rich and poor since slavery' I replied that anyone in the United States that was motivated could, through entrepreneurship, support themselves and break out of poverty. I added that while important it was not the disparity that mattered most, but rather the ability of anyone to become anything they dream.

Mobility was what truly mattered. A large pie unevenly distributed is much better than a small pie divvied up in equal proportion. As former Chinese ruler Deng Xiaoping once noted, "I can distribute poverty or I can distribute wealth." It is, in my opinion, better for there to be inequality and the worst-off person have two goats than there to be equality and everyone have just one goat.

In the United States there is not equality of opportunity in many cases. I still believe the opportunity is there, however, for anyone with enough desire and perseverance to reach the same heights as anyone born into money and a supportive family. While the system is by no means perfect, there are great opportunities in the economic system we have, and without the incentives provided within it, we would all be worse off and there would be a lot more of us in poverty. There is certainly some corruption and malfeasance within the economic system we have, it is much less that that in most other countries and in other systems.

Adding Compassion

I was completely sure of this view talking that day in psychology. I stood up there and vigorously and eloquently defended what I held to be dear. A girl came up to me after class that day, however; a girl named Allison. Allison just asked me to consider that perhaps many poor persons did not have the opportunity I had had.

It was true. I had two loving parents, a mom who always encouraged me to follow my dreams and be independent, and a supportive childhood during which I received a good education. I also had the luck to become good at web site development and web marketing and help build a company to a million dollars in sales my senior year of high school, providing at least some financial comfort for me.

I had never considered how difficult it would have been for me to start a business without loving parents supporting me. I had never considered how hard it would have been to start a business if my parents had not told me what I needed to know about sex and I had impregnated a girl at sixteen. I had never considered how difficult it would have been to obtain a good education without the encouragement to go to school and do well. And I had never considered how hard it would have been to succeed in business if I would have grown up with murder and drugs outside my door.

So did these considerations change my views on the competitive market economy and entrepreneurship? Not entirely, but they did add a bit of compassion to them. While we may not be able to start people out on the same footing, we can, through competitive market economies, entrepreneurship, education, philanthropy, and a little bit of compassion, provide any person who wants to take hold of it the opportunity to break the cycle of poverty and make something of themselves. It is up to that person to take the initiative. It is up to us to spread the word that this possibility is there. For me, this book is a start toward spreading that message.

On the topic of the role of government, there are cases that the justification of laissez faire simply should not be used. One such example is in early Industrial England when children were being shackled to machines in order to get them to work harder. The British parliament attempted to pass a law against this practice but many early capitalists lobbied the lawmakers to vote against the law, quoting Smith's work in saying that any attempt to interfere with the workings of the marketplace would be for the worse. While I am a strong proponent of the marketplace and of the competitive market economy, there are times when a government has to have a role.

There are other times, of course, when the government should have less of a role. Looking at the system setup during the communist era in the USSR provides a classic example. Communism failed because no human, or computer system for that matter, could properly plan and account for the dynamic nature of the marketplace. The market and resource directing information that prices provide simply could not be replicated by a team of a thousand researchers and planners at Gosplan with the best supercomputers.

While there are times when the government should be involved in the marketplace, there are many instances in which planners and bureaucrats would only harm us. In the end, it comes down to efficient and intelligent regulation, the ability we have as a society to root out corruption and promote ethics in business, our ability to strike a balance between protecting the consumer and worker while protecting commerce, and the ability we have as a society to instill ethical, non-corrupt leaders.

There are types of capitalists that I like and hold as heroes, and there are types of capitalists I consider criminals. The type of capitalists I don't like are those that exploited children in the mines and factories in the Industrial revolution, created monopolistic cartels in the 1880s, dumped toxic waste in rivers in the 1950s, and cooked their books in the 1990s. Those capitalists are the ones that give the market system a bad name and reduce, instead of increase the standards of living in our world.

Real capitalists, real entrepreneurs, promote innovation, bring efficiency into their industries, take on risk, drive competition, and build wealth for themselves as well as society. Let's commit now to bringing ethics, responsibility, and the ideals of the true entrepreneur into what we do. Let us succeed in building our million dollar companies because we find new efficiencies, build good teams, and take an innovative product or business model to market, not because we get in good with key government leaders, have the heads of our competing companies killed, report revenue on our books that doesn't exist, and save on disposal costs by dumping our waste in the ocean or in the river.

> "Real capitalists, real entrepreneurs, promote innovation, bring efficiency into their industries, take on risk, drive competition, and build wealth for themselves as well as society."

Without a competitive market economy, an incentive system, and a price system our lives would be terrible. There would be no incentives for teachers to teach, doctors to heal, bakers to bake, or workers to produce. There would be no chance for us to help the billions of humans in our world that presently are not able to enjoy our level of prosperity or improve their standard of living.

My dad, a retired Episcopalian priest has taught me that money is not the root of all evil. The Bible says it is the *love* of money that is the root of all evil, not money itself. Used and invested properly, money can create an increasing degree of comfort in the lives of all members of society. It's the excessive lust for and hoarding of money that is evil, not the building of wealth and reinvesting wealth to increase prosperity for all.

Chapter 5 The Global Entrepreneur

> "Globalization is not just a phenomenon and not just a passing trend. It is the international system that replaced the Cold War system. Globalization is the integration of capital, technology, and information across national borders, in a way that is creating a single global market and, to some degree, a global village."
>
> - Thomas L. Friedman, *The Lexus and the Olive Tree*

The International System

Beginning in the mid-19th century, as world trade was expanding rapidly, a global economic system began to develop. With the advent of the railroad and the opening of the trans-Atlantic telegraph wire in 1866, the first round of globalization had begun. This first round, however, came to a pause in 1914 with World War I. It revived slightly in the 1920s, and then came to a halt in 1939 with the start of World War II. As Thomas L. Friedman states in *The Lexus and the Olive Tree*, "The first era of globalization and global finance capitalism was broken apart by the successive hammer blows of World War I, the Russian Revolution, and the Great Depression, which combined to fracture the world physically and ideologically."

After World War II, a new structure was set up that completely changed how the international commerce and political systems operated. This structure was based on the Bretton Woods System, developed in 1944 in Bretton Woods, New Hampshire, and the General Agreement on Tariffs and Trade (GATT), established in 1947.

The agreement reached at Bretton Woods established two multinational organizations, the International Monetary Fund (IMF) and the World Bank. The IMF would maintain the order of the international monetary system while the World Bank would lend money to the European Nations to help them rebuild and later lend to developing nations. The agreement set forth a fixed exchange rate scheme, in which all nations would set an exchange rate based on the dollar.

The fixed-exchange rate system continued until 1973, when it broke down amid pressure of a dollar devaluation and increasing inflation in the United States.[4] Replacing the fixed system was the floating exchange rate system that continues to this day. The value of currencies would fluctuate based on the supply and demand in the market and currencies would no longer be convertible to gold. While the floating system offered many advantages, it also created new possibilities for problems. These problems became apparent with the Mexican Peso devaluation of 1994, the Asian Financial Crisis of 1997 and 1998, and the Argentinean Collapse of 2001 and 2002.

The GATT, on the other hand, was an agreement intended to increase trade by reducing tariffs and usage of quotas. If a member country felt that another country had unfair trade barriers in place, it would make a report to the Geneva, Switzerland based GATT administration, which would investigate and act to pressure the offending country into removing the barrier. Data show that the GATT was quite successful.

The GATT continued until December, 15, 1993 when President Clinton signed into U.S. law the Uruguay Round of GATT, which created the World Trade Organization (WTO). It is the actions of this organization, the WTO, that lead to much of the controversy that erupted onto the streets of Seattle in 1999 and Cancun in 2003. Many questions still remain for the organization such as what will be done about agricultural subsidies, currency volatility, worker exploitation, genetically modified food, and political corruption.

Today, liberalized trade, global financial markets, and new technologies have brought us into an era of globalization much different that that of 1850-1914. In one hundred and fifty years we've gone from news taking thirty days to taking $1/30^{th}$ of a second to reach Europe. In seventy-five years we've gone from a three-minute call between New York and London costing $300 in 1930 to $.01 with Voice-over IP. Microchips, satellites, fiber optics, Moore's Law, and the Internet have made their mark.

> "In seventy-five years we've gone from a three-minute call between New York and London costing $300 in 1930 to $.03 with Voice-over IP in 2006. Microchips, satellites, fiber optics, Moore's Law, and the Internet have made their mark."

Globalization has changed business in many important ways—ways that aspiring entrepreneurs must first understand before they can build a successful business. Today, if your business is to truly succeed, it must be global. Let's take a moment then, to be sure we understand the principles of the economy that globalization has created.

The Dynamics of the Information Age

Six years ago I was somewhat mad that I was born in 1984 and not 1979. I knew that if I had been born in '79 that I would have been out there in the late 90's with my own four hundred million dollar .com company. Staying true to the grass is always greener proverb, now, in 2006, I feel lucky to have been able to watch one of the greatest business lessons in the history of the world play out before my eyes, without losing the shirt off my back.

Back in 1999, many writers and journalists boldly proclaimed that new rules would require new strategies for businesses to effectively prosper. While they were partially right, business owners were not quite sure which rules were effective principles and which rules were just hyped up chaff. Magazines like *Business 2.0* and *Industry Standard* proclaimed that if you did not get venture capital funding in the hundreds of millions and spend it rapidly to gain market share you could not succeed. They seemed to have forgotten that most entrepreneurs that end up succeeding start out small, bootstrap their way toward success, and focus on profitability throughout.

Mark Brier, the former VP of Marketing for Amazon.com and CEO of Beyond.com said in his early 2000 book *The 10 Second Internet Manager* that "In the Internet World, it's all about mind share and market share. Profitability will come later." It's interesting to note that Beyond.com filed for bankruptcy on January 24, 2002.[5]

Even one of the most respected Venture Capitalists, Tim Draper from Draper Fisher Jurvetson, can be found proclaiming in a 1999 speech, "If you are on the Web, build market share fast. Grow. Move... Use whatever you can to be the biggest one fastest... Win. Grow big, fast, and just win. Be the winner. You don't want to be number two. [You] just don't.."[6]

It took a 77.9% drop on NASDAQ and a 35.4% drop in the Dow Jones Industrial Average[7] for people to finally overcome these years of "Irrational Exuberance," the term coined by former Federal Reserve Chairman Alan Greenspan in his December 5, 1996 speech.

According to *Fortune*, on September 27, 1999, there were eight American billionaires thirty-five or younger. Of this group, today, only three remain billionaires: Michael Dell of Dell Computers, Jeff Bezos of Amazon.com, and Pierre Omidyar of eBay.

So what did these entrepreneurs do right to propel their companies from an idea to household names? And how did they keep their company solid when so many other technology and Internet stocks were faltering?

Simply put, all three effectively implemented the benefits of ebusiness, managed their growth, and adapted their business models. Just as in the 1847 British railroad bubble, the businesses that played their cards right, came up with business models that actually made sense, and effectively leveraged the power of the new medium rose as champions.

Further, these companies did not make the mistakes of Beyond.com, Webvan, Etoys, Pets.com, Peapod. They did not overload on debt, they did not spend endlessly simply to gain market share, they did not make the mistakes of Enron and WorldCom; they kept their accounting clean, and they utilized the advantages of ebusiness while keeping within classic business logic.

The fundamentals of business are still very much the same. One must still have a source of capital to start up, provide a product or service that the market desires, build a quality team, market a product or service, and accurately account for sales and expenses.

While the advent of computers, the Internet, ecommerce, and ebusiness may not have changed the underlying fundamentals of business, the techniques used to execute the goals of a business have changed. The Information Age has brought improved supply-chain management, enterprise-class database solutions, better customer relationship management, and productivity-increasing Intranets.

While the fundamentals of marketing have held constant, the techniques used to manage the four Ps of marketing (product, place, price, promotion) have been radically altered, new markets have opened, laws have changed, and what was once the smart distribution method often is no longer the most profitable.

> "While the fundamentals of marketing have held constant, the techniques used to manage the four Ps of marketing have been radically altered, new markets have opened, laws have changed, and what was once the smart distribution method often is no longer the most profitable."

If you do not understand these changes, no matter if you are a Fortune 500 CEO or a small time entrepreneur you will be hard pressed to succeed. You will very soon begin to feel just like Mahathir Mohamad did in late 1997 after the Asian financial crisis had put his Malaysian economy in ruin. "This is an unfair world," he stated.[8] This new world is indeed unfair if you do not understand the changes Globalization (increasing free trade, capital flows, and interconnectedness of markets) and the Information Age have brought to markets and business over the past decade and a half.

Welcome to the Post-1989 World

On October 11, 1998, Merrill Lynch stated in a full-page ad in major newspapers, the world is only ten years old. "It was born when the Wall fell in 1989... The spread of free markets and democracy around the world is permitting more people everywhere to turn their aspirations into achievements. And technology, properly harnessed and liberally distributed, has the power to erase not just geographical borders but also human ones."[9]

Today, this world is approaching its eighteenth birthday. The Industrial Age ended and the Information Age began in 1989 with the fall of the Berlin Wall, and continued with the breakup of the U.S.S.R., the opening of new markets, the democratization of finance, the mass-utilization of the Internet, the advancement of telecommunications, and the spread of globalization.

Since we began to reap the benefits of the peace dividend, more or less intact since 1974, there have been three breeds of entrepreneurs. The first consists of people like Oracle CEO Larry Ellison, EDS billionaire Ross Perot, and yes, even Bill Gates, now over 50. These guys "got it" back in the day before the Internet. They were the "transformation entrepreneurs" and were integral in bringing the United States into the Information Age.

Next on the scene were the guys and girls that grew up with Commodore 64s, Atari, and Ronald Reagan. From this first breed of Internet Age entrepreneurs came people like Jerry Yang, CEO of Yahoo!, Pierre Omidyar of eBay, and Jeff Bezos of Amazon.com. All born more or less in the late sixties, these guys grew up watching the development of computers and were prepared to jump on the opportunity they saw in late 1994. They did well, and their companies tripled and quadrupled each year from 1995-1999. These guys were the frontrunners and were intelligent enough to see the possibility of the Internet twelve or thirteen years ago, perhaps the reason why all three of these companies are still around today.

The Joys of Irrational Exuberance

While these three companies have survived, there have been thousands that have not. On November 13, 1998, Theglobe.com was one of the first .com's to go public.[10] It offered its Initial Public Offering shares at $9. By the end of that day, its valuation was 605% higher at $63.50 a share. Today you'll see that highly sought after stock just eight years ago is now just a few pennies per share on the Over the Counter (OTC) market. In mid 2002 their web site proclaimed, "In 1995, theglobe.com confirmed the Internet's power to connect people worlds apart. Unfortunately, after six amazing years, theglobe.com closed its doors on August 15, 2001"[11]

During these high flying days, profligate spending on things such as Aeron® chairs, flat-screen televisions, game rooms, pizza parties, and massage breaks was the norm. It seemed like it would never end. Many thought it would not.

So what was it that caused the speculative bubble between 1997 and 2000? During this time, it was commonly believed that because of new technology, great gains in productivity, and the potential market size the Internet opened up, that company valuations, and in turn the stock prices of those companies, were not confined by the same Old Economy rules. Valuations were based upon multiples of hits to a web site instead of net profits.

Alan Greenspan, the former Chairman of the Federal Reserve, first noted the development of this speculative bubble in late 1996. Much mystique surrounded Greenspan during his tenure, and for good reason. He was the maestro of the United States Central Banking System from 1987 to 2006. Euphemisms referring to Greenspan ranged from simply "Superhuman" to "the Delphic oracle of global financial markets." He was perhaps the second most powerful man in the world during his time in office.

On December 5, 1996 at The American Enterprise Institute for Public Policy Research in Washington, D.C., Greenspan gave a speech in which he made the following important statement, "How do we know when irrational exuberance has unduly escalated asset values, which then become subject to unexpected and prolonged contractions, as they have in Japan over the past decade? And how do we factor that into monetary policy?"[11] Although missed by most in attendance at the time, press reviews and later remarks made it clear that Greenspan was implying that irrational exuberance existed in the market and that the financial markets were overvalued.

Between October 16, 1990 and the date of Greenspan's speech, the Dow Jones Industrial Average (DJIA) had increased by 170.3% and the NASDAQ was up 299.5%.[8] Further, at the time of his speech, the historical Price to Earnings (P/E) ratio on the Standard and Poor's 500, a key indicator of speculation, was 23, far above the historical mean since 1926 of 16.[9] The bulls of the markets had been out for the past six years and Greenspan was worried that irrational exuberance was creating a speculative bubble in the financial markets.

That night the Tokyo market panicked and closed down 3 percent, its largest loss of the year. Hong Kong fell almost 3 percent. Frankfurt dropped 4 percent, and London was down 2 percent.

However, the Dow recovered later that day and would continue its bullish streak. There were no reiterated warnings by Greenspan and for quite some time no monetary policy actions such as increasing interest rates were taken. In fact, the Federal Reserve did not begin to significantly raise the interest rates until August of 1999, nearly three years later.[8]

From the date of Greenspan's speech until March 10, 2000 the NASDAQ gained 288.3%, bringing the total gain since January of 1995 to 579.0%.[4] In layman's terms, this means that after Greenspan's speech, the market nearly quadrupled. The speculation continued, at an increasing rate.

This time, 1996 until 2000, in the United States was one of the most prosperous times in the history of mankind. With the advent of increasingly powerful computers, sophisticated software, the Internet, and other technological innovations, productivity and corporate profits were increasing tremendously and many thought we had entered a New Economy in which these gains could be sustained.

With the dot com era exploding, entrepreneurial ventures wildly succeeding, and trillions in capital flowing into U.S. markets, it would have been a very unpopular decision to try to dampen the economy. The bubble grew and grew, pushed by new rhetoric and a new culture of excess. If you could go one day without hearing the words paradigm or revolutionize somehow combined in the same sentence with CRM or ROI, you must have been on a deserted island.

"With the dot com era exploding, entrepreneurial ventures wildly succeeding, and trillions in capital flowing into U.S. markets, it would have been a very unpopular decision to try to dampen the economy. The bubble grew and grew, pushed by new rhetoric and a new culture of excess."

The Causes of the Dot Com Crash

After seeing two years of almost unbelievable growth, by mid 1998 almost every young MBA in America either worked at a .com or was thinking about starting one up. In a figurative sense, Silicon Valley was Mecca and hundreds of thousands of Americans had suddenly become Muslim. An associate of mine and Princeton graduate that I worked with made the trek in late 1999, only to go right back to the east coast six months later.

In the *Ten Second Internet Manager* Mark Brier, former CEO of Beyond.com, tells of his hiring away dozens and dozens of marketing MBAs from traditional consumer product firms like Coca Cola and Johnson & Johnson. He goes on to say, "You really can't demand that all your employees have Internet experience. It just hasn't been around long enough." From June 1998 until April 2000 there was an exodus of high caliber professionals from traditional firms to Silicon Valley. Enticed by stock options and the chance of an IPO, who can blame them?

We all know what has happened after April of 2000. However, many of us do not know why it has happened. You ask ten people and you may get ten different versions of the same story. In my view, there were four reasons that caused the overwhelming majority of Internet companies to fall flat on their face when the bubble popped. These were:

1. Their business plan. While often "inspiring" or "revolutionary", they were never based on sound market research.
2. They spent other people's money unchecked in an effort to gain market share as soon as possible.
3. They had inexperienced teams whose only goal was the fastest possible growth of their company, not long term success.
4. Their company may have made it in the end, but because of the failure of so many others their investor capital was pulled.

So what did we learn? First, it is better to be profitable with 50,000 customers than sinking in debt with 100,000. Rapid growth is not the way to build a solid company. There is nothing wrong with doubling the size of your company each year, but doubling the size of your company every month is generally not healthy for long-term prospects. If you're going to start a company that you hope to gross a billion dollars next year, make sure you have experience, an experienced team, and experienced advisors to guide you along the way. The problem for most companies was that the novelty of the Internet made it impossible to hire anyone with experience. It's not a good situation when neither your VCs nor your VPs understand what is going on.

This second breed of entrepreneurs has made mistakes, but they are learning from their mistakes and the successful ones are not repeating them. As I mentioned earlier, I feel lucky that I've been able to watch one of the greatest business lessons in history, prior to starting my career as an entrepreneur. Now that we've watched this lesson, we must make sure we do not forget it. Now we know what not to do, let's focus on what changed, why, and what to do.

The Power of Ideas in the World

Just after 9:00am on April 19, 1995 a bomb exploded in the Murrah Federal Building in Oklahoma City, Oklahoma. One hundred sixty-eight people, including 19 children, were killed. The building was damaged to such an extent that it was later demolished. The death and destruction demonstrates not only the power of the bomb but also the power of ideas. That day the power of neo-Nazi ideas about "white power," "racial purity," Jews, and other races and ethnic groups was shown.

Within business, many examples exist of the power of ideas. In the mid 1970s a nineteen-year-old by the name of Bill Gates came up with an idea that has made him the wealthiest man in the world; that computers would need software and an operating system. It was a computer company started out of a dorm by Michael Dell that has dwarfed the goliath at that time, IBM. How? With simply an idea – the idea to sell personal computers directly to customers instead of through distributors and retailers.

On a smaller scale, a lady by the name of Ruta Fox started a diamond ring company a few years ago. One would think that the barriers to entry and the competition in the diamond jewelry business would preclude a young lady with just $3,000 in savings from building a successful company. However, it is often not the amount of money, but rather the quality of the idea. Instead of going the usual route (developing a line of products and perhaps putting them in a catalog or trying to get her line picked up by department stores), she decided she would focus on one product.

Ms. Fox had an inspiration one day. She figured, "Married and engaged women had their rings, but what about the single woman?" She decided to do something about this and came out with the "Ah Ring" as she called it, the ring for Available and Happy single women.

A few weeks later, friends at fashion magazines invited her to their offices to present the rings for sale to staff members. One day while at the headquarters for "O," Oprah Winfrey's magazine, an editor liked the idea and sent a ring off to Oprah. It turned out that Oprah loved the idea and mentioned it in her next issue of "O".

By the end of that first year, Ms. Fox had turned her simple yet novel idea into a company with revenues in excess of $1 million. The point is simply, it is not how hard you work; it is how smart you work, how well you execute, and how good your ideas are. For anyone wanting to learn more about this concept, I would suggest reading a book by Napoleon Hill by the title of *Think and Grow Rich*.

The Democratization of Wealth

In the Information Age, it is not she who works the hardest that succeeds; it is she who has the best ideas and is able to execute best. While yes there still are considerable barriers to entry in many industries, no longer are the poor stuck being poor. With education (in the classroom or not), the right ideas, the courage to take calculated and educated risks, an entrepreneurial spirit, and a bias toward action almost anyone can become a millionaire (in US Dollars) and with a little more of the above ingredients, become a billionaire. Wealth has been democratized.

"With education (in the classroom or not), the right ideas, the courage to take calculated and educated risks, an entrepreneurial spirit, and a bias toward action almost anyone can become a millionaire (in US Dollars) and with a little more of the above ingredients, become a billionaire. Wealth has been democratized."

The Industrial Age paradigm of go to school, get a secure job, and work hard is very unlikely to make you very rich. MIT economist Lester C. Thurow argues in his book *Building Wealth* that the movement from the Industrial Age to the Information Age has created considerable economic disequilibria, creating the possibility for considerable economic gain.

The first step on this road to wealth is to understand what is occurring in our world today. This is why I wanted to spend some time on this topic before I delved into the specific business and marketing principles and techniques that will enable you to capitalize on this disequilibrium.

A New Generation of Entrepreneurs

Since the start of the technology age there have been three generations of entrepreneurs. The first generation consisted of people like Oracle CEO Larry Ellison, EDS billionaire Ross Perot, and yes, even Bill Gates, now over 50. These guys "got it" back in the day before the Internet. They were the "transformation entrepreneurs" and were integral in bringing the United States into the Information Age.

Next on the scene were the guys and girls that grew up with Commodore 64s, Atari, and Ronald Reagan. From this first breed of Internet Age entrepreneurs came people like Jerry Yang, CEO of Yahoo!, Pierre Omidyar of eBay, and Jeff Bezos of Amazon.com. All born more or less in the late sixties, these guys grew up watching the development of computers and were prepared to jump on the opportunity they saw in late 1994. They did well, and their companies tripled and quadrupled each year from 1995-1999. These guys were the frontrunners and were intelligent enough to see the possibility of the Internet twelve or thirteen years ago, perhaps the reason why all three of these companies are still around today.

There is a new breed of entrepreneurs that is already beginning to make their mark on our world. I am one of them. We are the eighties generation. We are as the music group POD says, "The Youth of the Nation." While yes, there are many of us who are disillusioned, uncaring, or depressed; I am seeing today something that creates hope. There is a subculture of youth in both the United States and in every country in the world that gets it.

I am very fortunate to have contacts in about forty countries. In 2000, I was lucky enough to receive a scholarship to go on a 53-day expedition to Spain, Florida, New Mexico, and Mexico called La Ruta Quetzal. On this trip I met three hundred fifty students from forty-three different countries. It has truly been priceless to be able to have these contacts. For example, during the Argentinean economic collapse in early 2002 I was able to jump on my computer and email Ana from Buenos Aires to see what the real situation was like. When a U.S. spy-plane was shot down in China in April 2001, I was able to email my friend Sonsoles in Beijing to get her take on the incident and her thoughts on what Jiang Zemin would do.

During the World Cup in June of 2002 I was able to chat live with my friend Kevin in Dublin as he grieved over each missed penalty kick in Ireland's overtime elimination defeat to Spain. For the pre-1980 people reading, would it not have amazed you when you were seventeen to have had the ability to chat live from Florida with your friend in Dublin while both watching the same penalty shot being taken at the exact same time in Seoul, South Korea?

This new breed of entrepreneurs, even if we all do not yet fully grasp the impact of globalization and how important the changes that are occurring today truly are, are either going through college right now or will in the next five years. The case studies they will have in Financial Management 202 will not be the rudimentary mathematical bores they perhaps were for many in their college days of old. They will be riveting tales of unlimited wealth, power, and innovation; in some cases collapse and fraud and in others extraordinary success.

I said a few paragraphs ago "there is a subculture of youth in both the United States and in every country in the world that gets it." But what it is that we get? We understand the following ten principles:

1. The world is global and interconnected. A negative economic report from one country can ravage the economy of a continent overnight, a trillion dollars can leave a country with the click of a few mice, and an explosion in Shanghai can cause bond prices in London to jump 10% within an hour.

2. Anyone with $1000 and some intelligence can either make a billion dollars or destroy the world.

3. In our economic prosperity, we must strive toward creating a sustainable existence or else the end of our lives and our children's lives will be years of difficulty and sacrifice.

4. Academic education is important, but at all but the best schools, an academic education will not give one the knowledge needed to be financially prosperous. As Thomas J. Stanley states in *The Millionaire Mind*, having a 1000 or 1500 on your SATs has no correlation to your likely net worth in twenty years. Just as important, if not more, is one's education and learning outside the classroom.

5. If one is going to become extraordinarily wealthy they better have integrity, ethics, and keep their accounting truthful and accurate.

6. Competitive market economies are essential to a high standard of living. An incentive system is necessary to get workers to work and a price system is necessary to properly allocate a limited supply of resources and goods. Competition is necessary to keep everyone honest and working efficiently to produce the optimum output with the minimum input. Although some believe capitalism creates inequities and is immoral, it is a few of the participants within this system that cause these unfair inequities. This lack of integrity among some participants will always be present. However, due to intelligent laws, regulations, oversight and the inherent positive properties of the market coupled with democracy such as transparency, freedom of the press, and a better educated proletariat this ethical problem is better now than in the days of centralized ownership of resources and dictatorships. Since there is no incentive to earn a profit or innovate, state-owned enterprises often breed inefficiency.

7. However, without honest, ethical, and compassionate people at the helm of a democratic and market system, or the proper laws and legal institutions to ensure this integrity, this system is no better than totalitarianism, autarky, or anarchy.

8. For prosperity to spread to developing countries we must not look to short run elixirs. It took 175 years to turn the U.S. into an economic superpower. The same change cannot take place in Somalia, Zimbabwe, or Afghanistan without the proper development of human capital, industrial capital, and a fundamental legal framework.

9. It is not he who works the hardest that succeeds; it is he who has the best ideas, works with the most intelligence, and builds the right team to help him accomplish his goals.

10. The ability to adapt to change and ability to learn quickly is as important as what you know right now. The world is going to change in tremendous ways over our lifetime.

Those that do not grasp these principles will have a hard time becoming successful or building a prosperous business. While the large majority of American youth do not (at least yet) have the faintest idea of what these principles are or what they mean, there is a growing minority that does. While progress is being made with the help of organizations such as Junior Achievement, the public secondary educational system of the United States, in many places, at times seems that instead of teaching the above principles it is teaching students to be provincial, closed-minded, economically-challenged, and financially inept. It almost seems if students in the American education system are taught from 1 st through 12 th grade to believe that the U.S. is the only country in the world, the only one that matters, and that our goal after we leave school should be to search for a secure well-paying job. These ideas will not produce the dynamic innovators and leaders needed to tackle the problems of this new century.

However, there is a growing minority of youth in the U.S. that does understand the world, globalization, a bit of history, and the basic concepts of business and economics. More importantly, the eighties generation throughout most of the rest of the world is not so provincial. On my 2000 Ruta Quetzal Expedition I was embarrassed to only know two languages. Most of the participants, all just fifteen and sixteen like I, knew at least four languages, and some knew as many as six. They not only knew the languages, but they understood the culture of whomever they were speaking with, whether they were Japanese, Swedish, Colombian, American, or Malaysian. The world is growing smaller by the day, and anyone who does not understand world culture, speak another language, or grasp globalization will have a glass ceiling in their profession, in their life, and in their business.

There has been some great progress on this front recently. Books such as *The World is Flat* and *The Lexus and the Olive Tree* by Thomas L. Friedman, *The Commanding Heights* by Daniel Yergin and Joseph Stanislaw, *Rich Dad's Guide to Investing* by Robert T. Kiyosaki, *Globalization and Its Discontents* by Joseph E. Stiglitz, and *Reinventing the Bazaar* by John McMillan enlighten us all.

This new breed of entrepreneurs did not grow up with 15% inflation, the Commodore 64, or Ronald Reagan (although I did love to play my Space Invaders game on my used Atari when very young). Instead, we have grown up with Nintendo and Sega Genesis, MTV, Bill Clinton, the World Trade Center attack, and most importantly, the Internet.

I was eleven, not twelve and not thirteen, but eleven. It was 1995 and I was helping people who were 40, 50, 60, 70, 80, and 90 learn to use their computer, send emails, browse the web, and write a letter without a typewriter. More often it is the four year old that is teaching her dad how to attach a picture to an email, or the seven year old showing his uncle how to burn a CD, than the other way round.

Right now I am 23. Anyone my age or younger will understand what I am about to say. I do not know what the world was like before the Internet. Let me repeat this—I do not know what the world was like before the Internet. Yes, of course I have memories before 1994, but to be honest I really didn't understand how the world worked back then. I did not read the paper too often then and only rarely watched Tom Brokaw or Dan Rather. I have grown up to know routers, Intranets, FTP access codes, HTML, and ecommerce.

This new breed of entrepreneurs; the investment bankers, analysts, economists, options traders, politicians, business owners, leaders, and entrepreneurs of 2005-2065, understand technology and they use it every hour of their waking lives.

We understand the above eleven principles. We know we live in a global interconnected village. We know the government will likely not be able to take care of us in old age. We know we must be responsible for our education and our financial well-being. We know that there is extreme suffering, sacrifice, and corruption in many parts of this world that will not cease unless we do something about it. We understand technology and understand the changes that have taken place in business and the business and economic lessons that have been taught to us over the past five years. In order to build a successful business you will need to understand these things.

This new breed will not be a typical, usual group. Who is to say that our generation cannot develop a more effective way at ensuring essential nutrients and enough food gets to those in need? Who is to say that we cannot double the standard of living in my lifetime or consign absolute poverty in developing nations to the dustbin of history?

This new generation is already doing remarkable things. Just read this excerpt from the May 29, 2002 issue of *Business Week*:

> Never before have teens had the know-how, the access, and the tools at their disposal to pursue business on an equal footing with adults. The number of teens doing some kind of business on the Net is already a lot bigger than many grownups would ever expect. For every teen millionaire, there is a veritable swarm of regular kids who routinely earn pocket money doing software work via the Net. It's impossible to pinpoint exact numbers, but they are large. Researcher Computer Economics Inc. in Carlsbad, Calif., estimates that 8% of all teens, about 1.6 million in the U.S., are making at least some money on the Net. "There's not a period in history where we've seen such a plethora of young entrepreneurs," says Nancy F. Koehn, associate professor of business administration at Harvard Business School.

The article goes on to talk about teen entrepreneurs that have made hundreds of thousands or millions of dollars over the past six years by creating popular web sites, developing software programs, and consulting for businesses. Personally, in my own work with the Carolina Entrepreneurship Club and the Collegiate Entrepreneurs Organization I have come into contact with many fellow young entrepreneurs. It seems to me that many in our generation surely do understand the great opportunity we have and the special time we are in. No matter what your age is, if you can learn these same principles we have learned, you will greatly increase your chances at building a successful business.

In the coming decades, new leaders will appear who have grown up with technology being a part of their lives for as long as they can remember. This new generation will intrinsically understand the principles of a global world and be much more effective in building successful companies than any person who does not. Whether or not you are in this generation, you better understand these principles.

> "There is only one way to make a great deal of money; and that is in a business of your own."
>
> – J. Paul Getty, once the richest man in America

The Role of the Entrepreneur in the Market System

Let's start things off with a question. What is needed to create wealth? Within the marketplace, there are many resources that go into the production of goods and services. These resources can be grouped into four categories. These categories are **land**, **labor**, **capital**, and **entrepreneurial ability**.

The resource of entrepreneurial ability is where you come into play. It is the entrepreneur that organizes and arranges the use of land, labor, and capital to create an output demanded by the marketplace. It is the entrepreneur's responsibility to decide on what amounts of each resource to use and then use those resources efficiently to create a product or service that is valued higher by the marketplace than the collective value of the resource inputs. As Campbell R. McConnell and Stanley L. Brue say in *Economics*, "Both a sparkplug and a catalyst, the entrepreneur is at once the driving force behind production and the agent who combines the other resources in what is hoped will be a profitable venture."

The entrepreneur is the catalyst that brings together the resources of land, labor, and capital to create valuable goods and services and in the hopes of building a profitable business. The word entrepreneur is of French origin and derives from *entreprendre*, which means to undertake. The American Heritage Dictionary defines an entrepreneur as "a person who organizes, operates, and assumes the risk for a business venture."

> "Without the entrepreneur and the system that provides incentives for entrepreneurs, we would have no printing press, no bifocals, no airplane, no air conditioner, no radio, no microwave, no computer, no telephone, no television, and no George Foreman Lean Mean Fat Burning Grilling Machine."

The entrepreneur plays a vital role in society. Without entrepreneurs, there would be no businesses, no inventions, no innovation, no progress, and no wealth. Without the entrepreneur and the system that provides incentives for entrepreneurs, we would have no printing press, no bifocals, no airplane, no air conditioner, no radio, no microwave, no computer, no telephone, no television, and no George Foreman Lean Mean Fat Burning Grilling Machine. In short, the standard of living would not be much better than that of 1450. The world would not be able to support the 6.5 billion persons it does, and the doomsday Malthusian predictions of overpopulation would have been realized many decades, if not centuries ago.

If it is your goal to become an entrepreneur, whether by running a small business in your home town or launching a high potential venture with VC funding, you should be commended. While being an entrepreneur is surely not for everybody, if you are the type who has a bias toward action, brings efficiency and innovation into everything you do, creates systems and processes, is not afraid to make mistakes, can build and inspire a quality team, and will persist until pigs fly in a frozen over hell while the cows come home and the Cubs win the pennant, you deserve a pat on the back. You are an entrepreneur. In mind, in body, in spirit, in soul—you are an entrepreneur.

How The System of Entrepreneurship Works

There are many different ways to become wealthy in our world today. You can become rich through inheritance, crime, entertainment, sports, or building a business. There are certain advantages and disadvantages to each method. Receiving an inheritance can be very helpful, but many do not have this option and even those who do often do not know how to properly manage and grow this money once they have it. As a criminal, you can make money fairly easily and very quickly, unfortunately your conscience may get to you, you'll destroy your reputation, and likely spend much of the rest of your life in a jail cell eating pre-packaged thawed lima beans.

One can surely make a lot of money through entertainment but unless you are extremely talented, are a white rapper, or win American Idol or star in Eurovision, the chances are slim you'll make it. Professional sports is an option. Again, however, the chances are very low and the chance of serious injury, numerous surgeries, and a life of chronic pain, worn cartilage, and sore joints does not sound too appealing.

That leaves being an entrepreneur. While there are many risks to being an entrepreneur, it seems that as long as one learns from his or her mistakes, keeps his or her ear to the marketplace, and persists, he or she will eventually succeed. The dynamic, always changing, life and the chance for significant personal gain make building a business the choice many make who wish to obtain financial security and become wealthy.

There are two ways to build wealth through entrepreneurship. The first way is to build a business and pay yourself a salary. If your business grows large enough to have an ample net profit margin, you can re-invest part in your company and still have enough pay yourself a large salary.

You may personally earn a few hundred thousand dollars per year, and may be happy with this amount, at all times maintaining majority ownership in your company and doing things the way you like to do them while still making time for other commitments such as a family. This method of becoming wealthy is often associated with that of the lifestyle entrepreneur, small business owner, family business owner, and the S corporation. It is surely one option and over time these types of companies can grow to become large organizations.

In order to have the potential to make tens of millions, you'll have to build a high potential company and make the majority of your money when the company goes public or sells to another company. To accomplish this goal, you'll have to develop a novel product or technology, protect your intellectual property, have a good business idea, and build a great team. You'll need to write a business plan and get the right introductions so you get in front of and when needed raise money from accredited private investors, angel investors, or venture capitalists, in turn giving up a portion of ownership to the investors.

You'll have to bring on a top tier team, in turn giving up a good part of the remaining ownership to your initial founders and top performers. You'll need to bring on additional products, build systems and processes, outsource operations across the globe, launch international marketing campaigns, use derivatives to hedge risk in overseas currency markets, and attract seasoned executives and newly minted MBAs to your growing firm.

You'll need to attract a solid Board of Directors led by representatives of your investors and industry leaders. And you'll have to reach proof of concept, raise a second and third round of financing, ensure your books meet GAAP standards, expand market share, and turn profitable.

"You'll need to attract a solid Board of Directors led by representatives of your investors and industry leaders. And you'll have to reach proof of concept, raise a second and third round of financing, ensure your books meet GAAP standards, expand market share, and turn profitable."

Finally, you'll have to attract potential acquirers or talk to investment bankers about going public. If a company wishes to buy your company, you'll go through a process of extensive due diligence and evaluation. If you choose to go public, you'll file form S-1 with the Securities and Exchange Commission, have a prospectus created, and go on an investor road show to pitch the merits of investing in your company.

Finally, you'll sell, part or all of your company—either to an acquirer or the public markets. Your equity, your ownership, will soon be liquid and you'll be able to cash in on the past six years of ninety-hour weeks. You may make $5 million or you may make $500 million—dependent on the market capitalization of your company and the amount of equity you were able to retain through all the financing rounds and option pool dilutions.

This is how, at the basic level, the system of entrepreneurship works. Going public or selling a company is a dream for many high potential entrepreneurs.

If you can start with a product that the market demands, raise funding, build a good team, establish market share, turn profitable, add additional products and revenue streams, and position yourself as a market leader in your niche, you'll make it. This process is not exactly easy, however, and more often than not, even the most experienced, well educated, well connected entrepreneurs fail at following this path. It can often take three or four tries, each taking 4-5 years of an entrepreneur's life, to take a venture public or have a highly successful exit.

> "If you can start with a product that the market demands, raise funding, build a good team, establish market share, turn profitable, add additional products and revenue streams, and position yourself as a market leader in your niche, you'll make it."

Which Type of Business to Start

Let's take a minute to analyze the pros and cons of starting a high potential and lifestyle business. Lifestyle companies include small consulting companies, local restaurants, laundromats, barber shops, hardware stores, or any kind of franchise. Generalizing, lifestyle businesses are local businesses that will likely never have yearly sales greater than $5,000,000 in a year.

The advantages of starting a lifestyle company include being able to control the company, being able to continue to do what you love without having too much risk, having a positive cash flow from the early going, only having to report to yourself, having a relatively constant cash flow, and being able to take time off whenever you want. Disadvantages include not being able to hire top talent (as talented people usually avoid companies that offer no stock options and only limited opportunities for personal growth) and not having the chance for huge gains.

High potential companies, on the other hand, generally are either developing a product (that they will sell internationally), are based on a technological breakthrough or change in regulatory environment, or are raising venture capital to explore a lucrative opportunity. These companies are usually C corporations, and if they succeed, have the possibility of getting to the $50,000,000 in annual sales within five years.

The advantages of starting a high potential company include the possibility for large returns on your investment, the ability to attract outside investment, and the ability to build a great team who will work with you to make your company succeed. Disadvantages include the usual necessity for the company to take on large amounts of debt or lose significant amounts of equity, a loss of control as investors and employees dilute the founder's equity, and the long wait to reach positive cash flow.

On the topic of lifestyle versus high-potential ventures, Harvard Business School researcher Amar Bhide, in his article "Questions Every Entrepreneur Must Answer" writes

> The company of a lifestyle entrepreneur does not need to grow very large. A business that becomes too big might prevent the founder from enjoying life or remaining personally involved in the work. In contrast, entrepreneurs seeking capital gains must build companies large enough to support an infrastructure that will not require their day-to-day intervention.

There is surely no right or wrong choice here. You just have to make sure the choice you make syncs with your goals. If you are able to take a huge risk and are shooting at a five year payout of $10,000,000 then you will need to start a business that fits within the high-potential category. However, if you are unable or do not wish to take a large risk, or are content making a few hundred thousand dollars per year with the potential for a larger return over an extending period, a lifestyle business may be for you.

To better analyze which is for you, take a look at the following chart that lists the key differences between lifestyle and high-potential companies.

Figure 6-1 – Differences between lifestyle and high potential ventures

Key Difference	Lifestyle Company	High-Potential Venture
Exit Strategy	None	Acquisition or IPO
Ownership	Founder is majority owner	No majority owner, CEO owns 5-30% of company
Financing	Bootstrapped, organic growth, or self-financed	Angel investors or venture capitalists for seed round. Additional rounds until cash flow positive or sold.
What is Sold	Services or products with low differentiation	Products with proprietary intellectual property or based on recent changes or new technology or high margin and value add services.
Family Members	Often part of business	Infrequently part of business
Entity Type	Sole proprietorship, partnership, LLC, or S Corporation	C Corporation, usually incorporated in Delaware
Market	Local or regional	National or international
Failure Rate	High	Very High
Founders Makes Money From	Net profits/Dividends	Liquidity event and sale of equity
Board of Directors	Composed of company members	Composed of investors, industry leaders, and one or two company heads
Systems	Fewer processes or systems. Often only make money while open.	Many processes and systems. Make money even while owners are sleeping or operated around the clock.
International sales	Few	Many. May be international offices and/or manufacturing operations.

Hopefully this chart will be of help to you as you align your personal goals with your business goals. On this topic, Amar Bhide continues to say:

If entrepreneurs find that their businesses, even if very successful, won't satisfy them personally, or if they discover that achieving their personal goals requires them to take more risks and make more sacrifices than they are willing to, they need to reset their goals.

If you have yet to do so, I encourage you to commit your personal goals to writing. Analyze the reasons you wish to start a business. Then take a look at the amount of risk you wish to take at this point in your life and the return you hope to achieve and go from there.

How to Get Out of the Middle Class

Let's analyze the key decisions that one must make in life to be on the path toward becoming wealthy. The large majority of persons (at least in the developed world) work at a job, earn $30,000-$60,000 per year and spend nearly all, if not more, of their incomes each year. At the end of forty years of working many of these persons must live the last years of their life dependent on Social Security and their 401(k). Many of these persons are content with such a life, which is of course fine. However, many are not. If you are not, then please read on.

The wealthy, on the other hand build assets, invest in assets, and have their assets work for them. Assets are items that generate positive cashflow. The wealthy certainly are willing to work at a job for a period of time, but the experience and contacts they gain from a position is much more important than the initial salary to them. They gain control over their expenses. What they save during a year is more important than the salary they earn.

The wealthy put off present consumption and purchase of luxuries like vacations, boats, and big screen televisions so they can invest in building an asset that will provide enough passive cash flow to buy twenty vacations, a cruise line, and a big screen television company in the future. They never go into debt for something that is for pleasure and not investment. They buy things like businesses, securities, options, bonds, and real estate. They intelligently use their businesses to pay many of their expenses, thus receiving numerous tax advantages. They use their expenses to make them richer, and have no fear of debt, as long as they are using debt to build an asset and not purchase unnecessary items.

The poor often live frugally, not realizing that time is more important than money. The rich realize that time is more valuable than money as with time one can make money but with money one cannot make time. They understand the principal of opportunity cost and do not hesitate to spend $1000 for someone to paint their house if during that time they can make $2000 working at what they do best.

The rich have their money work for them. They do their due diligence and research and invest it in public and private companies, and then sit back while their money makes them more money. They build companies that make them money while they are sleeping. Most mornings they will wake up richer than when they went to bed.

They realize the importance of developing multiple streams of income and creating passive cashflow—money that comes in whether or not they go to work. They stay out of the middle and lower classes by waiting, if possible, until they have consistent passive cashflow from their businesses and investments before they become married and have children.

While the rich may have to start off making money through earned income, they realize the advantages of and focus on building passive income from investments. The rich also know that they cannot become wealthy overnight, and they invest the time, gain the knowledge, make the contacts, and take the actions needed to become successful.

"The rich also know that they cannot become wealthy overnight, and they invest the time, gain the knowledge, make the contacts, and take the actions needed to become successful."

The rich keep close track of their cash flow. They have accountants and in the early stages use programs such as QuickBooks, Quicken, and Money to keep track of all of their income and expenses, both personally and in their companies.

The validity of the above principles is made clear to me each and every day in my life. There is a terrible disparity between the rich and poor, even in the streets of Chapel Hill, North Carolina. While certainly some of this disparity is caused by a lack of equality of opportunity, some of it is there for reasons beside differences in education and opportunity. Some of this disparity exists because those who are poor did not know the above principles.

The poor work for others and not themselves, will spend more money than they earn and go into debt for unnecessary items, will never delay present consumption to invest, never take the initiative to improve their financial literacy and business education, and are married and have children before they have a well paying job, let alone a stream of passive and portfolio income. Don't let your life go down this path, and if it has, learn and apply the above principles in everything you do and you will make it.

The Secret to Becoming Rich

Robert Kiyosaki states in *Rich Dad's Guide to Investing* that the secret to becoming rich is to "build businesses and then have your businesses buy other cash producing assets such as other businesses or real estate." This statement captures the essence of the process needed to become extraordinarily wealthy. I would modify this statement slightly, however. I believe the following:

> **The secret to becoming extraordinarily wealthy is to build businesses and then use the excess cash flow from your businesses and the capital gains from any liquidity events to invest in future ventures, early stage private companies, emerging markets, and other cash producing assets such as real estate.**

Please reread this statement a few times. This is the path I will follow throughout my life. I am currently in the process of building a successful business. Once this is accomplished and we're able to sell to the private or public markets, I will use the funds to make additional investments in early stage private companies, build additional companies, invest in real estate, and explore investments in other countries. I intend to make my first twenty million dollars by building companies. I'll make my next hundred million by investing half my assets in my future businesses, private equity, hedge funds, venture capital, and real estate, while keeping half of my assets allocated in small cap stocks, emerging market indexes, and commodity index funds.

It's important to remember that financial security and financial prosperity should be looked at as a **long-term game**. If you are 30 and are $40,000 in debt, make a goal to have this debt paid off by 35. Then by 40, make a goal to have $200,000 in bank. Then by 45, to become a millionaire. Take it one step at a time, work with five year plans, and each day make sure you're working toward your long-term goal. It will become easier and easier as you gain in experience and contacts and as you are able to leverage your existing capital to help create more capital.

If you're young, consider saving up what you can and opening an online trading account with E*trade or TD Ameritrade. In my experience, the easiest thing to do if you don't want to actively manage your investments is to put your assets in no-load index funds. I have put 50% of my overall liquid assets in a portfolio that is structured as follows: 35% in a small-cap index fund, 15% in a mid-cap index fund, 25% in an emerging markets index fund, and 25% in a commodities index fund.

While I am not qualified to give financial advice and I would certainly recommend consulting a financial advisor, if you can get $15,000 into a portfolio by age 25 that closely matches the market and not touch it until 65 and let the returns compound, you would have $471,000 after inflation by the time you retire (assuming an average inflation-adjusted annual return of 9%). If you can get $15,000 into a portfolio structured similar to this by age 25 and commit to putting $1,500 per year into the portfolio, you will have $1,023,000 after inflation by the time you retire. A little sacrifice early on can make a big difference down the road and allow you to feel safer taking larger risks such as starting your own business with the other 50% of the money you save.

Are You Right for Entrepreneurship?

Being an entrepreneur is not for everyone. Not everyone can handle the stress, risks, and responsibilities of having dozens or hundreds of persons' lives depending on your choices or reporting to a board of directors or panel of your investors. An analysis of the traits commonly found among successful entrepreneurs may assist in deciding if you are right to be an entrepreneur.

Here is a list of commonly noted traits of entrepreneurs. Put a check next to each one you believe you have.

☐ Initiative
☐ Bias toward action
☐ Vision
☐ Determination
☐ Courage
☐ Creativity
☐ Perseverance and persistence
☐ A Drive to achieve

☐ Orientation toward opportunity
☐ An Ability to deal with the abstract and ambiguity
☐ An Ability to prioritize
☐ Drive toward efficiency
☐ Ability to take feedback
☐ Tolerance for stress
☐ Decisiveness
☐ An Ability to deal with failure

☐ An Ability to learn from mistakes

☐ An Ability to delay gratification

☐ An Ability to plan

☐ An Ability to build a team

☐ An Ability to inspire and lead

Do you have these attributes? If you checked more than half, you may have what it takes to become a successful entrepreneur.

As part of a series of interviews I conducted with six successful entrepreneurs in North Carolina for this book, I asked the question, "What traits are most important for an aspiring entrepreneur to have." I gave the entrepreneurs fifteen options and asked them to number their choices 1 through 15 in order of importance. The results were very interesting. The most important trait for aspiring entrepreneurs to have, according to these five successful entrepreneurs, was "The Ability to Build a Solid Team". The second and third most important skills were, "Leadership & the Ability to Inspire," and "Persistence." The least important attribute of all, number fifteen, was "A College Degree." Here are the full results in order of importance.

1. Being able to build a solid team
2. Leadership & the ability to inspire
3. Persistence
4. Motivation & ambition
5. Integrity
6. Ability to communicate effectively
7. Confidence
8. Being able to execute
9. Having a bias toward action
10. Having a good idea or plan
11. Knowledge of marketing
12. Good networking skills
13. Having the right advisors
14. Knowledge of accounting & finance
15. A college degree

Would you work seventy hour plus weeks for months on end, sleep at the office when you get backed up, put your own money on the line when payroll is due and the bank has yet to approve a loan, be the janitor, the receptionist, the custom support representative, the bookkeeper, as well as

> "Would you work seventy hour plus weeks for months on end, sleep at the office when you get backed up, put your own money on the line when payroll is due and the bank has yet to approve a loan."

the President, and get up and present in front of a room of investors, after already being turned down by 50 other banks, angel investors, and venture capital firms? If you think so, then you just might have what it takes to become a successful entrepreneur.

There is no successful entrepreneur that would say building a successful company is easy and there is no one who would say that there is no risk involved in building a company. If building a company were easy, there were no risk, and it did not take years of dedication and persistence, everyone would be an entrepreneur. Unfortunately, the market has little compassion. It doesn't pull for the person who works the hardest or the person who has the best idea. It pulls for the person who works the most intelligently, sells what the market demands, puts together the needed resources, gets deals done, and executes.

Let's take a look at the best and worst things about being an entrepreneur.

Highlight 4: The Best & Worst Things about Being an Entrepreneur

Date of first publication: April 20, 2003, Reprinted from www.zeromillion.com with permission.

An alien lands on Earth. After a few days she finds out that she is going to need some money in order to purchase food and shelter. Daringdo has a choice. Should she become an entrepreneur or get a job? Let's examine the best and worst things about being an entrepreneur so we can help Daringdo make an educated decision.

According to InvestorForce co-founder Colin Wahl, the worst thing about being an entrepreneur is the loneliness. He says, "You are on your own and nobody supports you because it's hard for them to see what you see and feel the excitement that you feel in the early stages."

I would have to agree with Colin on this point. It can indeed be lonely sometimes. One can also become de-motivated after working so hard and so long on something for which the reward may be months or years away or perhaps never come at all.

KendallTodd, Inc. CEO Todd Ballenger says that the worst thing about being an entrepreneur is that you often work 80 hours a week as an entrepreneur to avoid working 40 hours a week as an employee. Posed with the same question, Inspire Pharmaceuticals CEO Christy Shafer says the worst thing is that you are constantly busy and stressed out and have less time for family. Best Friends Pet Care founder Randy Myer says that the worst thing is the impact on your health and your family.

With cash flow problems, having to lay people off, working eighty-hour weeks, the possibility of never being paid for your work, and loneliness, why in the world would anyone want to be an entrepreneur? An extra-terrestrial coming to this planet for the first time would surely choose the safety and security of a job in Corporate America. Or would she?

Before we can be sure, there is another side of the coin we must examine. Along with the negative, there are a number of positive things that go along with being an entrepreneur. While being an entrepreneur is not for everyone, let's examine the upside before you make your final decision.

So what is the positive side? Well, first you have freedom. You have the opportunity to use all your skills. Significant financial reward goes to he who succeeds. You have control over your destiny and will never have to worry about your or your family's financial security. Respect comes from your peers. You have the recognition of being a visionary. You have provided hundreds or thousands of people with jobs and they respect and thank you. You have provided value and efficiency to a market and improved the standard of living of many. Finally, there is no worry about being laid off or not being able to take care of yourself after the value of your 401(k) plan evaporates.

MCNC Chairman Dave Rizzo says, "You have control over your destiny, your calendar, and the vision is yours." Christy Shafer adds, "You are constantly challenged and have fun." Colin Wahl notes, "You have much more control of your own destiny and your entire life!' Randy Myer states, "The best part is the rewards -- financial and psychological."

So what will you choose? Well, in the end this lies with you. However, do remember that we only live once. If you have a good idea, the trust in yourself to execute, a basic knowledge of business, can bring together a good team, feel you are at the right stage in your life, and believe you can afford the risk, I'd highly recommend going for it. But you must get going and start moving.

There is a certain law of inertia that I often reference. A body in motion remains in motion. And while in motion it finds new people and acquires new knowledge that it would not have come in contact with if it was not moving. Once you begin on a quest, that quest will lead you to things unbeknownst to you at the beginning. Once you start on your quest, many new events and pieces of knowledge will fall into place. Inertia will take effect as new knowledge and possibilities create a snowball effect up the learning curve as you come closer and closer to your goal. One should not wait until all the traffic signals are green before he starts his journey.

In the end, it may take awhile to reap the benefits of being an entrepreneur. And you may experience much of the downside along the way. But if you get moving today and are adaptive, persuasive, self-confident, and a visionary, and have perseverance, have a bias towards action, and can inspire others with your leadership, you may just be able to enjoy this upside. As Colin Wahl says, "Go for it, it's an incredible chance of a lifetime – as the saying goes, better to have tried and lost than never to have tried at all! The riskiest thing to do is not to try…then the chance of success is zero. The downside: even if things don't work out you will gain amazing experience that will help you even if you end up having to go back to working for someone else."

So what is the final decision? Will our alien friend decide to be an entrepreneur or an employee? Well, after thinking things over, she decides that she'd be better off applying for a few scholarships, going to school, working on her English and business knowledge, making some contacts, and developing some business plans while interning at a company in the field she is interested in, and then venturing off on her own. Smart alien.

Now let's take a look at what motivates entrepreneurs. What is it, exactly, that makes them work ninety-hour weeks, wake up after five hours of sleep six days per week, and risk their savings and their livelihoods for their dreams?

Part Three:
The Ten Step Process for Building a Company to $1 Million in Sales

Chapter 7 Step 1: Find Your Core Motivation

"If you're alive, there's a purpose for your life."

- Pastor Rick Warren

The second step to building a successful company to is to determine your core motivation. Figuring out the reasons why—why you want to spend the next few years of your life building a company—is absolutely critical to your eventual success.

It takes at least five, maybe seven or ten years to build a successful company. If you are going to spend this much of your life, not to mention your money, sweat, tears, and reputational equity on building an organization—know why. Know that you have a reason to get up each and every day that is strong. A reason so strong that you will be passionate each and every day of your life about achieving your definite chief objective. It must get you out of bed, and it must inspire you to sacrifice.

When deciding which type of company you want to build, you'll have to take a close look at your personal goals. Do you want to attain a certain lifestyle, gain respect, create an innovative product, build an organization that will outlive you, contribute to your community, have an outlet for your talent, or be free from your job?

What are the reasons that you wish to start your business? Do you want to become extraordinarily wealthy, increase efficiency in an industry, have enough income to provide a comfortable life for your family, or travel the world as you grow your firm?

> "Do you want to attain a certain lifestyle, gain respect, create an innovative product, build an organization that will outlive you, contribute to your community, have an outlet for your talent, or be free from your job?"

Take time to write down these reasons. I'd caution going forward building your business without first aligning your plan with your personal goals. If you don't love what you do, it is very difficult to give it your all.

An entrepreneur's personal and business goals are closely linked. Unlike the manager of a public company who has a fiduciary responsibility to maximize value for shareholders, as the founder of a company you have some ability to build your businesses to fulfill personal goals. If you are unsure what these goals are, take out a pen and paper and write down every reason you have for starting a business and what your personal goals are.

Action Item 1 – Know Your Motivations and Goals

Write down every reason you have for starting a business and what your goals are for the business.

_____

_____

_____

_____

_____

_____

_____

Ask yourself, will I be passionate about going after this goal? If you can align what you love with what you do and what you do with what you're passionate about, you will be so much more successful in life and in business—however you define success for yourself.

> "If you can align what you love with what you do and what you do with what you're passionate about, you will be so much more successful in life and in business."

So ask yourself, "What is it that will motivate me to be willing to spend the next few years of my life constructing my vision into a thriving organization."

There can be many motivations. It is rarely one thing that motivates dedicated action within an individual. You could have a desire *to do* something or a desire *for* something.

What Will Motivate You?

You could have a desire:

1. To Create a Great Product
2. To Create Jobs
3. To Play the Game
4. To Change an Industry
5. To Help Your Customers
6. To Change the World
7. For Influence
8. For Recognition
9. For Respect
10. For Money

What's On Your Epitaph?

Here's a thinking exercise that can help you determine your core motivation. Let's assume for a moment that reincarnation does not happen and you only have one life to live. Now think, what words do you want to have on your gravestone? What do you want your epitaph to say? Let's assume you have 4 lines of up to 35 characters each. Here's an example:

Great Woman, Wife, and Mother	29 characters
Entrepreneur and Humanitarian	29 characters
Changed the World on a Global Scale	35 characters
Fought Poverty Through Love	27 characters

Action Item 2 – Start With the End in Mind

Take a moment and write what you want to be on your four-line epitaph.

_____

_____

_____

_____

By starting with the end in mind, you can ensure what you are planning on doing today and for the next few years will allow you to create the opportunities that allow you to reach your highest ambitions. At your funeral, how will those closest to you describe you? What will you have done? What will your accomplishments be? And what plans and direction should your life take to enable you to get to the point at which you can truly achieve great success.

One day your life will be done. And in your place you will have left something. What will that something be? How will you be remembered? What impact will you make? What will you create that continues on after you are gone?

> "One day your life will be done. And in your place you will have left something. What will that something be?"

Why I Am An Entrepreneur

So why have I have chosen to do what I do? There are six reasons.

1. I love the game.
2. I like being able to provide jobs.
3. I enjoy giving back to the local community.
4. I enjoy creating something that helps people.
5. I like the being able to be financially secure. .
6. I'm passionate about changing the world on a global scale.

I love to play the game of business. It is really what gets my blood going. I am a very competitive person, and I am passionate about entrepreneurship. I am glad we have competition, for it is competition that drives me. I have a desire to be the best.

At iContact and Virante we've created over 80 jobs in the past five years, and have the ability to create hundreds more in the next five years. We now have 41 children that we help support. Between our team members' spouses and their children, we help support over 170 people every month though our efforts so far.

At times having responsibility for and supporting so many people can weigh on you. I go into a bar and talk to a girl and tell her I'm 23 and support 41 kids and they run. It's something that is a really big responsibility, though it is something that drives me. It's something that gives me a reason to get up each and every day and work the hardest I can and be able to create something that is truly worth building for them.

We are able to give back to our community by sponsoring organizations like Nourish International, The Full Belly Project, AGRADU, Orange County Foster Care, the Chapel-Hill Carrboro Chamber of Commerce, Durham County Habitat for Humanity, and The Debian Project.

In terms of creating a product that helps people, I very much enjoy being part of a team that is developing an application that helps over 15,000 other businesses and 100,000 individuals more easily communicate online.

I do enjoy the opportunities, experiences, and positive influence that come along with having financial freedom. There are a few ways to make a good deal of money in this country and in the world. I could be a professional athlete, I could be a white rapper, I could move my way up the corporate ladder, or I could start my own business. Starting my own business is that path I chose for myself.

When I went into this business I had $12,000 to my name and that was going down by about $1,000 a month. I realized I had about 12 months to be able to make this thing work. My original salary was $50,000 but we didn't have any money so we couldn't pay it. So we accrued that salary up until on September 2004, when we could finally had enough to pay ourselves something.

From the beginning we knew that we weren't doing it for the money. That's not the reason we do business. We see money, cash flow and profits as the life blood of our organization, not the purpose of it. We strive for them only because they are essential toward fulfilling our true mission of creating jobs, creating a great product, and creating a great organization.

> "At iContact, we see money, cash flow and profits as the life blood of our organization, not the purpose of it. We strive for them only because they are essential toward fulfilling our true mission of creating jobs, creating a great product, and creating a great organization."

Today we are doing well and if we are fortunate enough to go public or sell to a strategic acquirer it looks like I will be financially secure for the rest of my life and allow me to focus my time and efforts on my true passion, reducing global poverty and changing the world through entrepreneurship, social entrepreneurship, and politics.

My true passion in life is working to reducing poverty in developing nations. I feel entrepreneurship is the best way I know for me to gain money and influence now so I can give back in a larger way later through social entrepreneurship, politics, and philanthropy.

The motivation came from a realization I had when I was seventeen. A couple years before, at age fifteen I went through a phase of rebellion. I had red hair, I was into punk rock music. I didn't really realize what the purpose of life was. I really didn't understand how I as a single individual could make a difference in this world. This got me down. I was in a rut.

With the support and the help of my parents and some of my teachers, and through some of the experiences I had, I was able to get out of that phase in my life and turn into someone that is very motivated and to get up every day.

There were also three books I read at seventeen that changed the direction of my life and truly got me out of that rut once and for all. The first book, *Rich Dad Poor Dad* by Robert Kiyosaki, taught me about financial freedom, how to build assets, and how to structure companies. The second, *Think and Grow Rich* by Napoleon Hill, written in 1928, gave me a personal philosophy centered around positive thinking, goals, and appreciation for life. The third, *The Lexus & the Olive Tree* by Thomas Friedman, opened my eyes to globalization and how the world worked and inspired my love for economics and reducing poverty through business, healthcare, education, and effective governance.

My Core Motivation

There are two facts that really disturb me and motivate me to do my best every single day so that I can work to change the realities these facts describe in the future. These two facts are:

1. 2.7 billion people in our world, 42% of the world's population, live on under $2 a day.[13]
2. 49,345 people (the majority of which are children) die each and every day in developing countries from preventable diseases and starvation.[14]

> "2.7 billion people live on under $2 per day. 49,345 people die each and every day in developing countries from preventable diseases and starvation."

These are two facts that once you know, you cannot pretend that you do not know. When I came across statistics like these in books like *The End of Poverty* by Jeffrey Sachs, it truly gave me added meaning, focus, and dedication toward my goals. And knowing that our generation, for the first time in human history, has the real opportunity to end the final travesties of mankind captivates and inspires me.

Ensuring a sustainable environment and reducing poverty, malnutrition, and hunger while improving access to healthcare, education, and opportunity are truly the issues I am passionate about and what I hope to work on over the next seven decades of my life through entrepreneurship, social entrepreneurship, public policy, and politics.

I have been fortunate to find my core motivation. My core motivation drives me each and every day to be excellent in everything I do. It is driving me to write these words write now. It drives all that I do, and all that I strive for. Finding this core motivation before I started iContact at 18 has been critical to getting me through the difficult and challenging times and finding the strength from within to persevere in the face of otherwise insurmountable odds.

Spend time thinking and meditating on your core raison d'être, your reason for being, and figure out what constitutes your core motivations for what you do and who you are. Know who you want to become and you can begin to direct your life rather than letting outside factors control you. Direct your life toward your definite chief aim. Let who you are and what you believe come out in all that you create.

Chapter 8 Step 2: Evaluate Your Idea

> "Entrepreneurs are simply those who understand that there is little difference between obstacle and opportunity and are able to turn both to their advantage."
> - Niccolo Machiavelli, 15th & 16th century Italian Statesman

Deciding on What to Sell

Before you can start a company, you must decide on what you will sell and how you will make your money. Experienced entrepreneurs often have a number of business ideas, that given the time, they would like to pursue. As an aspiring entrepreneur, you may not have an idea.

If this is the case, you'll have to develop an idea or partner with another aspiring entrepreneur that does have one. Business ideas often develop in entrepreneurs' heads over the course of years, often while working at a job. Almost always, business ideas are refined and modified as time passes and more knowledge is obtained and research done.

While teaching entrepreneurship to high schoolers at the Lead America conference in Chicago and Boston a few summers ago, we had to come up with a number of business ideas and then, over the course of a few hours, get the list down to two the team would create full business plans for. We began by filling the walls with blank poster paper and just letting the students shout out what came to their minds. You can do a similar exercise.

During a brainstorming session, write down whatever comes to mind, or focus on a specific industry you have experience in. Think about the products you use every day and how they could be better. Think about businesses you interact with and what you would improve if it was your business. Think about things that you would love to have if they existed. Consider the efficiency of the marketplace and attempt to find inefficient and bloated industries that you could enter into. Think about whether you would like to provide a service or sell a product. Consider the possibility of buying into a pre-existing franchise. Consider what you are good at and what people would pay you to do for them. Consider macro trends in the economy such as the aging population and advent of the internet.

Action Item 3 – Business Idea Brainstorm

Take a moment and write down any business ideas you have with a description of the product or service and the market you will sell to.

_____

_____

_____

_____

While idea brainstorming can be a helpful activity, the best ideas are often not generated while brainstorming. More frequently, they come through experience in an industry, from persons whom you know, or from a moment of inspiration. Don't be discouraged if you cannot come up with any ideas that you want to start a business around. It will take time. In the mean time, make sure you always are looking for opportunities and are networking with as many people and at as many events as you can make it to.

Here are five tips for coming up with business ideas:

1. **Continuously be aware** of the products you use everyday. How can they be better? What need or pain do you have that could be fulfilled by a product or service that is not currently being provided?
2. **Go to networking events**, seminars, and conferences like this one. You may find someone with a good product or a good idea that is looking for partners. Read magazines and publications that cover the industry you are interested in.
3. **Intern or get a job at a company in the industry** you are interested in. Work there to get experience and build contacts. Many times you will see product ideas in the course of your work that your company will choose not to pursue.
4. **Look for a franchise opportunity** that you can take advantage of to build a company around or inspire a business idea.

5. **Find a partner** with a business idea that you can join up with.

It's important to remember that opportunities are created when there are changing circumstances. Whenever you experience new things or the world around is changing, there will always be lots of opportunities. If you are lacking in ideas, you also may wish to ask around and see what internships are available at local entrepreneurial companies or apply for a job at one. Working at an entrepreneurial company with other entrepreneurial minded persons is one of the best ways to come up with new business ideas.

If you work at a larger company, I'd suggest talking with your manager to see if there are any new products or technologies the company is developing. By expressing interest in coordinating the development and launch of a new product, you may just get a promotion to being a manager with P&L responsibility for that product—allowing you to be an intrapreneur and leverage company resources while you build the new segment of your company.

How to Evaluate Your Idea

Once you are able to come up with a potential business ideas, the issue arises of determining whether your idea is a true business opportunity. One of the best ways to determine the potential of an idea is to screen it through an opportunity evaluation model.

Opportunities are simply good ideas. When an idea is timely, attractive, achievable, durable, fills a need, and provides value to the buyer it can be considered an opportunity. An idea is an opportunity only if there is reason to believe the market will validate the idea and the management team has the ability to execute the idea. Let's take a look at an opportunity evaluation model and see how our business ideas stack up.

> "When an idea is timely, attractive, achievable, durable, fills a need, and provides value to the buyer it can be considered an opportunity."

The MAR Model of Opportunity Evaluation

"All achievements, all earned riches, have their beginning in an idea."
- Napoleon Hill

In analyzing your ideas to decide on the one that you will select for your business plan, you must be able to pass these ideas through a test to determine if they truly are valid opportunities. I created the Market, Advantages, Return (MAR) Model to provide a screen through which you can pass your business ideas and see if they truly are opportunities with a demonstrated need, ready market, and ability to provide a solid return on investment.

Is the idea feasible in the marketplace? Is there demand? Can it be done? Are you able to pull together the persons and resources to pull it off before the window of opportunity closes? All of these questions must be considered and answered. Let's do evaluate a business idea in a methodical process.

To determine whether your idea has a good chance of being validated in the market place, it must analyzed based on a number of criteria. You must look at the need, market structure, pricing, market size, timing, cost structure, barriers to entry, intellectual property, the team, distribution channel, profitability, time to breakeven, needed investment, exit strategies, and return on investment.

Let's take these terms and turn them into an easy model that you can use to evaluate your business ideas you've come up with or your current business venture.

The Market – M

1. The Need. This is one of the most important questions to ask. Is there a big need for this product or service? Try to avoid ideas that sound novel or unique but have no real market. Make sure your product or service fills a need or solves a problem. Also make sure there is demand for the product or service in the location(s) where you will be selling or providing it.
2. Market Structure. Is the market a highly competitive market or more like an oligopolistic or monopolistic market? Determining the number and quality of competitors and type of market is important when developing your strategy to enter that market and determining the needed investment.
3. Pricing. What will you charge? Will there be a high enough markup? Is there enough demand in the marketplace to justify the price you intend to charge? What are your competitors charging? Settling on a

price that is not too low to be unprofitable but not too high to drive away the majority of your buyers can be a hard task.

4. Market Size. Is the market big enough to warrant entry? Is it growing or shrinking? Look for a growing market that will become of significant size.

5. Timing. Is the market ready for your product? You may have a great idea for flying cars, but if consumers are not ready for your product or the prerequisite infrastructure is not in place you may not be able to turn your idea into a successful business.

The Advantages – A

1. Cost structure. Who will your suppliers be? What will each element of your product(s) cost to source or manufacturer? If you can find a way to have lower costs than your competitors you'll improve your profit margins and have a big advantage.

2. Barriers to entry. Are there large competitors in the market niche? Are there regulations, patents, or large capital requirements that will get in your way? If there are many barriers to entry, it will be difficult to enter a market.

3. Intellectual Property. Do you have a proprietary advantage such as patents or exclusive licenses on what you will be selling? If so, you'll have an easier time raising funding, and if your technology is good, the chance to build a very successful company.

4. The Team. Who can and will you bring on to help you build your company? Will they be offered equity? How many persons will you need to get the company off the ground and what will be their roles? If you can convince an industry veteran to join your board or an experienced Vice President, COO, CTO, or CFO to join your team, you'll have a big advantage. Remember, if the management team does not have the ability to execute the idea, it is not a true opportunity.

5. Distribution Channels. How will you be selling your product? Will you sell it direct to the consumer via the Internet, sell it to wholesalers, sell it to businesses, sell it to retail stores, or sell through a network of partners? If you can develop a unique and efficient distribution channel you will surely have an advantage.

The Return - R

ZERO TO ONE MILLION

1. Profitability. Will your company make a positive net income? Will your revenues eventually be higher than your expenses? If not, either take a second look at your projections, or try another idea.
2. Time to Breakeven. Based on your projections, how long will it be before the company is cash flow positive? How long will it be until the company begins to have an aggregate net income and reaches cumulative break even? These are figures to know and two very important graphs to have in your business plan.
3. Investment Needed. How much money will it take to start-up this venture? Will it be $20,000, $200,000, or $2,000,000? How much money you need will give you an idea of where you'll need to go to raise funding? For under $50,000, friends and family and the bank are your best options. For $50,000 to $1,000,000 accredited private investors, partner companies, and angel investors are likely your best bet. Above $1,000,000 you'll have to look to venture capital firms or other companies that are willing to provide start-up capital for you. Do you best to minimize the amount of required capital it will take to start the business. If you are able, start with only your personal resources. Once you have revenues you will be able to raise investment funding much more easily and without having to give up as much.
4. Exit Strategy. Do you plan to sell the company or go public down the line? How will your investors get their money back? If you do not plan to ever sell your company or go public, you will not be able to raise equity capital.
5. Return on Investment. What is the projected return on investment for your investors based on your current projections? If it is not high enough, you won't be able to raise certain types of capital. Venture capitalists look for at least a 5x return over 5 years or less, with a target of closer to 10x. This is not to say you should make your projections higher. Rather, you may wish to explore alternative ideas, look at the possibility of taking less money at a lower pre-money valuation, or look at alternative financing such as angel investors and debt capital.

The MAR model for opportunity evaluation can be summed up with the following chart.

Table 1 – MAR Model for Evaluating New Ventures

Market	Advantages	Return
Need	Cost Structure	Profitability
Market Structure	Barriers to Entry	Time to Breakeven
Pricing	Intellectual Property	Investment Needed
Market Size	The Team	Exit Strategy
Timing	Distribution Channels	Return on Investment

Action Item 4 – Use the MAR Model to Vet Your Idea

Take a moment and evaluate your idea with the MAR model to determine if it is a true business opportunity:

MARKET	
What is the need for the product or service?	
What is the market structure?	
How will I price the product?	
What is the approximate size of the market?	
Is the market ready for the product?	
ADVANTAGES	
What will it cost to produce your product or service?	
What is the total start-up cost to get going?	

Will you need to acquire or protect any intellectual property?	
Who will be on your team?	
Will you sell your product to businesses or consumers?	

RETURN

What will your gross profit and net profit margins be based on your projections?	
How long will it take to reach breakeven and at what unit production level will breakeven be reached?	
How much money does the company need to get to cash flow positive comfortably?	
Will is my exit strategy? Do I intend to sell the company, go public, or make money off of quarterly profits?	
If my projections are correct, what can an investor expect to make for an investment in my company and what will be the payback period? Will the investor make money through dividends or a liquidity event?	

Once entrepreneurs have gone through this opportunity evaluation model, they are able to proceed with the venture, with the opportunity, in an educated manner, feeling confident that their idea will have validation in the market place.

So how does your idea stack up? Based on your answers from the above screening process, do you consider it to be a true opportunity? Is there a demonstrated need, a ready market, and the ability to provide a solid return on investment? If you believe so, congratulations. If not, I encourage you to follow the tips given earlier for generating and finding additional ideas and opportunities. Then use the model above.

The Ten Axioms of Opportunity

> The vitality of thought is in adventure. Ideas won't keep. Something must be done about them.
> - Alfred North Whitehead

I'd like to share you The Ten Axioms of Opportunity. I developed these principles while writing a speech that I presented to a group of high school students in Chicago in June 2003. They encompass the main points about knowing when an opportunity is a good opportunity, as well as the important principles that one must know in order to create good opportunities.

1. An idea is an opportunity when it is timely, attractive, achievable, durable, fills a need, and provides value to the buyer. An idea is an opportunity only if there is reason to believe the market will validate the idea and the management team has the ability to execute the idea.

2. To be a true opportunity a business idea must have a demonstrated need, ready market, and ability to provide a solid return on investment.

3. Opportunity-focused entrepreneurs and investors start with the customer and the market in mind. Then analyze the market to determine industry issues, market structure, market size, growth rate, market capacity, attainable market share, cost structure, the core economics, exit strategy issues, time to breakeven, opportunity costs, and barriers to entry.

4. Business ideas are a dime a dozen. What really matters is the execution and the quality of the team. It is not the idea. It is the people, and their ability to execute, that matters. Once you have the people and the execution, then your idea has the potential to become a true opportunity.

5. Too many people wait for opportunities to come to them. Don't wait for the opportunities to come to you. Create the opportunity for yourself.

6. If you are not ready for an opportunity during the short window it will be there, it will pass you by. You must make personal development a priority so that you will be prepared to take advantage of the opportunities.

7. Every adversity comes with a seed of equal or greater benefit. Through adversity, opportunity will come.

8. The world is filled with opportunities just waiting to be found by an energetic and intelligent person.

9. Making mistakes, learning from them, and being willing to put yourself out there is essential to finding opportunities.

10. With a positive mental attitude, a desire to succeed, a determined mindset, persistence, and enthusiasm you can find, create, and take advantage of any possibility and any opportunity that you can dream.

Why So Many Businesses Fail

According to a longitudinal study conducted by the United States Small Business Administration, approximately 60% of small businesses shut down within the first six years.[12] Small businesses fail for numerous reasons. The most common reasons new businesses fail are because their owners:

1. Grow their company too fast;
2. Have a poor concept;
3. Are not good at marketing or sales;
4. Fail to plan;
5. Start their company without enough money to get to breakeven;
6. Have an inability to differentiate;
7. Lack control of their finances and books; or
8. Don't build systems and processes.

Many entrepreneurs who end up unsuccessful do not build processes and systems and lack the ability or desire to sell. They do not carefully plan their business and often fail to raise the needed capital to sustain it until it is profitable. They do not focus on efficiency of operations or automation. They never make the investment in additional capital or employees needed to expand the company to the point where it can make a profit. As an entrepreneur, even if you have a great idea, you will have to plan well, build a good team, make sure you have adequate capitalization, build the proper systems, and execute your plan.

According to entrepreneur and adjunct business professor at UNC's Kenan-Flagler Business School Colin Wahl, there are certain critical success factors in building a successful small business. These include:

1. Vision of the management;
2. Passion;
3. A good idea;
4. Clean, focused business objectives;
5. A well thought through business plan;
6. Good organizational design;
7. Persistence;
8. Determination;
9. Strong work ethic;
10. Enthusiasm in the owners;
11. A good team;
12. Motivated employees;
13. Good cash flow management;
14. Adequate financial resources;
15. A clear understanding of market need; and
16. Execution of the management.

As you can see in the list above, a good idea is only one of many factors needed to succeed. As you can see in the list of business ideas a few pages back, ideas are a dime a dozen. Unless you have a Ph.D. and are doing cutting edge research at a top university, in most cases if you have thought of a business idea, someone else has thought of it too. The key to the success, then, is rarely the idea and nearly always good execution. To illustrate this principle, let's take an example.

In 1967, an angel investor, Fred Adler, received over 50 business plans from entrepreneurs who proposed to start microcomputer firms. Only one of the teams presenting this idea ever made it. Its name was Data General. But why did so many entrepreneurs pitching a plan to sell microcomputers either never receive funding or if they were funded, never succeed?

They didn't make it not because the idea was per se bad or didn't have the potential to be a good opportunity. It was a great idea and enormous opportunity. Rather, it was because the other entrepreneurial teams were unable to execute.

Think of the dotcom era a few years ago. Many had good ideas, but lacked in execution. I have heard many venture capitalists say they would rather have an A management team and

> "It is not the idea, it is the people, and their ability to execute, that matters."

a B business concept than an A business concept and a B management team. It is not the idea, it is the people, and their ability to execute, that matters. While a business that ends up being successful could be started with a so-so idea, a successful business will never be built without a good team.

By ensuring you pass your ideas through the MAR Model of Opportunity Evaluation, you'll be able to get a good idea of whether your ideas are true opportunities. But as you can see, execution is just as important, if not more important than the idea. So let's look at how to both plan for your business, and then execute based on that plan.

A Note for Entrepreneurs in Developing Countries

If you live in a developing country it may be more difficult for you to start your business. Many of the steps to starting and building a business listed here may be different in your country. If you are in a less developed country, you may not be able to easily access capital and the incorporation process may be entirely different. The business infrastructure may be in a less developed state, there may be corruption in some elements of the company registration process and you may be asked to pay bribes to obtain the needed permits. If this is the case for you, please know that I hope to spend much of my life working to make the ability to start a business open to anyone, anywhere.

If you are from a developing country and run into difficulties, I encourage you to continue as an entrepreneur, to learn about sources of micro-credit and assistance organizations, and to work to remove corruption and build the infrastructure necessary for innovation and progress to be possible in your country.

I encourage you to put pressure on your government to follow the work of persons such as Peruvian economist Hernando de Soto. It is my hope, however, that many of the general steps of this book will still be applicable and that within my lifetime it will be possible for all persons in all nations to have equality of opportunity and be able to express their creativity and passion through commercial entrepreneurship and social entrepreneurship.

Step 3: Plan for Success

The Business Plan

Until September 2003 I had not written a full-fledged business plan before in my life. I always planned informally, on one page checklists or handwritten sales forecasts. While we had operational plans and marketing plans, we didn't have a full business plan. I had never attempted to raise significant capital, and thus never needed a plan.

In early September 2003 I had a meeting with a potential board member for iContact. In reviewing our company, he asked to see our business plan. I said I would send it to him. That weekend I sat down and wrote for about twelve hours and finished it off, complete with executive bios, our fifteen page marketing plan, projected organizational charts, and a projected (pro forma) income statement.

While you will not need a business plan per se until you reach the point when you are ready to raise funding, it is good to have one right from the beginning. Writing the iContact business plan allowed me to take a step back from the day to day operations of the company and take a look at where we were, both financially and in the timeline of executing our strategies, and where I wanted us to go over the next two years.

It was especially helpful to take the time to write down all our current and projected expenses. It helped me determine if we needed to raise additional funding or if we would be able to organically grow from operations cash flow. The pro forma pinpointed the exact month, based on all my current knowledge of every expense and revenue source, that we would turn cash flow positive and the exact month we would reach cumulative break even. In short, it was a valuable experience for me to write that business plan and accompanying budget and pro forma revenue and expense projection.

If your idea is developed to the point you are ready to start a business around it, I'd suggest writing a business plan for it. Your plan will not be a static document, but rather a lively, dynamic work that changes and grows as your business grows. In your plan you should include the following basic elements:

The Executive Summary - A quick overview of all elements of the business plan, highlighting what exactly it is you will sell, how you are different from your competitors, why your team will succeed, how much money you'll need to launch the business, and what the expected return on investment will be for investors based on your projections. Here is the actual iContact Executive Summary from June 2007 for your reference:

Highlight 5: iContact Executive Summary, June 2007

Reprinted with permission from iContact

Executive Summary

Overview: iContact is a Durham, NC SaaS provider in the online communications space. Founded in July 2003 by serial entrepreneurs Ryan Allis and Aaron Houghton, the company has grown to 57 employees and an annual run-rate of over $6.3 million. The company's mission is to be the leading worldwide provider of on-demand software that makes online communications easy.

Financing: iContact was bootstrapped by its founders until May 2006, when it raised $500,000 in convertible debt from investor NC IDEA. The company has increased its monthly sales from $180,000 to $530,000 since the close of this round. The company has successfully identified highly profitable channels of customer acquisition that it can scale with additional funding. iContact is seeking to raise $3 million to $5 million in expansion capital in Q3 2007.

Products: The company has two product offerings: iContact and iContact Enterprise. iContact that makes it amazingly easy to create, publish and track email newsletters, surveys, autoresponders, blogs, and RSS feeds. As of June 2007, iContact has over 11,000 paying customers including market leaders like Vonage, Symantec, Century 21, Ford, Nissan, International Paper, Bank of America, Intuit, Re/Max, Centex Homes, and United Colors of Benetton. These and the thousands of other iContact clients generate over $530,000 in monthly recurring revenue.

Management: iContact has a world-class and fully built-out rockstar team—from a pair of serial entrepreneur founders who intimately know the market, to a technologist and marketer who are leaders in their fields, to a VP of Business Development with over 30 years of experience, to a CFO who helped raise over $100 million in the public markets for Broadband Technologies public in 1996, was the CFO for OpenSite—sold to Siebel in 2000 for $550 million in one of North Carolina's largest software company acquisition, and was most recently CFO of CipherTrust in Atlanta, which sold for $270 million.

Customer Acquisition: The average iContact customer pays $50 per month and stays around for 24 months, creating a lifetime value of $1,200. team has identified scalable methods of acquiring customers at a highly profitable customer acquisition cost, and has scaled its new customer acquisition rates from 300 to over 1100 new customers per month since July 2006. The company has over 1,300 Channel Partners.

Strategy: iContact is leveraging the base product to create the future of online communication, by creating a single central platform for businesses to manage all of their online communications. As RSS becomes mainstream during 2007, iContact is positioned as the easiest method of publishing content to a feed.

Vision: iContact's vision is to become the worldwide leading in on-demand software that makes communication easy by combining principles of the Software as a Service (SaaS) model with the web 2.0 trends of user-generated content and community engagement. The company is developing the first platform that makes online communication really easy for the masses, while redefining how consumers interact with content by becoming an engaging community, social network, and content depository on every imaginable topic.

Address:
2635 Meridian Parkway, 2nd Floor
Durham, NC 27713

Key Team Members:
Aaron Houghton, Chairman, Co-Founder, & Chief Innovation Officer
Ryan P. Allis, CEO and Co-Founder
Timothy K. Oakley, CFO
David Rasch, CTO
David Roth, VP Business Dev.
Brandon Milford, VP Marketing

Chuck Hester, Director of Corp. Comm.
Cindy Hays, Director of Human Resources
Amber Neill, Director of Customer Service
Robert Plumley, Director of Financial Operations

Number of Employees: 57
Bank: Bank of America
Law Firm: Smith Anderson
Auditor: Hughes Pittman & Gupton
Current Investor: NC IDEA
Board Structure: Ryan Allis, Aaron Houghton, Merrette Moore (NC IDEA)
Capital Raised to Date: $500,000 (5/06)
Financing Sought: $5M

Use of Funds:
Rapid scaling of customer acquisition for fully developed product

Key Points:
1. Rapidly growing 57 person company with 11,000 customers and $530,000 in recurring monthly sales.
2. Identified highly profitable customer acquisition model that is scalable with additional investment.
3. Company bootstrapped until $500k convertible debt round in May 2006.
4. Grew sales from $176,000/month to $530,000/month since last round.
5. Sustainable unique technological advantages that allow low-cost scalable technical structure.
6. Rockstar team with significant IPO, acquisition, and market experience.
7. Working toward becoming worldwide leader in on-demand software for online communication.

Financial Summary, Historical & Projected			
	2003 Actual	2004 Actual	2005 Actual	2006 Actual
Revenue	$11,964	$297,794	$1,314,136	$2,900,683
	2007	2008	2009	2010
Revenue	$6,366,564	$12,523,703	$23,393,447	$38,382,892

The Team – Explain who you are and who will be helping you build your business. What is their background and experience? Who else will come on board once you launch and/or receive funding? Why will your team fit together well? Who will be needed as your business expands? Within your team section, you'll want to include an organizational chart of what you envision your firm looking like in a year and then a few years down the road. As an example, here is the iContact org chart from when we had 15 employees (some persons fill multiple positions):

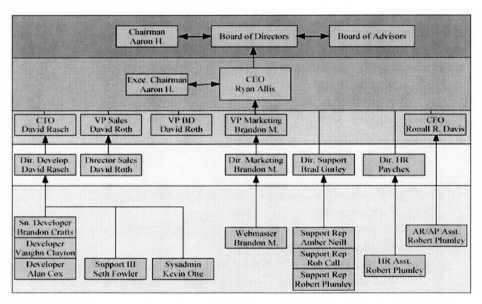

The Product or Service – What it is that you sell? What differentiates your product or service from those of all your competitors? What unique technology/intellectual property, if any, do you have? How does the product work?

The Market – Who are your competitors? What strengths and weaknesses do they have? What is the size of your market? Is it growing? What share of the market can you reasonably capture?

The Marketing & Sales Plan – How will you position yourself in the marketplace? What is your distribution strategy? Who is your target customer? What strategies will you use to make sales and build awareness of your company?

Challenges & Risks – What are the problems you may run into? What are the potential challenges you will face and how will you deal with these? What world events or competitor or government actions may impact your business? What are the risks?

Capital Use – How much money are you seeking (if any) and how will the funds be used? For product development? Buying hardware? Customer acquisition? Building a sales team? Explain how you will use investor funds.

Pro Formas Financial Projections – Create a full projected income statement, monthly through year two and then quarterly for years three through five. Here are the steps needed to do this:

1. Start by writing down all the categories of your current expenses and those in the future.
2. Fill out the actual dollar figures for any data to date and projections for the future, month by month for year one and quarterly through year five.
3. Project your sales volume and revenues for each of your revenue streams.
4. Subtract your monthly expenses from your monthly revenue to determine how much money you will lose or earn in each month. This is called your net monthly income.
5. Find the point where this number turns from negative to positive. That point is when you will have reached cash flow positive.
6. Below the net monthly income row, create a cumulative net income row in which you add up all the prior monthly (or quarterly) net incomes.
7. Find the point on this row where the number is the greatest to the negative side. This is how much money you will need, at minimum, to start your business, based on your projections.
8. To be safe, double this amount and make this amount your goal for how much money you need to raise to start your business.
9. Find the point where your cumulative net income turns positive. This point is called cumulative break even.

10. Finally, create a break-even analysis graph similar to the one we include later in this section to illustrate the time and money needed until your company turns profitable.

So you can visualize what your expenses might look like here is the actual projected expenses for the first six months of iContact:

Table 2 – Pro forma expenses for first six months of iContact

	Jul	Aug	Sep	Oct	Nov	Dec
Hosting	150	150	150	150	150	150
Servers	0	0	0	0	0	1000
Salaries	0	0	0	0	750	1000
Legal	0	1547	0	0	0	0
Rent	0	0	200	200	200	200
Phone	50	50	80	90	130	130
Computers	0	0	480	0	0	500
Internet	0	0	0	0	0	0
Furniture	0	0	0	0	0	0
Advertising	0	0	0	0	0	100
Utilities	50	50	50	0	0	0
Commissions	0	0	0	77	43	125
Office Supplies	50	50	50	80	80	150
Parking	80	80	98	160	160	240
Travel	0	0	0	0	0	200
Meals	0	0	20	50	50	100
Printing	0	0	20	50	100	100
Security	0	0	0	0	150	0
Merchant Acct	0	0	0	20	33	65
Gateway	0	0	250	20	30	30
Total	380	1927	1398	897	1876	4090

So you can see what the projections would look like of a more developed company, here are the projected expenses for iContact in months 19-24.

Table 3 – Pro forma expenses for iContact during months 19-24

	Jan	Feb	Mar	Apr	May	Jun

Hosting	1000	1150	1150	1300	1300	1450
Servers	1000	1000	1000	1000	1000	1000
Salaries	15000	18000	21000	24000	27000	30000
Legal	300	400	400	400	400	400
Rent	2000	2000	2000	2000	2000	2000
Phone	500	500	500	500	500	500
Computers	0	500	500	500	500	500
Internet	70	70	70	70	70	70
Furniture	200	200	200	200	200	200
Advertising	10000	10000	10000	10000	10000	10000
Utilities	200	200	200	200	200	200
Commissions	9500	10500	11500	12500	13500	14500
Office Supplies	200	200	200	200	200	200
Parking	560	640	720	800	880	960
Travel	1200	1200	1200	1200	1200	1200
Meals	500	500	500	500	500	500
Printing	200	200	200	200	200	200
Security	300	300	300	300	300	300
Merchant Acct	2730	2990	3250	3510	3770	4030
Gateway	30	30	30	30	30	30
Total	45490	50580	54920	59410	63750	68240

Putting the revenue projections and your expense projections together, you'll have your pro forma income statement. Here is the pro forma income statement for the first seven months of iContact.

Table 4 – Pro forma for first seven months of iContact

	Jul	Aug	Sep	Oct	Nov	Dec	Jan
Revenue	261	771	432	1250	2500	4250	7500
Expenses	380	1927	1398	897	1876	4090	4101
Net Income	(119)	(1,156)	(966)	**353**	624	160	3,400
Ag.Net Income	(923)	(2,079)	(3,045)	(2,692)	(2,068)	(1,908)	**1,492**
Available Cash	4196	4077	2921	1955	2308	2932	3092

Note the available cash line, where we kept track of how much money we had left in our bank account, assuming a starting investment of $5,000. It declines to $1955 by October, and then started to grow as we began to make more money than we spent.

The next thing you will need to do is create a break-even chart to graphically show when you turn cash flow positive and when you reach break-even. This is the actual initial break-even chart for iContact (we later went back into the red when we raised investment so that we could grow faster)

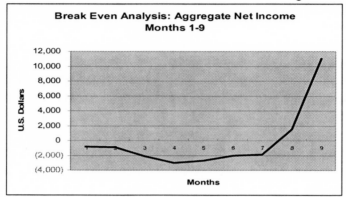

As you can see, the company went about $3,000 in the red before it turned cash flow positive. We were using our own funds to grow the business. If we would have been a traditional venture-backed company we would have a much larger initial loss. A usual break-even chart for a successful venture capital financed technology venture might look like:

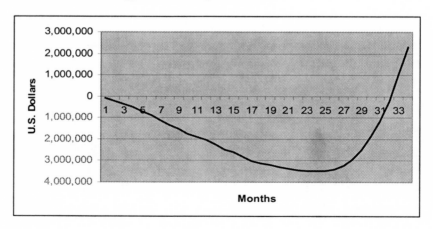

Once you have your business plan completed, if you are in the U.S. you may wish to schedule an appointment with the local chapter of the Service Corps of Retired Executives (www.score.org). They'll review your plan with you and provide feedback. If you know any business owners or successful entrepreneurs, ask them to lunch and for feedback on your plan. To protect yourself, if you do show anyone your business plan whom you do not know well, be sure to have them sign a confidentiality and non-compete agreement. Do note that venture capitalists and most investors will not sign these. However you are protected by the industry ethic.

Creating a Mission Statement

Once you have your business plan in place, there is just one more element of organizational planning to do. It is very important to create common mission statement for your business that all your team members can agree to and get behind.

As a new company owner, especially if there is more than one person working on the business, writing the mission statement for your business can be one of the most important things you can do. Often you will have rather different ideas among partners as to the direction and strategy of a company. By answering the questions below collaboratively and creating one document that all involved in the company agree to and sign, you will not only minimize headaches and arguments down the road but also be fully aligned on your goals and be able to work together efficiently.

The iContact mission statement encapsulates the overarching goal that we are attempting to accomplish for the organization. It reads:

> **iContact's mission is to be the worldwide leading provider of on-demand software that makes online communication easy.**

We also have a longer mission statement that we call the "iContact Manifesto" that resides on our web site and speaks to the reasons we are in business, our general strategy and positioning, who are customers are, the philosophy behind what we've built, an explanation of what we are trying to accomplish, and how we intend to be part of our community.

Mission statements can be short or they can be long, up to a couple pages. You may wish to come up with both a short mission statement that you'll show to all your customers and promote and a longer statement for internal guidance and planning. Here are three steps to coming up with a mission statement.

Step One: Identify the target customer

Step Two: State what you'll provide to customers

Step Three: State what differentiates your firm

Examples of short mission statements include:

Avis - Our business is renting cars. Our mission is complete customer satisfaction.

Eastman Kodak - To be the world's best in chemicals and electronic imaging

McDonalds – To offer the fast food customer food prepared in the same high quality manner worldwide, tasty and reasonably priced, delivered in a consistent, low-key décor and friendly atmosphere.

If you plan to write a longer mission statement, simply answer the following ten questions.

Ten Questions Your Longer Version Mission Statement Can Answer

1. What problem(s) do you solve? What need(s) do you fulfill?

2. What do you sell? How do you make your money? What is your revenue model?

3. How are you unique from everyone else out there? What is your unique selling proposition?

4. Who will you sell to? What is your target market?

5. What are your economic/financial goals?

6. What are your social/community goals?

7. What type of company do you want to create? Will you build a lifestyle or high potential company?

8. Where is the company going? What products/services/industries do you plan to venture into?

9. What is your five year strategy? Do you want to sell internationally,

> build an online store, franchise your business, build certain
> partnerships, develop additional products?
> 10. Do you ever plan on selling the company or going public? What is
> your exit strategy?

It may take weeks and multiple meetings and editing to get the responses to the above questions to be agreed upon by all parties and a single document created that all will sign. While it takes time, I cannot emphasize enough the important of having such a document. As stated above, it will not only dramatically reduce conflict and prevent arguments, but will also align all in your business with the same goals, in turn creating a much more effective team and much more profitable business.

Creating a Corporate Values Statement

At iContact we hold an "iContact Day" twice per year at an off-site location with all of our team members, usually at a hotel on a Saturday morning and afternoon. At the first iContact Day in January 2006, we developed our company's Corporate Values Statement together. This statement truly brings together the key principles we intend to follow as we go about attempting to accomplish our mission. Our Corporate Values Statement reads as follows:

Highlight 6: iContact Corporate Values Statement

Reprinted with permission from iContact

Corporate Values Statement

iContact's mission is to be the worldwide leading provider of on-demand software that makes online communication easy. While our mission is what we strive for, how we achieve the goal that it represents is just as important. With this in mind, we have established this Corporate Values Statement to serve a reference for us and those that come after us. In fulfilling our company mission, we will strive to always:

1. **Value People First** – We will respect and value our customers—for

it is they who allow us to survive and prosper. We will communicate openly with our customers, keep them in mind when making business decisions, and provide them with a high level of service and assistance.

2. **Build People Up** – We will respect and value each team member and work to build people up through positive reinforcement in a caring family environment. We will understand that mistakes are okay, as long as they are learned from.

3. **Be Competitive** – We will maintain a strong competitive ethic. We will strive to reach our goals by building a superior team, developing innovative products, and providing clear unique value propositions to our clients. We will work to keep sales high and expenses low, although we will always choose to invest for long-term benefit in both the company and our people.

4. **Be Innovative** – We will always be thinking about how we can improve what we're doing, what is coming next, and how we can create what is next in our markets.

5. **Be Quick Yet Thorough** – We will have a bias toward action, yet maintain standards of quality and excellence in all that we do.

6. **Have a Culture of Responsibility** – We will work together in collaboration with our team members and draw on the experience, skills, and knowledge of all to progress toward our goals. When we see a ball that may drop, we will do what it takes to pick it up and assist other members of our team.

7. **Work Hard, Have Fun** – We will always work hard and choose to go the extra mile when needed. In the same sense we will always remember to enjoy ourselves and keep our environment fun, dynamic, and energetic.

8. **Give Back** – As we succeed, we will give back in kind to organizations in our community, region, nation, and world that strengthen our society, provide resources that help us succeed, or help those in need.

Spend some time and thought developing your corporate values statement in conjunction with the other members of your team. The effects of a team driven by a "higher mission" can be truly revolutionary.

The Different Types of Businesses

There are many different types of businesses that you can start. All, however, will fall under one or more the four basic categories of manufacturing, wholesale, retail, or service. A manufacturing business actually makes the product, wholesale businesses sell products to stores, and retail businesses sell products to end buyers—which may be businesses or consumers. Service providers, on the other hand, sell their time and expertise instead of a tangible product.

My experience in business is in selling products at wholesale and retail and providing a service. In my experience, I have found that there is a very big difference between running product-centered company and running a service-centered businesses. My product-centered business is called iContact. We sell web-based email marketing and blogging software. My current service-centered business is called Virante. Virante does web marketing consulting for high potential companies and takes payment in cash, equity, and commissions on generated sales.

Whether you start a service-based or product-based business will have a large effect on the steps you'll have to take to build it to one million dollars in sales. I find that product businesses, in general, have a higher potential and are easier to grow exponentially, whereas service based businesses are nearly always limited.

While one can be making money while they sleep selling a product, in most service-based businesses, you can only make money when you're working. Your income is limited by the number of hours you can work. In order to overcome this, as a service-based business owner, you'll have to put the proper systems and processes in place and hire employees that can do the work for you so all you'll have to do is manage the company and set its vision.

You'll have to find high margin services in areas where you can truly add value for your customer. While services such as programming, web design, marketing consulting, and search engine optimization can be lucrative, it is rare that a one-person company makes more than $200,000 per year. To reach that $1 million dollar level in sales you'll have to stop working in your company and start working on your company—the classic advice of Michael Gerber in his book *The E-myth*.

> "To reach that $1 million dollar level in sales you'll have to stop working in your company and start working on your company."

Another difference I often find between product and service-based companies is that there is often only one founder of service based businesses—whereas there are more often than not three or four founders of product-based companies. This holds true with my companies. I maintain 100% of the ownership of Virante, Inc., but share the ownership in iContact with 11 others.

I consider iContact to be a high potential company that will hopefully sell for hundreds of millions of dollars in a few years, while Virante is a service firm, holding company, and tax advantaged business. This can be further seen by the fact that iContact is a C corporation—what most large corporations are—whereas Virante is an S corporation, allowing the profits of the company to pass through without being taxed twice.

By selling a product, one can automate much more of the business—especially if that product is delivered online or you can set up an autobilling system. One can easily automate an affiliate program, shopping cart, online merchant account—and then hire someone at $15 per hour to do the shipping and answer the phone. Further, there is much more ability to scale.

If you do decide to start a service based company, see if you can also develop a product based on your expertise in your niche—perhaps an ebook or informational product. If you can develop a product in addition to your services, you'll gain additional credibility and be able to develop a stream of income that will allow you to increase your revenue in a way that is not directly tied to the number of hours you work.

This concept is illustrated well by Robert Kiyosaki when he notes the difference between a small self-employed service provider with that of a business owner in his *Rich Dad's Guide to Investing*:

> Those who are self-employed will never become rich because they are not building an asset. If they stop working, they will stop making money. If a business owner stops working, he or she will continue to earn passive income from the asset he has built. At the core of assets are systems.

Entity Selection

To form your company, you'll first need to decide which type of entity to become. In the United States, you can choose to be a sole proprietorship, partnership, Limited Liability Company (LLC), S corporation, or C corporation.

There are different advantages and disadvantages to each depending on what your business will be doing and what your eventual goals are for the company.

A corporation is a legal entity which has a separate personality and rights from the collection of individual members it represents. The rights of a corporation include being able to sue, hold assets, hire employees and contractors, enter into contracts, and make bylaws that govern its activities. A corporation's general purpose is to develop and sell products and services and maximize the value of the organization for its shareholders.

It is generally accepted that Nevada is a good state to incorporate in for low taxes and privacy while Delaware is a good state to incorporate in if your intend to raise investment funding or sell your company, as it has business favorable laws, an extensive case history, and most corporate lawyers are familiar with Delaware law. Any U.S. resident can incorporate a company in any state he or she chooses. Definitely speak to a corporate attorney before you incorporate to get their advice and recommendation.

When you incorporate, you can do it yourself, with the assistance of an online incorporation mill, or with a lawyer. It will cost about $200 to do it yourself, $300 online, and $1500 through a lawyer, and perhaps quite a bit more if you have more than one founder of the company. In all, iContact paid our original law firm Hutchinson & Mason approximately $3000 for incorporation and all the initial start-up formalities. It was worth every penny for us, however, as we had six different founders and had a complicated capitalization table and vesting options.

To incorporate a company yourself, you'll simply need to know the name of the company, the number of shares you wish to create, and which state you wish to incorporate it in. Once incorporated, you will receive your Articles of Incorporation from the State Attorney's Office and a set of by-laws and stock certificates. Once this occurs, you contact the IRS to get an Employee Identification Number (so you can open a bank account and hire employees), choose whether to continue as a C corporation or file form 2553 to elect to be an S corporation, and hold your first board meeting.

I ended up meeting the iContact attorney through the Legal Issues for High Technology Start-ups MBA class I took in Spring 2003. If you do choose to go with a lawyer for incorporation and do not already know whom to choose, inquire about the following when evaluating each potential firm.

1. Reputation and references
2. Experience with start-ups/expertise (have they done it before)

3. Introduction to angel network
4. Access to venture capital firms
5. Library of precedents (firm as library of documents used before)
6. Potential employees/board members
7. Contacts in industry

Contracts and Agreements

In launching your company, there are certain documents that you will need in order to protect your idea and follow proper regulations. In forming iContact, between the five founders, there were over thirty-three different documents that we had to execute to launch the company. In forming your company, make sure you have all founders, independent contractors, and employees sign a non-disclosure, confidentiality and non-compete agreement. All consultants will need to sign a Consulting Agreement and all employees will need to sign an Employment Agreement. You'll also want to have a stock restriction agreement for all those receiving stock that has yet to vest.

Table 5 - Important Documents for Start-up Companies

Non-Disclosure Agreement - Initial document to be signed before any discussion of work commences. Prohibits passing on any information learned that is deemed confidential.

Confidentiality and Non-Compete Agreement - More comprehensive agreement that supersedes the original Non-Disclosure Agreement. Also contains a non-compete agreement with a provision that one cannot join or start any company in your industry for at least one (1) year after termination of relationship with the company.

Employment Agreement - For all new employees. Sets the salary, benefits, term, and scope of employment.

Consulting Agreement - For all new independent contractors. Sets the wage, term, and scope of the consulting relationship.

Stock Restriction Agreement - For all those receiving stock that has yet to

> vest. Sets the terms under which one may obtain and sell shares.

Securing Your Intellectual Property

Intellectual property (IP) is all the intangible assets of your company. These can be trademarks, trade secrets, copyrights, or patents. In the United States, the U.S. Patent and Trademark Office (USPTO) is the organization with whom you will have to file record of your IP. An overview of the major types of IP is provided here for your convenience.

Copyright

A copyright is the right to govern the use of creative works and obtain the economic benefits from the use of such work. One can copyright computer code, images, books, works of art, or any original works of authorship. However, one can only copyright the tangible expression of the work, not an idea behind such work. While the act of creation gives copyright, one can receive additional rights if he or she registers a copyright with the U.S. Patent and Trademark Office. In the United States, copyrights last seventy years after death for an individual.

Trademarks™ & Service Marks^SM

If you have a company or product name, you may wish to protect it with a trademark. One can trademark slogans (i.e. Where do you want to go today?), letters (i.e. HP), symbols (i.e. logos), and sounds (i.e. Apple Macintosh start up sound). You can register a trademark with either a state or with the federal government. To obtain protection throughout U.S., however, one should register with the U.S. Patent and Trademark Office. The USPTO bases its decision to grant a trademark based on distinctiveness and whether you are in the same industry as holders of similar trademarks or not. Once you receive your trademark, no one else can use that trademark without your permission. You can also file for a service mark if there is a special name for a service you provide. If you are in the United States, you can file for a trademark yourself at www.uspto.gov or use your law firm. The fee is $335 for a trademark.

Patents

Holding a patent can give a business a significant advantage over its competitors and be a big plus for potential investors. Patents give the right to a person or entity to be the only one that does something in a certain way. Most often it is new inventions or new processes that are patented. To be eligible to receive a patent, the idea or invention has to be novel and non-obvious. Obtaining a patent is not cheap, however. It usually costs between $10000 and $15000 and usually takes 18-24 months to be approved. Once you do receive a patent you have the right to be the only one to use your idea for seventeen years. In exchange for the patent rights, however, you have to make public the methods of how you created the process or patent.

Trade Secrets

One problem with a patent is that after your seventeen-year protection period, anybody can use your idea. As you have to explain the idea in detail when you file and these records are made public, a patent often does not offer the lasting protection a company needs. Due to this, trade secrets can often be better than patents as they never expire. A classic example of a trade secret is the Coca Cola® formula.

In order to protect a trade secret, there must be a high level of security. All employees must be forced to sign confidentiality and non-disclosure agreements, and information should only be provided on a need-to-know basis. Such protection is essential, as once a trade secret gets out, it is no longer a trade secret.

While it is important to protect your key trade secrets, consider carefully what you are willing to share. Corporate transparency can be appreciated by customers and allow you to get more press and build a more passionate user base and get more people talking about your company. This book is an example of willingness to have transparency within an organization due to the benefits of word of mouth and openness within a culture of bloggers in which the era of one-way megaphonic communication is clearly over.

> "Corporate transparency can be appreciated by customers and allow you to get more press and build a more passionate user base and get more people talking about your company."

Protecting Your IP

In order to protect your intellectual property, make sure you have all employees and contractors sign a non-disclosure, non-compete, confidentiality, and assignment of invention agreement before they start work. Make sure you make clear what is confidential information by always marking it with the word 'Confidential.' Also, when an employee leaves, be sure to hold a de-briefing session to remind the employee of his or her responsibility to not reveal your trade secrets and confidential information.

Chapter 10

Step 4: Raise Funding or Bootstrap

> "He who will not economize will have to agonize."
>
> - Confucius

Once you've found a good business opportunity or developed a good product and have incorporated, you may need some money to get off the ground. Depending on the scope of your plans, you may be able to afford to launch the company through self-financing. In other situations, you may need to raise a few thousand dollars from friends and family, apply for a $25,000 loan from your bank, raise $250,000 from angel investors, or bring in $3 million from a seed-stage venture capital firm. Your experience, sophistication, current revenue level, market size, location, relationships, competitive differentiation, and team will determine your ability to raise funds.

If you do need to raise money, you'll first need a good business plan. Once this is done, take a look at your pro forma financial statement and identify the cumulative short fall before you begin to turn cash flow positive. A good rule of thumb is to double this number, and then make this amount your goal for the amount of money you need to raise.

There are two types of capital that you can raise for your company—debt capital and equity capital. Debt capital basically consists of loans you have to pay back with interest whereas equity capital consists of investments for which you provide partial ownership in your company.

Here is a chart that summarizes the places to find capital based on how much you are seeking:

Table 6 – Where to Find the Money

If you're looking for	You'll most likely get it from
$1,000 to $25,000	Friends, family, your contacts, bank loans
$25,000 to $250,000	Angel investors, bank in some cases
$250,000 to $1 Million	Group of angel investors, Small VC Firms
$1 Million+	Venture capital firms

Debt vs. Equity

While staying with my brother at his apartment in Queens in March 2003, I had the opportunity to talk to one of his roommates by the name of Mitch. After finishing a dinner of an authentic New York City mushroom and cheese pizza, Mitch and I started talking about the business he wanted to start. He told me about his idea, the market knowledge he had gained so far, and how he hoped to bring his product to market. He also mentioned that he would need funding for the venture, and asked for some advice on how to obtain it. "I hope to obtain venture capital, but am not positive how it works," Mitch stated. "Do I sell them 49% of the company for their investment? What will be the valuation for the company if there aren't any sales yet? Should I go to a bank first?"

I explained to Mitch that while I had not yet raised venture capital myself, I had raised money from private investors for one of my companies, taken an MBA class on Venture Capital Deal Structure, and participated in the Venture Capital Investment Competition at UNC's Kenan-Flagler Business School.

I provided Mitch with an overview of the different types of capital available to an early-stage venture and how he might go about obtaining each. The following is essentially what Mitch and I discussed that night.

First, nearly all types of funding one can raise fall under one of two categories—debt or equity. Debt has to be paid back (it is a loan) whereas equity funding does not. In exchange for equity funding, the investor receives a percentage ownership (shares) in your company that grows proportionally to the overall value of your company. At a liquidity-producing event such as a sale of the company or an Initial Public Offering (IPO) to the stock markets, the equity holder could cash out their stock, ideally receiving a large return for taking the risk early on.

In his article, "Financing Instruments," attorney Michael T. Redmond explains the difference between debt and equity with

> Although there are certain exceptions, debt instruments generally represent fixed obligations to repay a specific amount at a specified date in the future, together with interest. In contrast, equity instruments generally represent ownership interests entitled to dividend payments, when declared, but with no specific right to a return on capital.

Debt Financing

Standard types of debt (short for debentures) include personal loans from family members and friends, bank loans, issued notes, venture debt, accounts receivable loans (called factoring), and corporate bonds. These financing loans are provided at an agreed upon interest rate and time period. Some debts, called convertible debts, can be converted to common stock later on, but most are paid back with cash on a set schedule or set date. Other types of debt such as venture debt, have interest accruing until the end of the maturity date, with upside provided to the lending firm (such as Silicon Valley Bank or Square One Bank) through options to purchase shares in the company.

Whether the receiver of the loan pays only the interest during the term of the loan and the entire principle (the initial amount of the loan) back at the end, or pays part of both the interest and the principle at each payment period, is determined in the terms of the loan. Debt instruments can be secured by assets of the corporation or personal assets, organizations such as the Small Business Administration, or unsecured (backed by a pledge of credit or equity in the company).

The advantages of providing debt capital to a business include a reduction in risk, as upon bankruptcy debts must be paid back before any assets can be distributed to stockholders, and a good chance of receiving the initial principle with interest back within a set period of time. Disadvantages for the issuing institution or person include not being able to participate in the value growth of the company in most cases.

The advantages to a business of taking debt capital include having less dilution and raising money at an effective lower cost. Venture investors generally require target annual returns of at least 35%, compared to between 7% and 14% for debt capital (depending on the current Prime Rate, your willingness to secure the loan, and the risk perceived by the lender).

There are many types and structures of debt. The below table reviews a few of the more common forms.

Table 7 – The Different Type of Debt

Friends & Family Loans – Loans from your friends and family, generally on favorable terms. Be careful taking money from your friends and family—it can make Thanksgivings a bit harrowing! iContact took a $5,000 loan from a

friend of ours to help us purchase server equipment early on.

Corporate Credit Cards – Many entrepreneurs use credit cards to finance their ventures early on. iContact presently has two credit cards with $100,000 and $60,000 lines of credit respectively. Credit cards generally have a much higher interest rate in the neighborhood of 12 % to 19% than credit lines.

Personally Secured Loans – Loans to your company secured by personal assets such as real estate.

Corporate Secured Loans – Loans to your company secured by company assets such as accounts receivable, inventory, company real estate, or machines.

SBA Backed Loans – Loans to your company secured in part by the U.S. Small Business Administration. iContact was able to obtain a $10,000 credit line (later expanded to $29,600 and $133,000) backed by the SBA. Our bank, Bank of America, was willing to provide us with a credit line equal to 10% of our prior year's revenue.

Convertible Debt – Loans to your company that convert into debt after a period of time. iContact raised $500,000 as convertible debt from local venture capital firm NC IDEA (later converting into equity in their IDEA Fund).

Venture Debt – Loans to your company from a Venture Debt firm such as Square One Bank or Silicon Valley Bank. iContact utilizes a $1,000,000 line of credit (LOC) from Square One Bank. Normally these firms are willing to lend an amount equal to your last two month's revenues—but generally only after you raise venture capital from an established institution. They also often take warrants (essentially the same thing as options to purchase equity at current fair market value) to increase their upside.

Corporate Bonds – Later on in the life of a company, when it is making millions of dollars in annual sales, it can set its own terms by putting together a memorandum and selling bonds to the public or private markets. The company will set the length and interest rate and then attempt to sell the debt instrument. Corporate debt is rated with letter grades based on risk by companies such as Moody's and Standard & Poor. The higher the perceived risk, the higher the interest rate the company will have to pay.

While obtaining funding can be a difficult process, there are a few things you can do to increase your chances. Here are some tips:

- If you are only looking for a few hundred or a few thousand dollars, you should first look to friends and family and then to the banks. If you have assets to back it up (such as cash in your bank account, a house, or a car) you should be able to obtain a loan with relative ease.
- if you do not have an adequate credit history or assets to back up the loan, the bank may ask for you to find someone (such as a parent or friend who does have adequate assets) to co-sign the loan. Remember, the less risk the bank feels it has, the greater chance you have of being approved.
- If you have an existing account, a good credit history and FICO score, and relationship at a local bank the process may not be any more complicated than meeting with a loan officer, discussing your plans, filling out a short form, and waiting a week for approval. However, if you have not established these relationships and history, now is a good time to start.
- If your are serious about raising more than a few thousand dollars of funding, you'll need at least some form of business plan. The more funding you are trying to raise, the more professional and complete this plan will need to be. At its core, you'll need to explain what you will be providing, what need/gap it fills in the marketplace, who you will be working with and who is on your team, your plan for making sales and marketing, and your financial projections including the time to break even. You may want to read some of the articles on developing a business plan on www.zeromillion.com for additional guidance or obtain a book on how to craft your plan.
- In general, you will be more successful obtaining financing if you have formed an entity (LLC or corporation) for your business. While it may still be possible to obtain a loan for your sole proprietorship, you will be taken more seriously and have many more avenues open to you as a corporation or other type of limited-liability company.
- If you are under 18, you will generally have to have a parent or guardian co-sign the loan. You should still be able to obtain a personal loan provided you have a well thought out plan, an

established relationship, and assets to back it up, or parents, relatives, or friends who are willing to co-sign and secure the loan with assets of their own. If you can learn the language, talk in terms of the bank's interest, reduce risk where possible, and show you have a grasp of accounting and general business knowledge, you very well may be able to obtain the loan you need.

- In the United States, another way to increase your chances of having your loan approved is to go to the Small Business Administration (SBA). If you can have your loan backed by the SBA, and hence by the Federal Government, it will be fairly easy to have your loan approved. One of the ways iContact was able to grow early on was through a $10,000 line of credit that the SBA backed.

- When applying for a loan, especially those for larger amounts or to finance large investments or expansions, be prepared to meet with the loan officers and underwriters for your bank. In short, expect to be drilled from every angle by these persons and have your answers ready. It is the underwriter's job to reduce risk, so expect hard questions.

- In general if you are looking for US$1000-$50,000 in debt funding, a bank should be able to help you. With the right relationships and assurances you may be able to raise more and at better terms. If you are looking to raise more than US$25,000 (and aren't willing to do a home equity loan) you may wish to look into equity financing.

Equity Financing

Equity financing provides stock to the investor in exchange for funds. This is usually the form of investment that venture capital funds, angel investors, or other private equity funds make. In exchange for the investment, the investor can benefit from the growth of the company and receive either common or preferred stock.

Diagram 1 – Calculating Ownership Percentages After An Equity Investment

Calculating ownership percentages:

Current value of company (Pre-Money Valuation) :	$40,000
Investment Amount:	$10,000
% You Own After Investment:	80%
% Investor Owns After Investment:	20%

Common Stock

Common stock is the most basic form of equity instrument. It represents an ownership in the corporation and includes an interest in earnings. Holders are also entitled to receive dividends (periodic disbursements to shareholders) based on earnings and the decisions of the Board.

Depending on the company or partnership's bylaws or charter, holders of common stock have the best opportunity to share in the company's growth, but also must take into account the increased risk of coming after holders of debt and preferred stock in the case of company failure and bankruptcy.

In the view of the business owner, there is one important advantage to issuing common stock in exchange for financing. There is no obligation to repay the amount invested. The investor's prime reward for taking the risk is participating in the value growth of the company and cashing out upon a liquidity event. Another advantage for the investor is the ability to vote for directors.

Preferred Stock

Preferred stock is a second form of equity instrument. While it is equity, it can have certain features that resemble debt that can make it attractive.

Most important to the investor, it has rights over common stock, reducing the risk of loss of investment. When issued, investors can also negotiate with the company whether it will be voting or non-voting stock and how dividends will be distributed. In short, it offers greater flexibility and reduced risk, and hence is preferred to common stock.

Preferred stock is usually the type of stock issued to venture capital funds upon investment in a company. Usually, the preferred stock will convert into common stock on a 1:1 ratio upon a private sale or public offering.

Equity funding tends to be a totally different ballgame than debt financing, and generally requires a greater level of sophistication to make it work. If you are looking for equity funding between US$25,000 and US$1,000,000, you should start by looking at individual angel investors or networks of angel investors. Angel investors are high net worth individuals and accredited investors (as defined by the Securities and Exchange Commission) who are able to risk relatively large amounts of money in risky ventures with a potential for a high return.

To attract these types of investors, you will need to have the right advisors (lawyers and accountants with the proper experience and contacts) and truly have an idea or business which has a potential for a high-return (US$5M and up, depending on the amount of funding needed).

To increase your chances of being funded, be sure you have a solid business plan, experienced advisors, and a team with market knowledge that has proven they can execute.

Venture Capital

If you are looking to raise US$500,000 and up and you have a business in the technology, biotechnology, energy, or consumer goods space with a potential return greater than $50M over five years, you may want to look into venture capital funding. At the seed stage (very early stage funding), you may be able to raise between US$500,000 and $10M (or potentially more if it is the right plan with the right people) in a Series A offering of your company's stock. To raise this amount of money and still maintain a good portion of ownership in your company, you'll need to have a high valuation before you accept the funding (your pre-money valuation).

For example, if based on your intellectual property, first mover advantage, unique idea, and experienced management team your business was given a pre-money valuation of US$10 million and provided with US$5 million in Series A venture funding, you will have given away 33% of your company.

To increase your chances of being funded by a venture capital firm, be sure to be introduced to the firm by someone they know. This includes entrepreneurs they have previously funded, investors they have done a deal with in the past, or an attorney they work with. Avoid sending in an "unreferred plan."

> "To increase your chances of being funded by a venture capital firm, be sure to be introduced to the firm by someone they know."

Most VC firms receive thousands of business plans per year and can only give a cursory (five-minute) look at most. If you can have a lawyer who works closely with the firm or successful CEO who worked with the firm in the past hand-deliver the plan you'll have a much better chance of getting in the door. When evaluating whether to invest, VC's generally look at the entrepreneurial leadership, the ability of a company to attract talent, relevant industry experience of the team, and for a marketing and sales orientation.

In summary, it can be difficult to obtain funding for your business as an aspiring entrepreneur. Many times you'll have to present to dozens of banks and investors before you can find someone willing to fund you. Other times, you'll have to bootstrap the company and grow it organically as your sales grow.

Eventually, around the time your company passes the $1 million in annual sales mark, associates from venture firms will start calling you! It was a great surprise to me in the Summer of 2005 when I got my first cold-call from an associate at a venture firm. These associates, many of them already having MBA degrees, work hard to drive qualified deal-flow for their partners so that they can become firm partners themselves a few years later.

The Seed Round

iContact first began the process of seeking venture capital in the Fall of 2005. We had bootstrapped the company since the beginning, using our own funds, a small loan and credit line, and reinvested company sales to build revenue. A friend of mine by the name Jud Bowman encouraged me to consider this path while having lunch with him in July 2005 at the local entrepreneur hangout Doce near our office. Jud was three years older than I and the co-founder and General Manager of the leading wireless content software provider Motricity—so I considered his advice seriously and agreed to have him connect me with a few local firms he had connections into.

The venture firms that we initially spoke to were Wakefield Group, Massey Burch, Southern Capitol Ventures, Aurora Funds, Intersouth, and NC IDEA. We received term sheets from Aurora Funds and NC IDEA, and were passed on by Wakefield Group, Massey Burch, Southern Capitol Ventures, and Intersouth. Intersouth and Southern Capitol Ventures came close to providing a term sheet. My friend Jason Caplain at Southern Capitol Ventures tells me that he regrets to this day he did not invest is us early on. While we are doing very well now, it is yet to be seen whether we will be able to successfully exit and allow us to rub it in. He is cheering for us regardless.

Initially, we were seeking $250,000 in funding. We talked to Southern Capitol Ventures in November 2005 and they indicated they might be willing to provide this amount at a $3 million valuation. This was much lower than what we were seeking, so we continued seeking.

By February 2006 we were able to receive a term sheet from the Aurora Funds at valuation closer to what we were seeking, but we were unable to agree on some of the terms such as founder revesting of shares, liquidation preference, option pool size, and board control—so we passed once again. It was very beneficial that we were cash flow positive as a company at this point, allowing us great flexibility.

It was not until May 2006 that we received a term sheet that gave us the valuation we were seeking at terms acceptable to us. We closed on a round of $500,000 convertible debt from Durham-based non-profit venture capital firm NC IDEA on May 17, 2006. The funds came to us in two tranches, $250,000 upfront and $250,000 at the end of the one year period at maturity with an acceptable interest rate. On May 17, 2007, the debt converted into equity at an agreed upon formula, and we were officially a "venture-backed company."

The Series A Round

By the time the NC IDEA investment converted into equity, we had already begun raising our next round of funding. Between the May 2006 funding and when the funds converted into equity, we had increased our sales from $176,000 to over $510,000 and our employee count from 22 to 55. We were a much larger company and now had an annual revenue run rate of over $6,000,000. We were playing a whole different ballgame now, and the venture firms were seeking us out.

We presented at three venture conferences in the Spring of 2007—at the Southeast Venture Conference in Raleigh, the AEA Venture Forum in Atlanta, and the CED Venture 2007 conference in Durham. In all, we had discussions with 39 firms during the process including NC IDEA, Southern Capitol Ventures, Intersouth, Aurora Funds, Wakefield Group, Frontier Capital, River Cities Capital, Bessemer Venture Partners, Pequot Capital, Scale Venture Partners, Noro-Moseley, HIG Partners, Core Capital, Valhalla, JMI Equity, Novak Biddle, New World Ventures, Capital Resource Partners, Battery

Ventures, Growth Capital Group, OCA Ventures, Symphony Technology Group, Edison Venture Fund, Summit Partners, Tudor Ventures, Open View Partners, True Venture Partners, Harbert Venture Partners, Ticonderoga Partners, Highland Capital Partners, Ballast Point Ventures, WWC Capital, Antares, General Catalyst Partners, MK Capital, Vantage Point, and the private equity groups Kayne Anderson, Alta Communications, and Housatonic Partners.

It did become difficult to stay in touch with all of the firms. I did use the help of our CFO Tim Oakley when I could, although he was occupied with finishing our annual audit until the last 3 weeks of the process when we had to narrow it down to the six firms that were most interested. At the end of the day, it was the venture firm that built the most rapport with us, introduced us to partners as well as associates, were willing to follow-up and seek us out, saw us for who we were becoming rather than who we had been in the past, understood what we were trying to accomplish, gave us the valuation and key terms we were looking for, moved the most efficiently, and were nice enough to come to see us at our office that got the deal.

> "At the end of the day, it was the venture firm that saw us for who we were becoming rather than who we had been in the past that got the deal."

In the end, after a competitive process we accepted a term sheet from Updata Partners out of Reston, Virginia, a firm with deep operational experience in the Software-as-a-Service space that we were competing in. We closed on a $5 million round on June 30, 2007, providing enough capital for us to continue to expand at a rapid pace and truly shoot for becoming a public company or having a $100 million or higher exit. Simultaneously, we accepted a term sheet for a $1 million line of credit from Durham-based venture debt firm Square One Bank. We are to date unsure if we will need or want to raise additional capital in the future. The possibility certainly does exist that we will choose to raise a Series B round in 2008 or 2009.

We will of course see what the end result is. We are attempting to grow as quickly as possible now while stay within the sights of profitability. We are taking more risk than before to have the opportunity for a bigger exit and the ability to create more jobs and give back in a more meaningful way to our community and world. We shall see what the final result will be. It could be $500 million, or it could be nothing at all. Such is the chance venture-backed entrepreneurs often choose to take in our fast-paced high-stakes dynamic competitive economy.

If we can reach at least $30 million in annual revenues profitably, we will likely be able to file our S-1 and take the company public, likely on the NASDAQ, AMEX, or NYSE, with the London Stock Exchange as a backup option. If we at least have a moderate exit and help our investors make money we will be able to raise money whenever we need to in the future. In our market system, the more money we can make for others and the more jobs we create in our community, the more we will be able to reinvest and continue the positive cycle of innovation and job creation.

We feel comfortable with real revenues and a world-class technology, and the expansion of private equity buyouts and alternate stock exchanges we will be able to have some form of positive exit. We are well aware, however, that market conditions are always susceptible to rapid change as we have seen before and at the time of this writing the markets are again good. Worst case scenario, at least we will know how to better play the Great Game of Business and have a few, perhaps premature, gray hairs of experience.

The 15 Step Process of Closing a Round

The process of raising venture funding generally goes something like this. Depending on the stage you're at, your experience and reputation, and connections some of these steps can be skipped:

1. **The Introduction:** You get introduced to a firm through a former entrepreneur they've invested in, an investor they've worked with in the past, a trusted attorney they know, or at a Venture Conference.
2. **The Initial Review:** An associate at the firm reviews your executive summary and gives a cursory look at your full plan and projections and if interested, schedules a call with you. It helps if you already have existing revenue or have had a previous successful venture.
3. **The First Call:** You speak with the associate by phone about what you are doing.
4. **The Partner Discussion:** If the associate likes what you are doing, he or she speaks to a partner at the firm about the opportunity.
5. **The First Meeting:** If you can get the interest of a partner, they will invite you to their offices to meet you, or meet at your office if you have an office, depending on their level of interest and your location. During this first meeting you will generally discuss your:
   a. Background and Experience
   b. Team Makeup

     c.   Competition

     d.   Product Differentiation

     e.   Market Size

     f.   Funding Needs

6. **The Valuation Discussion:** After the first meeting, if the partner remains interested, they may attempt to feel you out for the target valuation you are seeking. They also may choose not to discuss valuation and simply make an offer with the term sheet. If you are in a position of strength, you may wish to discuss valuation upfront yourself so you don't waste time. Be prepared with revenue multiples from both public companies that are similar to yours and private comparables. Depending on many factors (team, technology, industry stage, revenue growth, market size) one can expect to be able to raise funds at 2x to 10x your revenues from the trailing twelve months or 1x to 4x your projected revenues from the next twelve months. If you don't have any revenues yet, the valuation will be whatever you can negotiate with an investor and based upon your experience and any intellectual property you have. At the end of the day, the market valuation for your company is what an investor is willing to pay—and as such it is important to have multiple firms competing to invest in your firm if possible. Depending on the stage of your company, you may be able to raise funds at a 30% to 60% discount off the public market trailing or forward revenue comparables.

7. **The Partner Presentation:** Present to If you can come to general valuation range that you are both comfortable with, the partner may invite you to present in person or via videoconference to their full partner team. Prepare well and give a knock-out presentation. Invest in a graphic designer to make your presentation look nice and go heavy on actual examples of customer use and light on complex slides. I have seen a short flash product demo video or customer video interview within the presentation work well. Don't let any slide have more than five bullet points or fifty words. Your presentation is likely to be between 15 and 60 minutes.

8. **The Initial Due Diligence:** After the presentation to the full partner team, if the partners like the deal, they may ask for some additional due diligence items such as your full financials and want to speak with other members of your team and some of your customers.

9. **The Term Sheet:** If all goes well during the initial due diligence phase, the venture firm may provide you with a term sheet. A term

sheet is generally around two to eight pages and is an indication of interest in investing in you. With a term sheet, the investment firm attempts to create agreement around the general terms of the deal before the lawyers create the more extensive twenty to forty page investment agreement document. Depending on the amount of money you are raising, sometimes you will raise money from multiple firms at once in a syndicate deal. If this is the case, one firm will likely lead the deal and the other firm(s) will agree to the same term sheet. Often the first interested firm will be able to bring syndicate partners to the table, although sometimes you may need to find them yourself.

10. **The Attorney Review:** Once you receive a term sheet, have your attorney review it right away and provide feedback before you discuss it with the investment firm.

11. **The Term Sheet Negotiation:** Once you have reviewed the term sheet with your attorney, have a follow-up conversation with the partner or associate you are dealing with to negotiate the term sheet. Make sure you know which terms are the most important to you going into any negotiation (generally the valuation, option pool size, liquidation preference, participating preferred, founder revesting, and preferred stock veto rights). You may wish to have your attorney (or CFO if you have one) negotiate the finer points directly with the firm's attorney. At this point it is critical to have a top tier venture attorney on your side. These attorneys generally bill between $250 and $500 per hour depending on their experience and the market. Your negotiating power will be based upon:

    a.   how much you need the money;

    b.   the reputation of the firm;

    c.   your reputation as an entrepreneur;

    d.   any past successes you've had;

    e.   your experience;

    f.   the quality of your management team;

    g.   the members of your advisory panel;

    h.   the size of your addressable market;

    i.   your market timing;

    j.   the quality of your technology and IP;

    k.   your ability to walk away; and

    l.   whether you have other competing term sheets.

Know that it is generally taboo to provide specifics to one firm about another firm's term sheet, but you can often provide generalities or refer to wanting to have a competitive process in order to have more power in negotiating the term sheet. Do not sign the term sheet until you have negotiated it to your satisfaction and your attorney approves signing it. Once you sign a term sheet, it is very difficult to negotiate any changes in the final document. If you can create a parallel process and receive multiple term sheets you will have more power. It often will take three or four negotiation iterations to get a term sheet both sides are happy with. It can take a lot of time (and a few thousand dollars of attorney fees) to effectively accomplish this—and may be impossible without the right experience and revenues. We were unable to create a truly competitive process during our seed round, but did accomplish a competitive round in our Series A after we had $6 million in annual revenues, great technology, and rapid growth. While it can take six to eight weeks after the first meeting to get a term sheet from a venture firm traditionally, once you have an existing term sheet you may be able to get competing term sheets in as little as one to two weeks. Group mentality does at times take hold, causing the valuation to be bid up with multiple players in the deal and some of the secondary terms to be softened. This noted, at some point it can be unhealthy to push the valuation up. The highest bidders are not always the best firm for you to work with.

12. **The Term Sheet Signing:** Agree to the general terms of the deal and either digitally sign the term sheet or sign in person.

13. **The Full Due Diligence:** Once you sign the term sheet, a more extensive due diligence list will be provided to you. This list may include items such as:
    a. Detailed sales pipeline
    b. Revenue by customer type
    c. Detailed operational plan and budget
    d. Full business plan
    e. Hiring plan
    f. Detailed revenue assumptions
    g. Audited financial statements
    h. Bank reconciliation detail
    i. Product Pricing list
    j. Detailed product roadmap
    k. Customer, Employee, Insurance, and Lease contracts
    l. Relevant whitepapers and analyst coverage
    m. Details on IT infrastructure

n. Current partner list
o. Lead generation processes
p. Customer satisfaction survey
q. Customer reference list
r. Details on intellectual property
s. Current capitalization chart with options detail
t. Organizational chart
u. Salary and bonus structure for company
v. Employee turnover
w. Management background checks
x. Competitive analysis
y. Expected acquirers
z. Past board meeting minutes

14. **The Final Investment Documents:** Once this due diligence is complete, if all goes well, you will receive the final investment documents from the investment firm's lawyers. Have your attorney review it closely and negotiate any needed changes. Pay especially close attention to any representations and warranties you are making as an officer of the company and personally. The final investment documents generally include a:

a. Share Purchase Agreement
b. Investor Rights Agreement
c. Right of First Refusal and Co-Sale Agreement
d. Voting Agreement

15. **The Deal Signing:** Provide your company bank account information, close the deal, watch the funds go into your account, breathe a sigh of relief, send out the press release, and welcome your new investor(s) and board member(s) to the team with a celebration open house, exchange of company swag, and thank you card. Then get going on growing revenue.

As you can see, the process can be arduous and long, especially if you are dealing with multiple firms and trying to parallel process to create a competitive round. At the end of the day, even if a firm is not interested, try to build a relationship for the future.

Table 8 – The Key Terms of a Venture Term Sheet

THE OFFERING TERMS

- *Closing Dates: The target date for the close of the deal*
- *Investors: Which firm(s) will invest in the deal*
- *Amount Raised: How much money you are investing in*
- *Pre-Money Valuation The agreed upon value of your company before the investment*
- *Post-Money Valuation: The value of your company after the investment. Equal to the pre-money valuation plus the investment amount.*
- *Capitalization: The company's current shareholder list with the number of shares and options each shareholder has*
- *Use of Proceeds: How the investment money is to be used*

THE CHARTER

- *Dividends: The process by which dividends will be distributed to shareholders. Dividend distribution generally occurs at the discretion of the board. This section also includes the interest rate at which the investment funds will grow each year, on either a cumulative or non-cumulative basis. Try to negotiate out any interest or at least request no interest in the case of a successful exit.*
- *Liquidation Preference: The right for the investor to receive their money out first in a liquidity event before payment is made to common shareholders.*
- *Voting Rights: Covers the rights of the investor(s) to vote on certain items materially affecting the company.*
- *Protective Provisions: Describes what company changes need to be approved by the investor(s)*
- *Anti-dilution Provisions: The right of the investor to be protected from dilution in the event stock is ever sold at a price less than the current round (called a down-round). The broad-based weighted average is the method of calculating dilution that is most company-friendly.*
- *Mandatory Conversion: Describes the conditions and process by which the preferred shares convert into common shares.*
- *Optional Conversion: The right for the investor to convert their preferred shares into common shares at any point in time.*

- *Redemption Rights: The right of the investor to get their money back if they choose after a period of time, generally after five years. This is a rarely used provision, but be careful with it nonetheless.*

STOCK PURCHASE AGREEMENT

- *Representations and Warranties: The representations the company must make to be true and accurate for the investment to take place.*
- *Conditions to Closing: A general description of the due diligence area to be looked at prior to closing.*
- *Counsel and Expenses: Covers the maximum amount of money due to the attorneys to close the deal. Generally between $10,000 and $30,000 depending on the complexity of the deal. The company generally will pay this out of the investment amount.*

INVESTOR RIGHTS AGREEMENT

- *Registration Rights: Refers to the rights of the investor to register their shares during a public offering.*
- *Information and Inspection Rights: The rights of the investor to receive information about the company.*
- *Board Matters: The composition of the Board of Directors following the deal. Do you best to ensure there are more company representatives than investor representatives. You effectively lose control of the company if this is not the case. You may wish for your Board to be your CEO, Chairman or CFO, and one investor, or expand the size to five members and have your CEO, CFO, Chairman, and two investor representatives.*
- *Drag Along: The right of the Board and preferred shareholders to ensure all stockholders will agree to a sign if the Board and majority of the preferred stockholders agree to sell.*
- *Right of first Refusal: The right of the Company and/or the investor to purchase any shares that any shareholder chooses to sell.*

OTHER MATTERS

- *Bank Debt: Any related line of credit that the investor expressly approves.*
- *Employment Matters: A condition of closing requiring all employees to*

> *have employment contracts and non-compete agreements*
> - *No Shop/Confidentiality: An agreement not to tell anyone outside of company shareholders, the Board of Directors, and your attorney about the terms of the deal or to seek other term sheets during a period of usually 30 to 45 days while the deal is being closed.*
> - *Binding/Non-Binding Provisions: Any obligations that the term sheet will legally bind the parties to, whether or not the deal is executed, such as paying the legal fees of the investor.*
> - *Expiration: The date after which the term sheet offer is no longer valid. Don't let this date make you into signing the term sheet before you are ready.*

It takes time to learn about the many components of a term sheet. It can be very valuable to have an attorney or CFO who can advise you through the process. At the end of the day, don't sign the term sheet until you are fully comfortable with it and understand the provisions within. Here are twelve tips for anyone attempting to raise venture capital.

1. Get introduced through an entrepreneur or attorney the VC firm has worked with in the past. A good law firm can be very valuable for investor introductions, if you can convince them your business would be a good investment.
2. Talk to multiple firms at once. Create a competitive process and seek multiple term sheets if you are able.
3. Read up on term sheet terms and have a good understanding of them before you start talking to investors. The key terms are pre-money valuation, liquidation preference, participation, share revesting, dividends, board size, and protective provisions.
4. Be upfront about the general terms you are seeking to save yourself and the investor time.
5. Know that the pre-money valuation is only one of the important terms.
6. Get involved with organizations in your community that can connect you to other entrepreneurs who have done it before and then have lunch with those entrepreneurs.
7. Realize that it will probably take at least 9 months to raise money from start to finish your first time doing it.

8. Realize that until you have at least $1 million in annual revenue it may be difficult to get most VCs interested unless you have had prior successes or really unique technology.
9. Know that it may take 6 months of sustained product and revenue progress after your first meeting before a VC will consider your deal seriously.
10. Know how much money you are trying to raise before you begin discussions.
11. Know that it may be easier to seek angel funding or debt funding instead of venture capital early on.
12. Know that once you sign a term sheet it will be at least 30 days and up to 90 days before you actually close on the funds.

Bootstrapping

It is certainly possible to create a successful company without any initial investment other than time and energy. This is often the only option available to young entrepreneurs. Here's what you can expect if you go this route.

1. Be prepared (and able) to work 70+ hour weeks for a year or more without any salary.
2. Be prepared to wear multiple hats including CEO, CFO, COO, VP Marketing, VP Business Development, and Chief Executive Janitor
3. Be prepared to offer ownership in your company to other team members until you can pay them a market salary
4. Be able to look at creative ways at getting legal and accounting advisors to provided discounted help including offering them a small piece of the pie.

Highlight 7: CEO & Chief Executive Janitor

Reprinted from www.zeromillion.com with permission.

When a company is started, unless there is ample financing, often the owner will find himself or herself all alone for a while until sales start picking up and cash flow can support hiring help. My friend and business partner Aaron Houghton once told me, "As a start-up CEO you are the Chief Executive Officer, Chief Executive Painter, and Chief Executive Janitor." Now, clearly this is not the case if you are backed by venture capital or have enough funds to bankroll a staff. However, many people simply do not have much capital they can invest, do not have access to venture capitalists, or simply wish to avoid going into debt or selling off part of their company. Office space for these people, at least at first, often consists of dorm rooms, garages, or third bedrooms.

So how does one get past this start-up phase? What are some ways to start building cash flow? And at what point does one invest in things like office space, intellectual property protection, accounting software, inventory, or employees?

As I told the story in Chapter One, in August 2001, I met a man who had founded a number of companies, and was working on his next. When I came aboard, everything had been put in place and the groundwork had been done. The business owner had developed the product and had spent the past year laying the foundation for the company that would sell that product. Only a few hundred dollars in sales had been made to that point, but things were ready to take off.

As I told before, by a year later the company was nearing $200,000 in sales each month and close to passing the $1 million in sales mark. This company, however, never raised a dime of venture capital and never even took any debt. This was a bootstrapped company from start to finish. In June of 2002, I had a chance to interview the owner of that company. Here's what he said on the topic of bootstrapping his company.

> First of all, if you are on a tight budget, be ever mindful that the last thing you need is overhead. Don't put the cart before the horse. Find a product. There are products out there. Look through the classifieds. There are people out there who have wonderful products but do not know how to market them. Contact these individuals and make them an offer. Give them a small piece of the action and buy the product out from them or license it. If you do not have money, find investors. Just make sure you retain control of the company. There are books available that can show you how to draft sample agreements like this.
>
> The small entrepreneur simply needs to learn that much can

happen in his or her own garage. You can take a product, spend a minimal amount of money to get a label on it and packaging and take it out door to door to small shops. Go to these shops and tell them you'd like to put the product in on consignment basis. Here you may run into trouble with stores asking for credit, but do what you can and extend credit if you are able to get some initial cash flow.

Then take your product and sell it to your friends. If your product is as good as you say it is those same friends are going to be telling their friends. You can build off a simple little platform like this.

Then build your web site, get an affiliate program going, and go from there. The key is finding a superior product that can be manufactured at a very low cost. The typical successful television product needs a seven times markup, 700%. Educate yourself about markups and costs.

Packaging is essential. Spend more on your packaging and written materials. If you cannot write, go find a copywriter that can. Get out and talk to people and get feedback on your product as often as you can.

If you have a superior product, you'll win the battle. If you do not, odds are you are going to lose.

Learn to do what you can yourself. Don't walk into a lawyer's office and spend $2500 needlessly. Find an incorporation mill that can do it for $250. Learn how to write copy, that's really essential.

If you make a mistake, be sure to learn from that mistake. If you fail, be sure you learn from the failure. I've not known a successful entrepreneur that didn't have four or five failures. I might be a notable exception. I've only failed two or three times [laugh].

Just keep punching. It's tenacity that wins.

Very powerful words from a man that built a very successful company. If

ZERO TO ONE MILLION

you find yourself in a position without too much money, but do not want to take on debt or sell off stock, internalize these words.

Doing the foundational groundwork for a new company can take time. Common jobs include sourcing products, filing articles of incorporation, printing letterhead, business cards, and brochures, writing sales copy, finding office space, developing a web site, negotiating contracts with suppliers, purchasing an initial inventory, registering a trademark, and buying office supplies, among many others.

In August 2001 when I began working with the nutraceuticals company, there was not enough cash flow to hire any employees yet, so the owner and I had to do everything. The CEO and janitor saying rang true indeed for the owner, while I was a jack-of-all-trades myself. I handled all the emails, the phones, the packaging of orders, the marketing, the walk-in customers, the affiliates, and the web site. The owner handled the bankers, the forms, the accounting, and the most important customers. By no means were we in Silicon Valley in 1999 and by no means did the company have millions of dollars of venture capital.

After incorporating, the company went five months before obtaining office space and eleven months before bringing in any outside help. After bringing me on as an independent contractor, no one else was hired for three additional months.

Soon, however, we were lucky enough to begin to have enough orders for the product to require a part-time person to package the orders and take them down to the post office. This position soon became full-time as more and more orders came in. This person also kept track of the inventory of all supplies and reordered items as needed.

By February, the company had grown to the point where I was spending much of my time answering the phones and emails instead of marketing. At this point, the company hired someone to take care of customer service. This person took over all the customer service emails and answered the phones, allowing me to concentrate on growing sales. In April, the company hired an eventual replacement for me - someone that I could train in my marketing methodology and practices before I left for college that August.

Finally, in July the company brought on an accountant to take over as Chief Financial Officer. The company at that point was having trouble with the merchant account processor and the expenses were starting to grow. The CFO handled payroll, took checks to the bank, and went over the expense reports and merchant account figures with a fine-toothed comb.

Start with a good product, do the groundwork and due diligence well, don't skimp on good advisors, put the proper marketing systems into place, get the right people on your team, then mix in a little time and an ounce of perseverance. Finally, just remember as you toil away endless days and endless nights on your dream, on your baby, on your future million dollar company, that the entrepreneurial gods are with you, and cheering you on every step of the way.

Step 5: Develop Your Product

> "Never before in history has innovation offered promise of so much to so many in so short a time."
>
> - Bill Gates

If you want to make a lot of money in business, in general, you have to do one of two things. You have to either create a new product or create a new business model—or invest in a business that is doing this. You have to innovate or be an innovation-enabler. Michael Dell

> "If you want to make a lot of money you have to do one of two things. You have to either create a new product or create a new business model."

created a new business model with his direct-to-consumer distribution of personal computers. So did Ford with his mass-production assembly line, Rockefeller with his vertically integrated oil empire, Ray Kroc with McDonald's, and Pierre Omidyar with eBay. Others however, from Edison to Wally Amos have made their money from product innovation. In this chapter, we'll talk about the steps involved in developing a product.

The Perfect Product

While most established businesses have more than one stream of revenue, it is often sales of products that contribute most to this cash flow. The product(s) a company sells will be a huge factor in whether they succeed. The right product can propel any company to fortune and the wrong product can make even the most exhaustive efforts unprofitable.

So what are the attributes of good products? As we learned in the MAR Opportunity Evaluation Model, one of the most important requirements of a product is that it must fulfill a need or want. Does the product ease a pain, fulfill a dream, make life easier, or make life better? If not, you better start searching for a product that does. The first part of the Executive Summary in any business plan is the need. What is the need, and how does your business/product fulfill this need?

The second part of the executive summary is an overview of the market. What is the market for the product? Is it a business to business product or business to consumer? How big is the market? In some cases, having a product with mass market appeal is a good thing. For example, if you wanted to have your product featured on the Home Shopping Network or market it using infomercials, then you want your potential customers to be everyone or at least a large part of the population. Products with a mass-market appeal that have been successfully marketed through infomercials include George Foreman Grills, Ginsu® Knives, and OxiClean® cleaner. On the other hand, it is unlikely that you would be successful marketing a book analyzing the cerebral cortexes of llamas via a mass-market infomercial.

Other times, however, it is beneficial to have a product that is geared to a niche market. It is much easier to become a real player with niche products than with products that appeal to everyone. There is generally less competition, plus you are able to focus your marketing and advertising on a pre-determined demographic group. In most cases, there will already be trade journals, web sites, and magazines which the market segment you are targeting pays attention to, making it much easier to develop brand recognition and a product-following. Word of mouth, also known as viral marketing, also tends to spread faster with these niche products, and it is quite likely that someone with a specific need knows a few other people with the same need.

The Importance of an Ample Margin

Sufficient markup is crucial attribute that a good product must have. Generally, it must be at least 2:1. However, the best products have markups of 5:1 or more. This translates to a 400% or more markup. You might say, "If I raised my prices that high no one would ever buy." This may be true, depending on your product and the competition in your industry. However, there are a number of things you can do to increase your markup, and hence your per product profit margin, without reducing the number of sales.

First, let's define what a markup is. Markup is simply the sale price of the product divided by the cost of the goods sold. This equation has two components and can be worked on from two angles. The first angle is to lower your cost of goods sold. How? Do everything you can to get the lowest possible price with your supplier(s). Renegotiate terms, offer incentives, tell them you'll be sending some business their way; whatever you need to do to get their lowest price. Second, increase your sale price. How can this be done without hurting sales? Simple—increase the perceived value of your product.

Perceived value is what customers think your product should cost, or more specifically, what value they think it has to them and what they would be willing to pay for it.

Improving perceived value

Here are eight ways to improve the perceived value of your product.

1. Emphasize quality;
2. Display success stories on your web site and in your marketing materials;
3. Tell of your top quality customer service;
4. Stress convenience;
5. Improve the design of your product's packaging and labeling;
6. Distinguish your product from your competitor's product and tell why yours is best;
7. Develop your unique selling proposition; and
8. If you are selling this product from your web site, make sure the site is nicely designed, easy to use, and typo-free.

After you've improved the perceived value of your product, you should be able to increase your price without causing a decrease in net profits.

One-Time-Sale or Continued Sales?

J. Paul Getty, a former billionaire oil baron and once the richest man in the world, is known for emphasizing the importance of selling products that give continued sales. Most products are single-sale items (vacuums, beds, ladders, videos, etc.), and it is more difficult to build a business selling these as you are always spending money and time trying to attract new customers. If you have your choice of products, look for those that can be sold multiple times to the same customer.

The pharmaceutical industry can afford to spend the billions it does on research and development. Why? Simply because most often they produce treatments and not cures for diseases and ailments. Treatments must be taken continuously. Other health products like nutraceuticals and vitamins are also repeat-sale products. Anything that needs to be refilled or reordered within a relatively short time frame can be considered a repeat-sale product. The majority of services (phone, water, electricity, hosting, etc) are on this auto-bill and auto-deliver system. See if you can find a way to put your product on an auto-bill and auto-ship system. And if you can't, find a product or service to sell that you can.

Up-Sell & Cross-Sell Ability

A good marketer knows the value of upselling and cross-selling. In a business there are three ways to increase your revenue. One, increase the number of customers you have, two, increase the frequency at which your customers buy from you, and three, increase the amount they spend on each purchase. Upselling and cross-selling work on increasing this third pillar. Essentially, upselling is encouraging (usually though an incentive like a discount or free gift) a customer at the time of sale to purchase more of your product than they had originally intended. Cross-selling is selling the same customer a related product to the one they are buying that they either were not intending to buy in the first place or didn't know you offered.

Here's an example of an upsell and a cross-sell. For Christmas one year in high school, I wanted to buy a small turtle for my girlfriend Kristina. So I drove to the pet store and walked in with the intention of buying a turtle, some turtle food, and a fish bowl to put her in. Well, eighty-seven dollars later I walked out with a lovely new turtle, a glass aquarium, an automatic filter, an aquarium heater, two bags of stones, turtle pellets, and some dead crickets. Walking out, I realized that I had been both up-sold and cross-sold by an experienced salesperson.

Also, often related to upselling and cross-selling is the back-end product. The back-end product is a related and often more expensive product offered to customers after they've purchased their first product. Using back-ends, cross-selling, and upselling is a great way to strengthen your bottom line. Therefore, before deciding to sell a product, it is necessary to determine how easily a product can be upsold and cross-sold and if there are any suitably-related products to offer your customers after they've made an initial purchase.

The Perfect Product in Review

The perfect product has the following attributes…

1. Fulfills a need or want;
2. Has either niche market appeal or mass-market appeal;
3. Has at least a 2:1 markup; 5:1 or higher is optimal;
4. Has a high perceived value;
5. Must be replenished or repurchased by the customer often;
6. Is easily upsold and cross-sold; and
7. Has a related back-end product.

On August 1, 2001 I first met the owner of the health company that I worked for my senior year of high school. He had found a great product and had worked the past year laying the groundwork to create the company that would sell that product. I wasn't sure at the time just how good his product was. A year later however, as we neared the $1,000,000 in sales mark, I knew.

The market size was huge. The demand for the product was large and increasing. The product was of very high quality. The product was unique and could be distinguished easily from competing products. The product was effective. The product gave significant benefits to the consumer. The product had to be reordered every thirty days. The product could be obtained at a relatively low cost, which supported a large markup. Finally, there were few serious competitors selling similar products.

In short it was a great product. But how do you know if your product is great? And if you are in search of a product to sell, what questions must you ask to determine if it is great and will sell well?

Well, there are two factors that must be assessed when selecting a product. These are the inherent qualities of the product and the state of the marketplace. Here is a list of questions to ask in examining each of your products or potential products.

How to Tell If Your Product Is Great: The Inherent Qualities of the Product

1. Is the product of high quality?
2. Is the product effective?
3. How valuable are the benefits the product gives to the consumer?
4. Does the product increase pleasure, increase utility, or reduce pain?
5. Must the product be reordered?
6. Can a back-end for the product easily be developed?

How to Tell If Your Product Is Great: The State of the Marketplace

1. Can it be obtained or produced for a low cost so as to support a high margin?
2. What is the current demand for the product?
3. Is this demand expanding?
4. How many other competitors are selling the same or similar product?
5. How many serious competitors are there?
6. What are the sales figures of these competitors?
7. What are the products substitutes?
8. Are there any factors that may increase or decrease sales of substitutes?
9. How hard will it be to differentiate the product from competing products?

Creating Your Product

The first step in creating a product is to determine whether you will be manufacturing your product in-house or outsourcing your manufacturing. In cases where production requires heavy and expensive machinery, you'll want to outsource production initially. In cases where the needed equipment can be purchased fairly inexpensively, it may be less expensive to purchase the equipment yourself.

If you choose to produce your product(s) yourself, you'll need to source (find suppliers for) all the parts and machinery you'll need. If you will be outsourcing everything to a manufacturing partner, you'll need to submit a request for quote (RFQ) from potential manufacturers. You'll describe exactly what you need done and then evaluate the possibilities based on the information and price quotes you receive in return. Here are two stories of young entrepreneurs I've met who have developed products.

When I first met a current friend of mine by the name of Erik Severinghaus, he was developing a product that would allow, at the touch of a button, information to be passed from a small hub to a PDA device. Erik envisioned that the device could be used at trade shows to quickly transfer information from a company to a prospect or from a prospect to a company, between business persons, or at the front desks of hotels. He had incorporated a company to sell the product by the name of FastCAT, Inc. and had spent over a year developing his product.

Erik used his skills learned as a network and systems engineer to take a computer chip process and modify it to load and wirelessly transfer the needed information. He then constructed a half-sphere case out of a light cover and a piece of PVC pipe. He then sourced a press button and connected the button to the chip. He learned about the transfer standards with the major PDA operating systems, and finally, after over a year of work, got the device to function.

His next step was to raise the funding he needed so he could hire a graphic designer to redesign the graphic casing to make it look less like a science project and more like a high technology device, locate a manufacturer, and outsource the production of a functioning prototype with the new design. Unfortunately, Erik was unable to find the funding, and he soon moved on to other ventures. His story provides a good illustration of just how many steps there are in developing a product.

In February 2003, I met Dan Bowman and Chirag Nanavati. Dan and Chirag had been working on developing a technology that provided a more efficient, healthy, and tasty way to remove fat from potato chips. While Dan was a first year MBA student at UNC Kenan Flagler Business School, he was working for the Office of Technology Development and was looking through UNC's intellectual property portfolio. Within, he found out that professors at UNC and NC State University had developed a method of using carbon dioxide to extract the fat from snack foods. Dan talked to the Technology Transfer office and obtained permission to build a company to commercialize this technology.

The first step was to choose the application. After completing market research, Dan decided that he would start-up by building a machine that would take the fat out of potato chips. He went through the process of finding a manufacturer that could produce such equipment and worked with them over many months to develop a working prototype. During that time, he brought on partners Chirag as well as Randy Diefenthal and came up with the company name of Singras. Finally, just in time to present at the Venture Capital Investment Competition in February 2003, the manufacturing firm came up with a prototype machine needed to produce the chips. They were excited to bring their first batch to the competition.

These quick stories can only begin to illustrate the number of steps and difficulty of creating some types of products. From naming a product to obtaining a trademark to designing label and packaging to evaluating manufacturers to going through the patent process it surely can become complex. If you have the right team, a good technology, and a good partner in your supplier, it can be done however. The benefits are often worth it.

In your case, you may be developing a product that is not so difficult to produce. Perhaps you are starting a t-shirt printing company or writing an ebook you will sell online. Or perhaps you are not selling a product at all. This is fine as well. Just make sure that if you are developing a product you keep in mind the key points above regarding creating a good product.

The Product Management Process

One of the biggest perils of being a new company as it grows from being a fledgling organization into a multimillion dollar corporation, and eventually into great worldwide company is developing a product or service over multiple product cycles from the first iteration into the next version. Whether it's in software and you're working with versions or you're providing a consumer goods product and you're improving a feature or changing the design or functionality, getting the ongoing process of product development correct is key to a company's success. There's a process of innovation you must go through. You can do this process correctly and you can do this process incorrectly.

Whether you're able to put it in place the right product innovation processes and R&D processes within your organization is going to make a big impact on how successful in the long term you're going to be. It is possible to build the first version of a product and make a few hundred thousand dollars in sales, and not continue to innovate. Within a year to eighteen months, however, a new product cycle will come along in the market. Regardless of the business you are in, if you're not reinvesting part the money you're making into improving your service, improving your product, and listening to your customers so that you know how to improve your product and service, you are going to fall behind in a fairly short period of time.

The first principle of creating a great product management process is to listen to your customers. Survey your customers. Ask them, what do they like, how can you improve the features that you already have, and what features and services can you provide in addition to what you're currently providing? Asking these questions is critically important.

> "The first principle of creating a great product management process is to listen to your customers."

Within iContact we hired our chief technical officer in February 2004. We brought him on as a lead developer, and he was our fourth employee. He started out right away writing code and putting in the product, and within a month we had a new surveying product, and within another month we had a new autoresponder feature. The process was fairly quick since we had only one programmer. Over the past four years our technical department has evolved from having just one developer into having a team of fourteen full-time developers, a user interface engineer, a database administrator, a quality assurance team, and a systems administration team.

Now, out of necessity, we go through a formal iteration process. We have a formal product wish list, a tracking tool called Xplanner to monitor our progress, a bug tracking tool called Bugzilla, and product stories submitted by employees and refined by Directors,

We go through an iteration process and have a monthly sprint review process in which we review all the work we've done over the past four weeks. We have a sprint planning meeting where we plan for the next four weeks, and what we're going to develop. We have a product management meeting every two weeks. We are constantly seeking input. We seek data through customer surveys, customer focus groups, feedback forms within the web site and application, and competing products. This allows us to ensure we are aware of the customer requested features as well the features we need to create to lead the market with the version of our product.

Our product management process is a more agile process now. We use sticky notes, note cards, voting systems, surveying tools, and different meetings and processes. This flexible innovation process for us has been critical to our success. We used to have a six month development cycle in which we would create a big Products Requirements Document of thirty or forty pages. We would say this is what we want, we'd give it to the developers, and they'd have six months to develop that. What we ended up seeing when we released is that we would not have the quality assurance level that we needed we were losing so much dynamism by having such a long process. In response, we ended up switching to a four week sprint and a scrum style of development that has been very helpful to us.

Regardless of the type of company that you are building, think critically about how your product innovation process and your product management process can work together to create a system of constant improvements. This is what capitalism and what the competitive market economy is all about, and what the real role of an entrepreneur is—to consistently improve. There's this Japanese theory of "Kaizen" which means consistently improving, always improving. If you can take something you have today, and over time as money comes in,

> "This is what capitalism and what the competitive market economy is all about, and what the real role of an entrepreneur is—to consistently improve."

reinvest that money to make it better and better, you will be able to provide a better quality service or product at a lower cost. This constant improvement will allow you to be able to expand the scale of your marketplace and create a lasting and very large organization that is profitable for yourself and your shareholders, as well as the customers using your products.

Step 6: Develop Your Marketing & Sales Strategy

> Two shoe salesmen find themselves in a rustic backward part of Africa. The first salesman wires back to his head office: "There is no prospect of sales. Natives do not wear shoes!" The other salesman wires: "No one wears shoes here. We can dominate the market. Send all possible stock."
>
> — Akio Morita, Sony

What is Marketing?

Marketing is everything you do to place your product or service in the hands of potential customers. The purpose of marketing is to get the word out about your product—and in turn to make sales of your product or service. While sales is the act of converting a prospect into to customer, marketing is the process that makes sales possible including brand development, partnership creation, publicity, and advertising.

Marketing is the background work that gets prospects in the door. Sales is the process of converting those prospects to lifetime customers. The cause of the failure of many businesses is a breakdown in, or lack of, marketing. You can develop a wonderful product or provide a high value-add service, but if no one knows about it your business will not succeed.

While marketing can be complex, the basics of marketing are simple!. Here are the key questions to ask as you develop your marketing plan:

1. Who is likely to buy my product or service?
2. Where do these people look for products or   services like mine?
3. How can I get in those places?

There are two different types of marketing. The type you'll learn in most business schools can be generally defined as corporate marketing. In a business school class on corporate marketing, you'll learn about things like branding strategy, demographics, and positioning statements. While these subjects are important to know, they will not be of great benefit to the bootstrapping entrepreneur who does not have a million dollar budget, ten ad designers, and a sales force of one hundred. The other type of marketing is entrepreneurial marketing. In entrepreneurial marketing, instead of concentrating on brand recognition you concentrate on sales. Without much money to spend, the return on investment (ROI) of every ad, of every campaign, is that much more important.

In this chapter, I will present the basics of marketing, the core of much of what corporate marketing is based on as well as a complete step-by-step entrepreneurial marketing strategy to launching your business and building it to one million dollars in sales at a low cost.

Table 9 - Important Definitions for Marketers

B2B – Business to Business.
B2C – Business to Consumer
Brand – The aggregate representation and reputation of your business across all those who interact with it. Includes much more than simply the logo and corporate identity.
CAC – Customer Acquisition Cost
CRM – Customer Relationship Management
CTR – Clickthrough Rate
Demographics – Data on customers and prospects such as gender, location, birth date, past purchases, income level, marriage status, and birth date. A marketer can better target their promotions with good demographic data.
Direct-to-consumer – Selling a product directly to the buyer without any middlemen.
Distribution Model – The levels of companies through which a product is sourced, manufactured, and then sold.
Distribution Strategy – Where and how a company positions itself in the value chain, including what type of distribution model it follows.
LTV – The Lifetime Value (of a customer).
Market Research – research about a market including the competitors and competing products, its size, and growth rate.
Retail – Selling a product to an end buyer
ROAS – Return on Ad Spend
ROI – Return on Investment
Target Market – Who your business will be targeting with the promotions for your product. Those that are most likely to buy.

USP – Unique Selling Point, also known as the value proposition; what you do that differentiates you from your competitors.
Value Chain – A representation of the distribution model based on the value added by each type of business at each level.
Wholesale – Selling of a product to another business who will later resell it.

The Four Ps

One of the most basic and most important concepts in marketing is known as the Four Ps. The four Ps are product, price, place, and promotion. If you can develop a good product at the right price, position it in a place where buyers are, and promote it well to create desire in the customers' mind, you'll quickly succeed in making a lot of sales.

Product

As we talked about before, your product is crucial to your success. If you have a good product, getting the other three Ps right will be that much easier. The 'product' includes both the actual physical product as well as product decisions such as function, appearance, packaging, labeling, and warranty. The word 'product' also encompasses any services you may provide. The service you provide is your product.

Price

If your price is too high, not enough people will be able to afford it. If your price is too low, you will not make any profit. On the other hand, if your price is too low, many will not buy it because they may see it as an inferior good. To best manage these forces and optimize your net profits, you will have to test many different prices of your product(s).

Place

Place is essential to building sales. Place essentially rests on **positioning**—the positioning of your marketing message and the positioning of your product. In both retail stores, the corporate market, and online, how to properly position your product is a very important skill. Without proper positioning, no one will know you exist. If you are hidden in the back corner of a store on the bottom shelf and your web site is number 3425 in the search engines for your targeted keywords, you likely will not make many sales, no matter how good the product is. We'll talk more about how to position your product both online and off later in this chapter.

The positioning of your product is also known as your **distribution strategy.** A distribution strategy is developed by determining where on the **value chain** you want your business to be positioned, and who the buyer will be. You may sell your product to a retail store who then resells it to the buyer, a manufacturer who sells exclusively to jobbers and regional representatives, or directly to your end consumers. We'll talk more about distribution models and strategies later in this section.

Promotion

Promotion is an essential part of the marketing process. Promotion decisions include those related to communicating your message, advertising, and public relations.

Market Research & Competitive Intelligence

As noted earlier, when you write your business plan, you will need to complete research on the state of the marketplace. Four good sources for quality market information are Hoover's Online, Lexis-Nexis, Factiva, ZoomInfo, and Dialog. These are all paid services, but can be worth the investment if you can properly leverage the information in their extensive databases. And if, by chance, you are a university student, contact your librarian as you may have free access to these services. If you are not, make a visit to your local library. Many libraries will either have subscriptions to these services or static versions of the databases on CD.

To complete your market research, it is always a good idea to talk to potential customers. You can create a survey and send it out to potential customers using a tool such as iContact, or hold a focus group with a related organization in your area. If you have a prototype of a product you are working on, you can ask potential customers about everything from design to functionality. As an aspiring entrepreneur, many people will be willing to help you. Be sure to take advantage of this.

Generally, your research will help you uncover several target markets that you can reach with your product or service. It is important to, as specifically as you can, describe each of your target markets. You may define one of your target markets as married males 30-45 living in Hoboken, New Jersey or all persons over the age of 60 that suffer from type 2 diabetes. You can surely have more than one target market, known as market segments. For example, your product may be effective for senior citizens and athletes. Surely, you'll want to have different marketing materials for each segment.

If you can, attempt to determine who you customers are, how many there are, where they are, what needs they have that currently are not being met, why they buy, and from whom they buy.

At iContact, we have created five personas that represent each of our distinct markets. These personas are:

Carl – The contract web designer living in a big city
Karen – The work-at-home mom who scrapbooks in her free time
Frank – The President of a ten person company
Joe – The Vice President of Marketing at a one hundred person company
Eileen – The Director of Emarketing at a Fortune 500 company

Action Item 5 – Create Your Target Personas

Create three to five personas who are likely buyers of your product or service. What is their name? How old are they? Where do they live? What type of company do they work at? What is their job title? Where do they look for products like those you provide?

1. _____

2. _____

3. _____

4. _____

5. _____

Creating Your Distribution Strategy

To get a product from parts to consumer in the old economy it would often take five or more companies. There would be a parts supplier, a product manufacturer, a jobber, a wholesaler, and a retailer who would finally sell to the end consumer. With each middleman there would have to be another markup. There was great inefficiency and prices were high.

Many companies today, however, are turning toward a Direct-to-Consumer (DTC) model. Instead of five or six companies in the distribution chain there are two—the Supplier and the Manufacturer. Now, because of the Internet and mail order, companies that once focused solely on creating, can also built competencies in selling. All the manufacturer has to do is set up a web site, get it to the top of the search engines, and hire a few people to ship out orders. And now, instead of a 40% markup it can charge a 400% markup—all because of a shift to a DTC strategy.

I learned this lesson very well working with the nutraceuticals company in 2001 and 2002. When I got there, the company was focusing on selling to local retailers. We soon shifted toward focusing on DTC internet sales, taking the markup from 3x to 7x. Here is a comparison chart between an old and a new distribution model:

Diagram 2 – Old vs. New Distribution Model

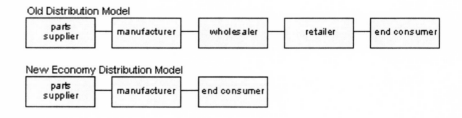

As you can see from the diagram, the new model is much more efficient. By selling direct to your customers instead of going through middlemen whenever possible, you'll be able to increase your price while keeping your costs the same, greatly improving your gross and net margins.

In addition, by developing your consumer channel first, you'll create demand at the retail level. This is what happened with Icy-Hot when marketing expert Jay Abraham got on board with the initial product developer to sell directly to consumers via mail-order. Before they knew it, they had created a huge retail business in addition to their direct-to-consumer business. It's a lot easier to get into the GNCs, Wal-Marts, and Sears of the world when they have dozens of customers every day coming to them asking why the store does not stock your product.

While it may make sense in some cases to sell through traditional channels as a wholesaler, I'd encourage you to at least consider the possibility of selling your products direct, either via the Internet or via mail order. Of course, if your product is a high-ticket item or you are selling to businesses, you likely already have a sales force doing just this.

Building The Lifetime Value of a Customer

"The real and effectual discipline which is exercised over a workman is not that of his corporation, but that of his customer."
- Adam Smith (1723-1790)

Many companies see the value of a customer as simply the value of all the purchases that customer has made to date. So if Sue has only bought one product worth $39 they would see Sue as being worth $39 to them.

Looking at the value of a customer in this manner is dangerous in that it really cannot give you any indication of the true lifetime value of your customers, or the average expenditure of a customer with your company over the period of time between their initial and final purchases. Assuming an average customer of yours purchases more than once from your company, this value will be higher than the value of the first sale. Your goal is to make this value as high as possible, of course.

Having a good idea of the true average lifetime value (LTV) of a customer is essential to knowing how much you are able to spend in acquiring each of your customers. For instance, if your average customer purchased a product worth $39 ten times from you then their lifetime value would be $390. Knowing this information, you may in fact be able to spend more than $39 in acquiring each customer and still make a profit in the long run depending on your Cost of Goods Sold and Operating Expenses.

Another great reason to determine the lifetime value of an average customer for your company is so you can have a quantifiable goal. Once you have a quantified figure you can create goals such as "In quarter three I want to increase my average LTV by 10%." These type of specific goals have much greater chance of being accomplished than if you were to say, "I want to increase the lifetime value of my customers."

Essentially, increasing the lifetime value of your customers comes down to three objectives; increasing the length of time a customer buys from you, increasing the amount they spend on each purchase, and decreasing the time between purchases. Here are three steps designed to increase the lifetime value of your customers by working on these three objectives.

Step one: Personalize the Relationship & Build Rapport

Building rapport with customers is a very important thing. Too many businesses are commoditizing their product. You may have a product and feel it is the best in the world - and it may well be. But there are lots of other companies out there and lots of other companies producing nearly the same product. You need to differentiate both your product and your company. You need to build a personal relationship between your customer and a figure in the company, say for example, the owner. You need to develop a relationship and build rapport and trust with the customer for both the company and that person. Personalize the interaction.

Instead of saying, let's do business with XYZ Corporation, the customer will think, "You know, I'm gonna do business with Joe. I like Joe. Joe's been emailing me those great tips every month because I subscribe to his newsletter. I have a good relationship with Joe. He followed up with me and made sure I was doing okay. I talked to Joe on the phone last month, he gave me some great advice. I'm gonna stay with Joe. Just because this other company's product is a few bucks cheaper, no matter, I know Joe, I trust Joe, I am going to stay with Joe."

It's no longer "I'm going stay with XYZ Corporation". You have succeeded in de-commoditizing your product and have taken a very positive step towards increasing the lifetime value of your customers.

Business is about building relationships and you build these relationships through effective communication. You communicate with your suppliers, your employees, and your affiliates; but you also have to effectively communicate with your customers.

Now I've been saying customers to this point. But in fact you do not want customers. Let me say it again. You do not want customers. What you do want are clients. What you want is to turn your customers into clients. Because once that person is your client they will value the relationship more and stay with your company a lot longer. The lifetime value of that person will be exponentially higher.

How do you turn a customer into a client? Well, along with your product you must offer a service. You must offer the valuable service of your advice and care. You must be an expert on your product and the benefits your product offers, take that customer under your guiding wing, and offer them only your best advice. You must have a Strategy of Preeminence in which you align your interests with your clients' interest and advise them in making the decisions that will best benefit them, no matter what the effects on short term profits.

Instead of having a commoditized product with customers buying on the basis of price only, you need to have a differentiated product. Your customers need to have a personalized relationship with someone within your organization; and you need to turn these customers into clients by offering them quality advice.

Say you are selling a nutraceutical product that treats fibromyalgia. Instead of saying "buy my product, it is the best" say "buy this product, it will do this and this and this and also be sure to exercise this joint and this joint and you may wish to do this stretch and oh yes I found this stretch to be good as well and you may wish to drink a bit more water and be careful of these foods in your diet." You want to help the customer and give them good advice. Take their interest to heart at all times and develop rapport with them so they learn to trust you.

Once your customer develops trust in you or an employee in your company, you are well on your way to turning that person into a lifetime client and passionate user. Do note, however, that trust is crucial. Offering bad advice or advice that benefits you in the short term but hurts your customer will be detrimental to developing this relationship. Always have your customer's interests at heart and even if this means a short term decrease in your profits it will greatly increase them in the long term. So let's look at the best ways to follow up with customers, build stronger relationships, and turn your customers into clients.

> "Once your customer develops trust in you or an employee in your company, you are well on your way to turning that person into a lifetime client and passionate user."

Step two: Make Yourself Available and Answer Questions

Although a phone call will always be more personal, email can be a very effective tool for building relationships with your customers. If you can, be sure to answer your incoming emails with a quality reply and quality advice.

Make your email address accessible. This is a great first step in building a strong customer relationship. Betty in Iowa will be so surprised that the owner of the company responded to her personally that she just might tell her friends about your product. Word of mouth is priceless.

Eventually, you'll find that you just do not have enough time to respond to every email and comment individually. When this happens, make sure you have a very, very well trained support person or support team to take over from you. Make sure they are well-read and very knowledgeable on the subject - as much as you are if possible. Then, allow them to answer questions and comments about the product and have them do it in your name. This will continue to build strong relationships from the outset while you are off managing and strategizing.

<u>Step Three: Follow-up with Your Customers</u>

To really begin to develop good relationships with your customers, try the following strategy in the beginning stages of your firm. Once per month, send a follow-up email to each of the customers that have purchased from you recently. Although it will change depending on your product, it is always good to give a month or so for clients to evaluate your products. So if it was June 15, for example, I would send a follow-up email to all the customers who had purchased one of my products between April 15 and May 15. Adjust this to the specifics of your product. However, do not email all your customers every time, just those who purchased within the interval.

You could send a follow-up something like the following:

Subject: How is [product] doing for you?

[firstname],

I wanted to personally thank you for purchasing [product] on [date]. How is it doing for you? Have you been pleased with the results?

Do let me know if I can answer any questions or be of any assistance.

Warm regards,
Joe Smithers, President

XYZ Corporation
joe@xyzcorp.com
1-800-242-4231

Do note that I used the mail merge fields [firstname], [product], and [date]. These fields are stored in a spreadsheet or database for each subscriber. Using these makes it much easier to personalize each email and save hours of time. You'll need to use an email manager with mail merge capabilities such as iContact to be able to use these.

In practice, I've seen this email double sales totals for the day it was sent out. Much more important that this, however, is that it enables you to develop a personal relationship with your customers and continue the process of turning them into clients. The response from the email will tell you how your product is performing, how your product can be improved, and what else your customers are wanting, This information is truly valuable. The method is also a great way to obtain wonderful testimonials. One company I used to work with collected over 250 testimonials and success stories through the use of this email alone.

Now, you may be thinking to yourself, "This can't be good. This is going to remind people about my product and increase returns." First of all, if you are worried about this then you need to go back to square one and critically look at the quality and efficacy of your product. Second, in truth, yes, this follow-up may remind a few people about your product who wanted to return it but had forgotten. In practice I saw that this happened to about 1 in 400 recipients who received the follow-up. However, the added lifetime value of the strengthened relationships you have built will far outweigh one or two returns. If you are confident in the quality of your product and you truly believe your product does what your sales material says it does you should have no worries. If you do not, it will be difficult to succeed for one can always tell when a salesperson does not truly believe in his products.

Creating this loop of client feedback is essential to knowing what the market wants, keeping your competitive edge, and constantly refining and improving your products. If you want to increase your market share and grow your company obtaining and analyzing customer feedback is crucial.

So in review:

1. Instead of creating customer to company relationships, create client to person relationships. Personalize each transaction. Offer the valuable service of your advice and take care of your customers. De-commoditize your products. Build trust and rapport and begin to turn your customers into clients.

2. Make yourself available, make yourself open to questions. Answer emails and questions on orders personally or have trained support persons answer each question and provide quality advice in your name. Impress your clients with your level of sincerity and quality of advice.

3. Send out a monthly email follow-up to all clients who have purchased from you between one month and two months ago. Creating this loop of feedback is essential to improving your product and knowing what your customers want, will be a powerful step in building relationships with your clients and increasing their lifetime value. Plus it is a great way to obtain testimonials. You may also want to send out a monthly email newsletter with quality related content to further build rapport and trust. Use a form on your site to allow visitors to subscribe or unsubscribe and a program like iContact to manage the subscribe and unsubscribe requests, send out personalized and mail merged emails, and be able to obtain detailed reporting on your campaigns.

Once you have these three practices in place you will begin to develop strong relationships with your clients, greatly increase their lifetime value, and have turned fickle customers into evangelizers who will encourage their friends to buy your product too. Once you have developed strong relationships with your clients and sown the seeds of success by encouraging word of mouth you'll be well along the path toward a million dollars in sales.

> "Once you have these three practices in place you will begin to develop strong relationships with your clients, greatly increase their lifetime value, and have turned fickle customers into evangelizers."

The Art of the Sale

"The customer only wants to know what the product or service will do for him tomorrow. All he is interested in are his own values, his own wants, his own

> reality. For this reason alone, any serious attempt to state what our business is must start with the customers, his realities, his situation, his behavior, his expectations, and his values."
>
> - Peter Drucker

The skill of sales is one of the most-prized attributes that an aspiring entrepreneur can have. The ability to lay out the reasons why someone should buy from you and not your competitor, in a customer-centered fashion—and then go for the sale at the exact right moment, is more difficult than one would imagine.

In your company, you may have a long or short sales cycle. You may sell a product directly to consumers via the Internet and not have to have any interaction with customers at all before they buy. On the other hand, you may be selling a service or product that costs thousands of dollars, and requires the approval of multiple departments.

You may have to present to school boards or Fortune 500 companies. It may take nine months between the time of first contact and time the sale is closed. If your sales cycle is long, you'll have to compensate for this in your projections. It can become very frustrating to sell a high ticket item or service that takes months of presentations, discussions, and contract revisions to sell.

Here are eight questions to answer to get you started on your sales plan.

1. How will the product be sold? In a retail store, online, by direct mail, by catalogs, by infomercials, through distributors, or by a combination?
2. Will you sell your product at wholesale, at retail, or both?
3. Is your main market businesses or consumers?
4. Where do customers currently go to look for the product?
5. How can we be positioned so that we're in these places?
6. Could the price point support a telesales force?
7. Could the price point support a direct sales force?
8. What is my unique selling proposition? What will make my product so different that customers will buy it rather than competing products?

Take for example my good friend Erik Severinghaus' former company MainBrain, Inc. MainBrain sold web-based school administration software that featured grade and recordkeeping for teachers, the ability for parents to view the grades, tardies, and absences of their children online, a web-based interface for teachers and coaches to maintain an web page for their class or sport, school closing information, event calendars, faculty and staff profiles, school message boards, and a staff directory. The software sold between $5000 and $25,000 depending on the requested modules and features.

The sales cycle for MainBrain was much longer than that of iContact. From the time MainBrain contacted a school and sets up its first appointment, it could be six months before they got a signed contract. They often had to present to a school board or school administrators multiple times, negotiate the details of each contract, and then wait for funding to be available for each school or county that it sells to. iContact on the other hand, selling web-based software that costs between $10 and $699/month, instead of $5000 to $25,000, has a sales cycle of less than a week in most cases, and in some cases, no sales cycle at all. Approximately one half of our customers sign up without ever contacting us.

I find it easier on the psyche to sell short-sales cycle products. If you do choose to sell a more expensive product that will have a longer cycle, make sure you are very good at the sales process or have a sales team that is. While we can rely on my web site, frequently asked questions page, and free trial to make most of my sales for iContact, you will have to take an active role, experiment with direct marketing, and keep detailed follow-up spreadsheets. Either way, learning to sell will be a big benefit.

> "If you do choose to sell a more expensive product that will have a longer cycle, make sure you are very good at the sales process or have a sales team that is."

Even though the iContact sales team rarely goes on sales visits, each one of us has to know how to sell. For the half that does contact us before they purchase our product, we have to know how to sell via email and via phone. We have to know our product inside and out, be able to answer any questions, talk on the phone with confidence, be enthusiastic, listen to the customer's needs, and emphasize our competitive advantages.

Napoleon Hill, in his book, *Succeed and Grow Rich through Persuasion* listed eleven traits that the successful salesman must possess. I have adapted these traits, and created my own Nine Traits a Successful Salesperson Must Have:

1. Knowledge of merchandise
2. Belief in the merchandise or service
3. Knowledge of the prospective buyer

4. Ability to make the prospective buyer receptive
5. Ability to know the right psychological moment to close the sale
6. Initiative
7. Persistence and the ability to follow-up
8. Ability to listen and respond to the customer's needs
9. A good memory

In making your sales, you'll have to set certain factors such as price, return policy, warranty, length of required contract, etc. If you are the owner of the company, try to give your salesman a selection of things they are authorized to offer if they feel they need to close the sale. For example, if my Enterprise Sales Rep needs to close a sale, he knows that he can offer up to a certain percentage discount to get that sale.

As far as return policies go, in nearly all cases, the longer and better your return policy is, the more money you will make at the end of the day. Sure, if you have a lifetime guarantee you may have 1% of your orders returned instead of .5% with a 30 day guarantee, however, you'll also increase your sales by 50%.

You may lose $5000 from the solid guarantee in additional refunds, but gain $500,000 in additional revenue. If you are selling an item that doesn't depreciate rapidly (such as technology items) and have anything less than a 90 day guarantee, experiment for a couple months to see how much your sales will increase by offering a 90 day, or even a lifetime guarantee. Run the numbers and at the end of the day, nine times out of ten you'll be way ahead of the game.

The importance of listening to your customers' needs cannot be emphasized enough. If your sales are not taking off the way you'd like them to, a reason may be that—for one reason or another—you're not selling what anyone wants to buy. If you are going to become a good salesperson and a successful entrepreneur you must always keep your ear to the ground and listen to both prospects and customers. You must know what makes your customers buy and what is keeping your prospects from buying. If you can determine, and then overcome, the major buying obligations of your prospects, you'll greatly increase your sales—and the size of your wallet.

If you choose to sell your product online, much of your success will ride on your sales copy. If you will be writing your sales copy yourself—either for your web site or for any marketing materials—be sure that you emphasize benefits of your product or service and not the features. People don't care all that much that your Superturbo Lawnmower 5000 has an over-size fuel tank, auto-sensing cutting, and extra-sharp blades. They will care however when you tell them that their lawns will be cut in one third the time and the lawnmower will cut their lawn without their supervision, saving them lots of time and making their lives easier. Always address prospect concerns, tell why you are unique and better, and use things like case studies and testimonials. If you can remember to always keep in mind the acronym AIDA, you'll be all right. Start by attracting <u>A</u>ttention. Then develop <u>I</u>nterest, create <u>D</u>esire, and spur <u>A</u>ction.

Building a Sales Compensation Plan

To be able to support your future revenue projections you will need to show how these sales will be made. If all the sales are coming through your web site you will only need to show your current traffic levels, rates of traffic growth, your visitor to customer conversion ratio, and your average sale size.

If you are selling your product to other businesses however, either via telemarketing or direct sales, you will need a sales force and account managers that are compensated on customer acquisition and customer retention respectively. You can view your sales force as the hunters that bring in the contracted revenue and the account managers as the farmers that sow the relationships with the client, work to get the client to renew the business at the end of the contract term, and advise the client on what other products or services the client may need from your company.

Your sales plan and your sales compensation plan tie back into your sales coverage model, a spreadsheet that reconciles your projected revenues with the sales team and account manager count and cost. Being "at plan' refers to hitting your projected sales figures. Try to come up with a plan that has realistic sales goals, yet will require your team to stretch to hit them. To create a sales compensation plan, start by identifying and making assumptions for the below variables:

1. Leads generated by channel by month
2. Lead to customer conversion ratio
3. Average upfront revenue per sale
4. Average ongoing monthly or annual revenue per sale
5. Number of leads one sales rep can manage
6. Length of the sales cycle in weeks

7. Percentage sales commission paid to lead generation source (generally on contracted year one revenue), if lead generator is separate from closer

8. Percentage sales commission paid to closer of the lead into a customer (generally on contracted year one revenue)

9. Target new contracts per month per sales rep

10. Base salary for a sales representative (usually between $30,000 and $75,000 depending on market, type of sales, commission rate, and experience)

11. Number of accounts one account manager can manage

12. Average upsell revenue per client per year (sold by the account manager, above and beyond the original contract revenue)

13. Percentage commission paid to the account manager on account renewals

14. Target percentage of accounts that will renew each year

15. Base salary for an account manager (usually between $25,000 and $40,000)

Once assumptions for these variables are in place, you can create your spreadsheet such that it outputs the following information:

1. Base salary to commission ratio (many companies do 50% base, 50% commission for their "at plan" compensation)

2. Target total annual compensation "at plan" for a sales representative (usually between $50,000 and $150,000 depending on market, type of sales, and experience)

3. Target annual compensation "at plan" for an account manager (usually between $45,000 and $75,000 depending on market and experience)

4. Number of sales representatives you will need to have to hit plan

5. Number of account managers you will need to have to hit plan

6. Revenue from sales at 75% of plan (worst case projection)

7. Revenue from sales at 100% of plan (expected case projection)

8. Revenue from sales at 125% of plan (best case projection)

"When the time is right to build out your sales team, ensure that you have a CRM tool in place to track and manage your lead generation rates, sales funnel, sales cycle length, customer retention rates, and commission payments."

Building out a professional sales plan will allow you to determine the breakdown in people that you will need to hit the revenues you have projected as well as allow you to share with your sales reps and account managers what you expect of them. When the time is right to build out your sales team, ensure that you have a CRM tool in place to track and manage your lead generation rates, sales funnel, sales cycle length, customer retention rates, and commission payments.

Obtaining Publicity

Obtaining publicity is similar to obtaining free advertising, except better, as the advertising comes in the form of a trusted third party recommendation or mention. Third party endorsements have great credibility to viewers, listeners, and readers and can generate many more leads than a paid ad.

Good media relations require planning and time, however. You cannot decide on Tuesday that you want to get a press release out by Thursday and expect to get coverage. You need to build and cultivate relationships with editors and reporters as journalists tend to rely more on their Rolodexes than press releases when writing their stories.

Before you launch your publicity campaign, you'll need to decide whether you'll be doing it yourself in-house or outsourcing it to a public relations firm. If you do decide to hire a PR firm, you may wish to contact the business editors at local newspapers or trade journalists and ask them which firms they respect and work with often. It is also a good idea to ask for client references and have your firm present a plan with a budget and timeline. Most firms will work on a monthly retainer. It is important to keep in mind that a one or two month press campaign is not likely to produce results. In my experience, you will need to commit to at least a six month spend of at least $3,000 per month to get any results worth mentioning. If you do decide to do your publicity campaign yourself, here are a few tips.

1. **Know Your Audience.** First, know who your audience is and what types of media they pay attention to. Then build relationships with these publications and outlets.
2. **Personalize Your Emails.** Instead of sending a press release directly, begin an email message with, "I enjoyed your recent story about _____." This will improve your chances of getting noticed.

3. **Become a Source.** Instead of sending out a press release when you are ready to launch your campaign, send out an introduction message a few months before stating who you are and what you are an expert in. Offer to answer any questions the reporter or editor may have on these subjects.

4. **Build the Relationship First.** Instead of sending a press release out of nowhere, start a few weeks in advance by dropping a short email to the relevant editors and reporters at your local papers letting them know that the company will be making an announcement in the future. State that you believe that based on your knowledge of that person's work, you believe they are the right person to contact and you wanted to confirm this before sending any unwanted press releases. If that person is not the right person, he or she may let you know the proper person to contact. If that person is the right one, there is a good possibility that he or she will take the chance to inquire a bit further about your company and upcoming news.

5. **Create a Proper Media Kit.** Invest time in creating a professional media kit, printed in color in a nice portfolio folder. Include company information and history, product information, executive bios, case studies, past press coverage, names of prominent clients, and high-resolution pictures of your product(s) and executives on a burned CD. Mail this kit in advance to publications or trade press that have covered stories similar to yours in the past.

6. Use resources such as Vocus, MediaMap, and Bacons to build a list of media contacts in your area and utilize press release distribution services such as prweb.com, businesswire.com and prnewswire.com.

At iContact we did our first campaign in the Fall of 2003. Our Director of Marketing Josh Carlton created a press kit and a press release and mailed it to the editors at newspapers in our area. We were able to get an article in the Chapel Hill News through which our Vice President of Business Development David Roth found us. Over time we built relationships with the editors of local publications such as the Raleigh News & Observer, LocalTechWire, Triangle Business Journal, and TechJournalSouth so that now whenever we have an announcement it is nearly ensured that it will get coverage.

Our second campaign was done through a local firm called Maverick Endeavors in 2005. They did a good job for us, but we were not aware that we would have to stick to it for at least three months to get good results. We gave them a one month contract for $3,000 to see what they could do, allowing them to re-do our press kit but not giving them enough time to actually get coverage.

When we got to a size that was large enough, in July 2006, we hired a full time Director of Public Relations by the name of Chuck Hester. Chuck has done a tremendous job for iContact and gotten us countless podcast interviews and blogger reviews, coverage on the cover of Fortune Small Business Magazine and Success Magazine, a mention in the Wall Street Journal, Women's Edge Magazine, and CIO Magazine, and in all the local newspapers and trade journals multiple times. In my opinion, when you get to the point that you can spend $5,000 per month or more on public relations and press coverage, hire a person in-house. Their focus on your business and cost of $30 per hour instead of $100 per hour for a firm will get better results at a lower cost.

> "When we got to a size that was large enough, in July 2006, we hired a full time Director of Public Relations."

Chapter 13 · Step 7: Launch Your Web Marketing Strategy

> "Selling to people who actually want to hear from you is more effective than interrupting strangers who don't."
>
> - Seth Godin

I've been in the web marketing business essentially since age 14. At 17, I was managing a monthly marketing budget of $50,000, learning everything I could about email marketing, affiliate programs, search engine optimizations, and ecommerce.

I began in 1998 not knowing a thing about marketing on the Internet. After taking an HTML class in seventh grade, I began working with a lady by the name of Lois who sold pearls and wanted to sell them online. I designed her web site, added the products to the site, integrated an online shopping cart, and started a monthly newsletter. Within a few weeks, we began making a few sales. While that business ended up not working out for Lois, I gained invaluable experience in web site design and had learned a few lessons about online marketing.

In 10th and 11th grade, I continued to put these lessons to use with the clients of my web site design firm, Virante Design & Development. During this time I began reading the articles and courses of some of the more well known online marketing experts. By the time that I received that fateful call from the business owner with the nutraceuticals product, I had gained quite a bit of knowledge about online marketing.

Over the next year, as we took that company from $200 in sales/month to $200,000 in sales per month, I learned more about marketing and web marketing than I could have imagined. With the significant financial resources of the company behind me, I could try out new ideas and purchase the proper software I needed to be an effective web marketer.

I learned how to effectively use co-registrations, interstitials, autoresponders, and newsletter software. I learned how to manage our customer database and promote back-end products and special offers. I learned how to maximize ROI on pay per click engines and increase the lifetime value of a customer. And I learned how to get a site to the top of the search engines and how to build an affiliate program that produced an additional $45,000 in sales each month for the company. In short, the experience was again invaluable. I was 17 and had full control over a $50,000 per month marketing budget. I learned many lessons, and through trial and error began to develop the system that I will share with you here.

Web marketing is not something many business owners are used to doing or for that matter very good at. However, it is something that can launch a business from nowhere to doing tens of thousands of dollars in sales per week in a matter of a few months. If you have a product that is sold to consumers or small businesses and sells for under US$500, this plan is tailored to your type of business and will allow you to grow your sales without spending much upfront. If you run a service-based business, this plan will help attract new customers both locally and nationally. If you run a business that sells a product that costs more than $500, the strategies below will help you generate thousands of leads each week.

There are five lead generation and conversion channels that the system is based upon—techniques that have proved their efficacy time and time again in both my businesses and every business I know that has properly executed them for their company. These channels are search engine optimization, affiliate programs, permission-based email marketing, CPC and CPM advertising, and social media marketing.

Properly maximized, these five channels will allow your business to be launched with very little upfront cost. They are the same channels I used at the nutraceuticals company and the same strategies we have used to position iContact as a market leader in the email marketing and online communication industry. The key is proper execution and investing the needed time.

The great thing about search engine optimization (SEO) is that once you are positioned in the top of the search engines for your targeted keywords, you will receive a stream of thousands of unique, highly qualified prospects to your sites, newsletters, and autoresponders each week—all completely free of charge.

The great thing about reseller and affiliate programs is that you only pay out after a sale is made. You already have the money in your bank account before you have to write the check for the commissions, completely eliminating any risk for you.

With permission-based email marketing, you can leverage the traffic on your site to obtain tens of thousands of subscribers to your newsletters, and then use software such as iContact to send out a weekly or monthly newsletter with quality content and your marketing message.

Online advertising via Cost Per Click (CPC) and Cost Per Mil (CPM, which essentially means Cost Per 1000 Impressions) channels does cost money upfront to test, but if you can make either channel provide a positive return you can greatly scale it. iContact now spends over $300,000 per month on Cost Per Click advertising alone, most with Google Adwords, generating over 35% of our monthly customer acquisition.

Social media marketing comes down to blogging on your site to generate content, getting visitors to subscribe to your RSS feeds, getting other bloggers to review your product or service, participating in online forums, commenting in related communities, creating groups on social networks, creating and posting viral videos and podcasts about your business, and generating exposure for your company by creating a useful tool or controversial news. You will know you've succeeded with social media marketing when you have created interactive conversations with your customers and visitors rather than one-way broadcasts.

These strategies come down to one thing—positioning. You don't have to beat your competitors by having a better product or more money than they have—you simply have to be better positioned than them. So let's get started with the details.

Search Engine Optimization

Search engines are the market makers of the Internet. They connect consumers with providers at the very moment of consumer interest and enable all of us to find exactly what we want, when we want it. They bring great efficiency to the Internet and our lives and shall exist as long as the network of servers and computers we call the Web is around.

The first purpose of search engine optimization is to be positioned in the places where your customer is looking. The second purpose is to be positioned better than your competitors in these places. In the world of search engines, better means higher, and higher means a much greater probability that an individual will click on your link. Approximately 70% of users, if they click, will click on one of the first three listings in a search engine. So how do you get there?

> "The first purpose of search engine optimization is to be positioned in the places where your customer is looking."

Step one is to determine which keywords you wish to target. Ask yourself, which keywords a potential visitor is likely to type in when trying to find your web site or product. Once you have determined this, work to increase the number of times this keyword or keyphrase is on your home page. Make sure you page title contains this term and that you have lots of content on your web site about this topic. The three most important factors in your search engine ranking is the number of times your target keyword appears on your home page, whether the keyword is in the title, whether you have content on your site about this topic, and whether there are other related web sites about the same topic linking to your web site.

The majority of web site owners have under ten incoming links to their sites. The search engines view incoming links as verification that your site has quality content. The more related links your site has from other sites (with the underlined clickable text including your targeted keywords), the higher your ranking in the search engines will be. Here is a more in depth, step-by-step overview of this entire SEO process.

1. **Select your keywords.** Use tools such as the Overture Search Term Suggestion Tool, Google's Search Term Suggestion Tool, and Wordtracker to determine which related keywords or key phrases it would be best to optimize your site for. Once you have a list of potential keywords, go to Google and type in those keywords. Then see how many incoming links the top few sites have. You can determine this number by typing in "link:http://www.competitordomain.com." Take a look at whether the first few sites have the targeted keyword in the domain name, in the title, or often on their page. Use this information to estimate what it would take to get your site above the current sites in the rankings.

2. **Ensure your site has those keywords on it.** Make sure that the keywords you are targeting are on your home page at least five times. Having a 5% to 15% keyword density for your targeted search term on your homepage is optimal. Also ensure your title tag and image alt tags have your targeted keyword it in. Add your targeted term to a H1 header tag for added prominence.

3. **Build good quality content on your site.** I call this phase the 'content campaign.' Either write articles yourself for the site or go through the search engines to find related content. If you find an article on another site you'd like to publish on your site, send an email to the author, site owner, and/or publisher to request permission to

syndicate their article(s) on your site. Present it as a win/win quid pro quo in which you receive good quality content and the author/publisher receives free exposure and a link to their web site in the byline of the article. I'd suggest having at least twenty-five quality articles on your site before going forward. Optimize your home page for the two or three target most competitive terms. Optimize your in-site pages for the more unique and less competitive terms. You can also outsource the creation of this content to copywriters using a service such as elance.com for about $30 per 400 word article.

4. **Build links to your web site.** Without incoming links to your site, it will never have a chance at being at the top of the search engines for competitive terms. Use the research you did earlier on the number of links the sites at the top of the listings have or your targeted keywords to set a goal for how many related incoming links you want to build to your own site. To obtain links, go through the search engines and find related web sites, then contact the owners of those sites and offer to exchange links. Add their link to your website and email them to let them know that you've linked to their site and would appreciate a reciprocal link. I'd suggest contacting them first via email and then via phone if necessary. In your initial email to site owners, include the URL and description of your site, as well as the location of where there link is and which site of theirs you are referring to. I'd suggest creating a resources section of your site and placing your link partners in the appropriate category within. You can also build links naturally through press releases or by having great content, a useful tool, a viral video, or an interesting blog. If you have more money than time, you can also purchase relevant links from quality web sites through a service called LinkExperts or purchase reviews with links from sites such as PayPerPost, ReviewMe, and Blogvertise. Ensure whatever links you build to your web site have your target keyphrase in the anchor text, the words that are clickable and underlined. Finally, text links are much more valuable than image links as the search engines can follow text links and associate the link text with your web site, but not image links.

5. **Continue building your site's reputation.** Once you have built a few related incoming links, the search engines will find and index your site. If your site is new, it can take up to nine months for Google to allow it to show up for competitive search terms. During this time,

continue building good quality related content and work to build as many incoming links from related web sites as you can.

Building a Partner Program

At iContact we have over 1500 partners that send us visitors and customers for a 25% to 35% lifetime commission on each referred sale. We have approximately 1300 affiliates, 150 marquee resellers and 50 global resellers. Affiliates receive 25% commission. Our marquee resellers are required to sign a reseller contract but receive a higher 30% commission and cobranded landing page at theirname.icontact.com. Our global resellers are companies that have more than 10,000 small business customers who can refer us substantial business. These resellers receive a higher 35% commission and special support in working with us to maximize referred sales. Approximately 15% of our overall sales come through our partner program, and we are working hard to grow this percentage.

Developing additional lead generation channels is an important part of growing your sales. Depending on what you are selling, a partner program may be able to help you increase your customer acquisition rates. Partner programs typically have different tiers. Affiliate partners can sign up directly on the web site without any required review, while reseller partners often get additional benefits but must sign a reseller contract.

Partner programs are essentially Cost Per Acquisition (CPA) programs in which you pay a set amount or set percentage to acquire a customer. Once you know what your customer lifetime value is, you can easily determine the maximum amount that you are willing to spend to acquire a customer. This amount is called your maximum Customer Acquisition Cost (CAC).

> "Partner programs are essentially Cost Per Acquisition (CPA) programs in which you pay a set amount or set percentage to acquire a customer."

If you are selling a product online you can have an automated affiliate program in which you track the exact number of referred visitors and pay a commission for any visitors that turn into paying customers. An affiliate program uses web based software that tracks the source of referred visitors to your site through cookies and databases, and then connects with your shopping cart to calculate commissions to the referring affiliate when a visitor they referred in the past ends up purchasing your product(s).

Affiliate programs have been very useful for Internet entrepreneurs. It seems that not a single successful online company is without one. The first step in launching your program is to obtain affiliate software. You can either purchase affiliate software like 1ShoppingCart, AssocTrac or MyAffiliateProgram, use an open source platform like OSCommerce, have custom software developed, or join an Affiliate Network that provides both the software and the connection to advertisers who can promote your product like CommissionJunction or LinkShare. While launching your affiliate program may cost between $1,000 and $5,000 if you can properly build and promote your program your return on investment will be many times this amount.

Once you've purchased your software, installed it, and ensured that it works with your shopping cart and merchant account, you'll need to decide on the level of commissions you will pay. Most programs pay between 10% and 35% of each sale. Keep in mind that the higher you pay out, the more affiliates you will attract. However, if you are losing money on each sale, it will not matter to you how many affiliates you have.

Once your commissions are set, you'll need to create banners and images for your affiliates to use. If you are not good at graphic design you can visit www.guru.com, www.smarterwork.com, or www.elance.com to find freelancers. You'll also need to create a guide explaining how to link to your site, instructions on how to view sales statistics, a sign up form, and sales copy encouraging affiliates to sign up. When you have all this done and have tested everything, you can begin to promote your program.

To promote your program, you can follow the same general method that was used in contacting link partners. Use the search engines to find related web sites and contact them via email and phone to encourage business owners to partner with your company. Once you have this list, contact the potential affiliates. Make sure you do it individually and customize your message for each prospect. Encourage them to learn more about your program at your site. Finally, be sure to follow-up about a week later. You can also list your affiliate program on sites like Refer-It and AffiliatePrograms.com, or join a network like Share-a-Sale, CommissionJunction or LinkShare.

Many affiliate program owners have a great affiliate program but fail to promote it. During the months you are waiting for your search engine rankings to come in, it is a great time to promote your affiliate program. You should be able to build at least 200-300 affiliates during this time frame, depending on your product and the commissions you are offering. This should be enough affiliates to get a steady stream going of a few sales each day.

Once you have a couple hundred affiliates and a few months of data, you can go after larger partners that can bring in $10,000 per month or more in sales. First, determine what your overall visitor to sale conversion rate is on your site. Using this data, figure out the average payout per visitor sent to you. If you can show empirically that it makes financial sense for larger companies to partner with you, you'll have a much easier time convincing VPs of Marketing to take on the risk and establish an alliance with your company and put ads for you on their site on a Cost Per Acquisition (CPA) basis.

To establish these larger alliances, you may have to increase your commission, sign contracts, guarantee minimum payouts, and get on planes. This has been the exact work that my VP of Business Development David Roth has been doing for the past four years to build our Global Reseller Partner list and I am sure he would tell you that it is not easy but the benefits are significant to partnership building. Do whatever it takes within the realms of profitability.

In addition to a traditional affiliate and reseller program, some of the larger ad networks such as Google Adwords offer CPA program in which you set what you willing to pay for a certain action (lead signup, whitepaper download, purchase, etc) to occur. This can be another effective channel for acquiring customers at a predictable CAC.

Permission-Based Email Marketing

> "Email marketing is fast, effective and dirt cheap — a godsend for marketers in an economy that has crunched advertising budgets."
>
> - Time Magazine

iContact began in 2003 as a permission-based email marketing application. At the application's core, it allowed you to upload a list of contacts that had requested to receive emails from your organization, add a sign-up form to your web site, select a template, paste in your content, distribute your newsletter, then view the opens and clicks while managing the bounces and unsubscribes.

Today, iContact has evolved into an online communications platform that makes it easy to create, publish, and track email newsletters, surveys, autoresponders, blogs, and RSS feeds. While RSS, blogs, and social media is becoming an increasingly important method of communication online, email remains the top method of communicating with your customers and prospects.

Starting a monthly email newsletter allows you to collect prospect data and stay in touch with your customers and most interested prospects. The effects of a monthly or weekly newsletter with quality content including an increased visitor to sales conversion rate and better brand awareness in your industry and with your customers and prospects.

The first step to starting your own email newsletter is to select the email list management software you'd like to use. You can choose web based or desktop based software. If you want subscription and unsubscription requests and bounce backs to be handled for you, I'd recommend web-based software as opposed to desktop-based software. In your software look for features such as open and click-through tracking, the ability to send HTML messages, bounce back handling, unlimited list creation, multiple message autoresponders, and message scheduling. You should also look for a tool that also allows you to easily distribute your message to other channels such as RSS or blogs.

Once you select the software you'd like to use, add the sign up form to your web site. Most services will provide you with the HTML code you need to do this. Without a sign up form for a newsletter on it, you are losing valuable prospect data. When a visitor goes to your web site, they are often looking for a product or information you provide. Many of these visitors are willing to sign up for a newsletter with good quality content and more information on your industry and products.

Once you have your sign-up form up decide how often you'd like to send out your newsletter and what content will be in it, and create an information page with archives and a sign up form on your site. Finally, log into your newsletter software and send out your newsletter on the schedule you decided on.

I usually send out my newsletters on same day once per month, but it is up to you how often and when your newsletters go out. As far as content, you should include at least one good quality article in your newsletter. Intersperse recommendations for your products and case studies or testimonials. As a final step, once your newsletter has been sent, add it to your archives page so new subscribers can see what past issues were like.

If you can properly execute a permission-based email marketing strategy, you'll greatly improve your contact and relationships with your current and future customers. You'll build your reputation in your industry, and tremendously improve your visitor to sale conversion rate, meaning more sales, more often, for higher amounts.

Especially if you are able to get your site to the top of the search engines, you'll be able to build an opt-in list of thousands of subscribers within a couple years and turn these subscribers into passionate evangelizing customers. The nutraceuticals company I worked with in 2001 and 2002 was able to build a permission based email list of 30,000 within twelve months. The wonderful thing was, every time we sent out a newsletter, sales would jump by $4000 to $6000 that day.

> "You'll be able to build an opt-in list of thousands of subscribers within a couple years and turn these subscribers into passionate evangelizing customers."

At iContact, we have a company newsletter, The iContact Marketing Monthly, that we send out on the 28th of each month. We currently have about 80,000 subscribers to the newsletter. Whenever we sent out our monthly message, we add 50 to 60 new additional customers, generating about $30,000 in new annual revenue for us. We're able to increase revenues by $30,000 by sending out an email that would cost around $250 to send if we were paying our own prices. By implementing a similar strategy for your permission-based communications, you'll soon be able to see the same noticeable impact on your bottom line.

CPC & CPM Advertising

Online advertising has a drawback. You have to pay for the ads upfront (compared to lead from affiliate ads in which you pay only after the customer is acquired or leads from search engine optimization which are free after the upfront work is done). This noted, if you can make the numbers work, online advertising through Cost Per Click (CPC) and Cost Per Mil Impressions (Known as CPM, Mil is Latin for 1000) can be a scalable method of growing your sales to the one million dollar mark and beyond quickly.

With CPC advertising, you set a maximum bid for what you are willing to pay per click and then based on the competition and the Click-through Rate (CTR) on your ads the exact cost per click is set. The major Cost Per Click ad networks at the time of writing are Google Adwords, Yahoo Search Marketing, and MSN AdCenter. The market share is approximately 65% Google, 25% Yahoo, and 12% MSN, through there are presently some discussions about

Yahoo and MSN merging their ad networks. The other second tier CPC networks include Miva, Kanoodle, Business.com, and 7Search.

At iContact, we have scaled our online CPC spend from $15,000 per month in June 2006 to over $300,000 per month today. We scaled it in-house until we got to $150,000 in ad spend and now have outsourced our CPC management to a nationally known and very high quality firm called ROI Revolution in Raleigh, NC. They have greatly improved our results by using multivariate landing page optimization, ad copy testing, integrating the tracking with Google Analytics, and expanding the number of keywords we bid on. It is important to be able to track your advertising back to the actual sale so you can determine which campaigns are working and which are not. You can do this through a free tool like Google Analytics or through your affiliate software.

CPM advertising allows you to purchase build text and banner ad impressions at a cost per one thousand impressions. At the time of writing, the major CPM networks are 24/7 Real Media, Advertising.com, Tribal Fusion, aQuantive, AdBrite, and ContextWeb. Standard ad sizes in pixels are:

468 x 60 Banners   336 x 280 Large Rectangles
728 x 90 Leaderboards   300 x 250 Inline Rectangles
250 x 250 Squares   120 x 600 Skyscrapers
200 x 200 Small Squares   160 x 600 Wide Skyscrapers

Costs per 1000 impressions generally range from $1 to $10 depending on how targeted your ads are. Run of network (RON) ads are generally at the lower end of the spectrum with behaviorally targeted premium sites at the higher end. CPM advertising is generally better at brand advertising and not at generating profitable customer acquisition in the near term, but if you can make it work you can scale quickly.

Social Media Marketing

Social media marketing revolves around creating interactive conversations with your visitors, often through new mediums such as blogs, videos, podcasts, and social network communities. It is a relationship building, and not a promotional, form of building your brand.

Blogging can be one of the most effective ways at building quality related content and incoming links to your web site, as well as creating a transparent participatory discussion with your customers. You can blog using tools like Blogger, Wordpress, TypePad, or iContact. With iContact we wanted to create a tool that allowed you to blog at the same time as sending out your email newsletter.

"Blogging can be one of the most effective ways at building quality related content and incoming links to your web site, as well as creating a transparent participatory discussion with your customers."

A normal blog has its content in reverse chronological order with datestamps, a commenting system, a method of tagging and categorizing posts, a method of archiving posts, and a method of subscribing to the blog's feed. Some blogs utilize a tool like Feedburner or iContact to track the number of their subscribers as well as to distribute their blog posts automatically as email.

Most blogs show the most recent content on the home page with archives by week, category, or individual post. At the bottom of most blog posts are interactive buttons that allow a user to share the post on a number of Web 2.0 services such as Digg, Facebook, iGoogle, MyYahoo, Reddit, Del.icio.us, StumbleUpon, Technorati, Fark, Furl, Ma.gnolia, Newsvine, Slashdot, Spurl, and TailRank.

Blogs can also utilize widgets that allow additional interactivity by showing information such as the avatars of the community members (MyBlogLog), recent videos (YouTube), photostreams (Flickr), slideshows (RockYou), bookmarks (Del.icio.us), favorite blogs (called a blogroll) favorite music (Last.fm), social network updates (Facebook, LinkedIn, MySpace), what the blogger is currently reading (Goodreads), or what the blogger is currently doing (Twitter). Other forms of social media marketing include:

1. Creating a community of your users through a off-site social network like Ning, Facebook, or MySpace, or an on-site installed tool like Drupal, Shark, OneSite, CommunityZero, or CommunityServer.
2. Creating a presence in virtual worlds such as SecondLife (yes this is being done);
3. Creating a unique or controversial story and submitting it for exposure on Digg and Netscape.com;
4. Claiming your blog and building up reputation for it on Technorati.
5. Exchanging blogroll links with other related bloggers;
6. Adding a discussion forum to your site;
7. Participating in online forums that discuss your field;

8. Adding information about your company on Squidoo, ZoomInfo, or Wikipedia (if it is noteworthy enough, that is);
9. Creating interesting videos showing what you do and posting them on video sharing sites such as YouTube and MetaCafe; and
10. Creating podcasts and then distributing them via iTunes and Odeo.

Through all these methods you can go from being a company that communicates via a one-way broadcast tool into a company that builds authentic open dialog in a democratic participatory manner.

Bringing It All Together

Let's quickly review your web marketing plan in step-by-step form:

Phase One: Get Your Site to the Top of the Search Engines

1. Select your keywords.
2. Ensure your site has those keywords on it.
3. Build good quality content on your site.
4. Build links to your web site.
5. Continue building your site's reputation.

Phase Two: Get hundreds of affiliate web sites to promote your product

1. Purchase affiliate software
2. Install affiliate software and connect with shopping cart
3. Decide on commission rate
4. Create an affiliate central with statistics, images, and linking instructions
5. Create sign up form and sales copy
6. Contact potential affiliates – this will be the step that takes the longest
7. Send out monthly newsletter to affiliates with best practices and stories of successful affiliates
8. Mail out checks monthly to affiliates who have made sales.
9. Build a reseller program of larger partners.
10. Understand your conversion rates and average commission and then pitch larger potential partners by showing them in advance what they can expect.

Phase Three: Turn Your Prospects into Lifetime Customers with a Regular Email Newsletter

1. Sign up for web based email list management and marketing software such as iContact.
2. Add a sign up form to your web site to begin collecting the information of prospects.
3. Send out a daily, weekly, or monthly newsletter to stay in touch with your subscribers, provide quality content, recommend your product(s), and tell of successes with your product.

Phase Four: Test and Then Scale CPC and CPM Advertising to Grow Sales

1. Sign up for accounts with Google Adwords, Yahoo Search Marketing, and MSN AdCenter.
2. Set up a tracking system with your affiliate program or Google Analytics so you can track the exact return from your ad spend.
3. Bid on keywords on each of the network.
4. Adjust your bids depending on performance.
5. Test new match types, geographic targets, landing pages, and ad copy to maximize the return and scale your spend while maintaining the same Customer Acquisition Cost.
6. Create a few graphical creatives in the standard sizes.
7. Do a tracked test on one of the major ad networks: 24/7 Real Media, Advertising.com, Tribal Fusion, aQuantive, AdBrite, or ContextWeb.
8. If the test is profitable, scale it.

Phase Five: Create a Transparent Discussion with Your Customers Using Social Media

1. Add a blog to your web site using Blogger, Wordpress, TypePad, or iContact to build related content and incoming links.
2. Post to your blog often.
3. Utilize Feedburner or iContact to track your RSS feed subscribers and automatically send email updates to them.
4. Utilize Technorati, Squidoo, Wikipedia, MyBlogLog, Del.icio.us, Zoominfo, iTunes, Odeo, Digg, and Netscape.com to get more exposure for your social media content.

5. Utilize off-site social networks like Facebook, Ning, and MySpace or on-site social network applications like Drupal, Shark, OneSite, CommunityZero, or CommunityServer to build an interactive community of your customers.

6. Participate in online forums and comment on blogs that discuss your field.

Now that we can see the full five phase plan, let's show how each of the channels interact and work together to produce a winning web marketing strategy. The diagram below summarizes the relationships and flow of traffic.

Diagram 3 – Your $1 Million Web Marketing Flow Chart

In essence, the search engines provide traffic to your site, which converts visitors to prospects with product recommendations and obtains their contact information with an autoresponder ecourse and free email newsletter. You continuously stay in touch with your prospects and customers with your email newsletter, blog and RSS feed, building your reputation as an industry-leader. Through this process, highly qualified leads are generated for the product site, which is also receiving traffic from the affiliate program and your CPC and CPM ads. Your product site is optimized to convert visitors to prospects, prospects to customers, and then customers to lifetime customers that you can build an organic and transparent interactive dialog with.

Highlight 8: The Twenty Keys to Web Marketing

Reprinted from www.zeromillion.com with permission.

Below are the twenty keys to successfully marketing your product, service, and business online.

The Twenty Keys to Online Marketing

1. Have a professional, easy to navigate, quick loading design. Hire a professional design firm or at least use a good site template.

2. Have lots of quality related content

3. Build lots of links to your web site

4. Build credibility and rapport

5. Start an email newsletter and send out at least once per month with quality content.

6. If you are selling a product, have an affiliate program

7. Once you have an affiliate program, don't forget to promote it.

8. Do whatever you can do profitably to attract large affiliates and form key strategic alliances.

9. Position yourself well in the search engines.

10. Use Cost-per-click (CPC) engines but make sure you know the lifetime value (LTV) of a customer and that you do return on investment (ROI) checks often

11. Supplement your affiliate advertising with both online and traditional

advertising, but track results and always do ROI checks.

12. Advertise using CPM channels to build brand recognition, but put profitability before brand recognition.

13. Offer yourself as a resource to the media as an expert in your niche.

14. Hire a great publicity firm or bring an experienced publicist in-house.

15. Use autoresponders to maintain constant contact with prospective customers

16. Remember that business is all about relationships and communication. Always work to build more relationships and once they are built, make sure you are in continuous contact with your prospects, customers, strategic alliances, suppliers, investors, and the media.

17. Encourage word of mouth among your customers.

18. Have superior customer service and have staff to answer all incoming emails within 24 hours

19. Send out periodic email follow-ups making sure your customers are happy and asking them for feedback on your product and the service your company has provided

20 Blog frequently with quality content

Chapter 14 — Step 8: Build Your Team & Become a Manager

> "The secret of the success of Standard Oil was that there had come together a body of men who from the beginning to end worked in single-minded cooperation."
>
> - John D. Rockefeller

How to Build Your Team

You've spent months and perhaps years of hard work getting your business to the point where you are nearly ready to make your first sale. You've developed your business idea, closed on deals with suppliers, ordered your inventory of products, wrote your business plan, incorporated, and raised the money you need to get started. Before you can truly begin to grow quickly, you'll have to build your team, infrastructure, and put a few key systems into place. When you can afford to bring your first employee on, do so. If you never hire anyone you'll be doing all the work yourself and be creating a job rather than building a business.

Many aspiring entrepreneurs have asked me how they can find a business partner. I always answer that a partner is not someone that you can find overnight or in a few weeks. It usually can only be someone that you have been friends with for a while and have developed trust in and established trust with, someone that has worked for you for some time, or someone you've worked with in the past.

The skills of my business partner Aaron Houghton complemented mine. Aaron was a tremendous programmer and technologist, while my core skills were in marketing and building a company. Together, we were able to work together to create something greater than either of us could have created separately.

Having a business partner can be very helpful. Partners can help with financing, industry contacts, or taking over roles you have less experience in. They can allow you to get twice the work done in half the time, and can give you that needed motivation when things are tough. If you do wish to find a partner, start networking. Join your local Chamber of Commerce and volunteer for committees and in your community. If you are a student, join business clubs or business fraternities. Talk to people about your business whenever you can. Put up flyers looking for a partner in an entrepreneurial business. If you receive any replies, meet with that person and if you feel it would be good to do so, start them in a role where they can begin to learn and show you their commitment. After a few months, you may be ready to offer them part ownership in your company.

I have found that one of the toughest conversations to have with your partners is the discussion regarding equity distribution—what percentage of ownership each partner gets. But it is a necessary conversation to have upfront. It is often hard to negotiate with someone who is a close friend of yours. Because of this, some partners simply decide to split things equally. Unfortunately, it is a rare occurrence that all persons involved contribute equally to a company. If the proper steps are not taken, such an occurrence—when one partner is not living up to his or her end of the deal—can destroy long lasting friendships.

> "One of the toughest conversations to have with your partners is the discussion regarding equity distribution. But it is a necessary conversation to have upfront."

To protect against this, I would highly recommend two things. First, no matter how difficult it is, have a serious conversation with your partner(s) about who should get what. Base your discussion on the following four factors:

1. Work completed in the past;
2. Monetary investment into the company;
3. Who will be doing work in the future; and
4. Experience and contacts in the industry.

Secondly, I'd very much recommend vesting your shares and having a stock restriction agreement. Vesting is the granting of ownership over time, instead of all at once. For example, if you give a partner 30% of your company without vesting his shares and he leaves a month later, he'll leave with 30%. On the other hand, if you vest that partner's shares over 3 years, he will leave with only 0.83% of the company. In this case, he would have to work for the full three years to receive the 30%. Vesting is used often by venture capital companies to put 'golden handcuffs' on top executives. If you do use vesting, you'll need to have a stock restriction agreement that spells out these terms, including the terms of sale and transfer.

Before you launch your company, you may wish to bring additional persons onto your Board of Directors. You may wish to ask industry veterans or key investors to join. Simply keep in mind that you should have an odd-numbered board at all times, as decisions will not be able to be made with an even number since a majority vote is needed. In order to attract experience to your board, you may need to offer stock options or a yearly stipend for members. You also may wish to set up an informal Advisory Board for your company.

As your company grows, you will have to add on certain professionals and outside advisors to your team. You'll want to have a good accountant, attorney, financial advisor, insurance agent, and banker. These important advisors will be a big part of your company's success or failure. As Robert Kiyosaki says in *Rich Dad's Guide to Investing*, "First dream of having a team of full-time accountants and attorneys. Then you can have the big boat and the free time."

As you grow your team and begin hiring employees, you'll have to quickly learn to evaluate applicants and resumes, and do interviews. I evaluate the two most important qualities that a good worker can have— initiative and work ethic. You'll quickly learn that no matter what someone's experience, if you can find someone that has a bias toward action, takes initiative, and has a solid work ethic, you'll have found someone that you'll want on your team permanently.

Originally, I conducted all interviews. Today, our Director of HR screens the applicants and the manager within a specific department conducts the first interview. If the manager wishes to submit the candidate as a possible hire, I will then interview them. The manager ensures the applicant is qualified, has the needed experience and capabilities, is able to start the position within a reasonable time period, and is within the salary range we are offering. Generally I am simply checking to make sure the applicant is sane, has a good work ethic, and can communicate well. At the risk of giving a slight edge to future applicants who read this book, my favorite interview questions to ask are:

1. Tell me about yourself? Where are you from and what is your passion in life? (You can't ask where they live, but you can ask where they're from)
2. Tell me about what you did at your last position?
3. Why are you no longer at your last job? Or why do you wish to leave?

4. What have been your failures and the mistakes that you've made in life?
5. What adjectives would you use to describe you?
6. What are a couple experiences in your life that have changed you and made you who you are today?
7. What were the most difficult periods of your life?
8. How did that experience change you?
9. As an individual, what are the things that you believe in?
10. Are you familiar with what we do?
11. How would you describe what we do?
12. What are your favorite books?
13. What do you like to do outside of work?
14. What are the goals that you have for your professional life?
15. What are the goals that you have outside of your career?
16. What do you see yourself doing in three years?

We have grown very quickly since we had two employees in a 700 square foot office in Chapel Hill. We now have over 70 employees and 25,000 square feet of office space in Durham. We added to our management team in the following order:

1. Chief Executive Officer – Ryan Allis, Jul 2003
2. Chairman – Aaron Houghton, Jul 2003
3. Director of Marketing – Josh Carlton, Sep 2003
4. VP of Business Development – David Roth, Nov 2003
5. Chief Technical Officer – David Rasch, Feb 2004
6. Director of Customer Service – Brad Gurley*, Apr 2004
7. VP of Marketing – Brandon Milford, Aug 2004
8. Chief Financial Officer – Tim Oakley, March 2006
9. Director of Corp. Communications – Chuck Hester, Jul 2006
10. Director of Human Resources – Cindy Hays, Mar 2007

*Our current Director of Customer Service Amber Neill joined us in May 2005. Brad works for us part time now while he goes to school.

This group of nine people (Josh left us in April 2004 to go to graduate school) is our core Director team that I meet with every Monday at 10:30am to review the Director report from the prior week. Around employee number twenty five, we also began developing a secondary layer of management. We added a:

1. Senior Accounts Manager – Rob Call
2. Software Development Manager – Alan Cox
3. Software Maintenance Manager – Geoff Catlin
4. Systems Manager – Jay Faulkner
5. Billing Manager – Rainy Kolar
6. Design Manager – Alan Underwood
7. Deliverability Manager – Justin Rauschenberg
8. Customer Service Manager – Richard Oliver and Dave Walker
9. Operations Manager – Carl Carpenter
10. Enterprise Sales Manager – Bruce Woods

We also made use of interns from UNC, NC State, and Duke as we needed to in our marketing, development, and systems administration departments. We hired the best team we were able to and used job boards such as Monster, HotJobs, TriangleJobs.com, and Craigslist, local networking groups such as RTP 2.0, the Triangle Linux Users Group, Triangle Internet Workers, and Triangle PHP Users Group, local university career centers, and social networking tools like Facebook and LinkedIn to spread the word about the positions.

After raising our seed round of funding in May 2006 we were able to begin to use recruiting firms such as HireNetworks, The Select Group, and FullScale Solutions to fill positions. These recruiting firms charge us between 10% and 15% of a placed employee's first year salary as their fee. This cost can be between $3,000 and $10,000 depending on the salary and rate, so it can get expensive quickly.

Setting Priorities as a Manager

As your company grows and you enter the role of a manager, you'll need to gain new skills. You'll need to learn how to manage people, delegate responsibility, identify leaders, and set priorities. Here is a simple model that can be used to assist in setting your priorities.

Diagram 4 – Business Impact & Investment Priority Setting Model

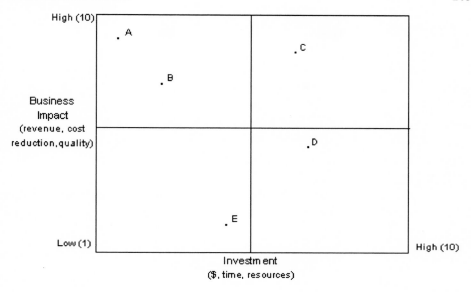

Whether you are planning out a long term strategy, or setting priorities in the midst of a crisis, the above model can help you order which tasks or projects should be done first. To use the model, simply plot the impact each project will have on your business on the vertical axis and the amount of money, time, and resources it will take on the horizontal axis. Do this for each project you must prioritize.

As you can see, projects which are plotted closer to the top left will be those that you should pursue first. They are the ones that will have a big impact on your business without costing much to implement. In this example, you would aim to complete project A first. This same model can be used to prioritize any type of to-do list and assist you as a manager in ensuring your time is being spent in ways that will most benefit your business.

There have been days over the past five years when I have felt like everything was on fire and a model like the above would have been of no use whatsoever to me. On a day-to-day basis, I use Outlook 2007 and a legal notepad to keep notes. I put an A with a circle around it next to any task that is an action item, and meet at least three times per week with our Executive Assistant Michelle. Michelle helps me keep my list of ongoing projects and tasks I need to get done, as well as transcribes my voicemails, writes correspondence, books travel, and fills out purchase orders and reimbursement forms for the Director team. We hired Michelle as employee fifty-two which was way after she was needed.

Ten Management Lessons

Over the past five years as iContact and Virante have grown, I've learned a lot about managing people. A business is little without the people behind it. As I mentioned in the section on building a team, the two most important things I look for when hiring are initiative and work ethic. I cannot overestimate the importance of bringing on good people to the eventual success of your business. But once you have these good people, how do you manage them?

I would certainly submit that I have much left to learn about leadership and management, but here are a few tips I've learned that may be of some use.

1. **Have a Vision and Communicate It.** Make sure you clearly communicate your vision for the company. No one follows a leader who cannot communicate the way in which the company will succeed. Each employee's future is tied closely to the success of your company. Make sure they believe in your company, what it stands for, and its products and services and make sure they know that the hard work they are putting in now will pay off.

2. **Show Respect.** Treat people, including your customers, suppliers, partners, and employees, with respect at all times.

3. **Share Your Success.** Make sure your employees share in the success of your company. As the company is able, provide additional benefits such as healthcare and dental coverage, a stock options plan, and a 401(k) plan. As an employee's skills and abilities grow, reward them with fair compensation. Finally, consider incentivizing your top employees and managers with ownership in the company. Few things can make a person work harder than a piece of the action.

4. **Don't Be Too Serious.** Make the business environment fun at times. While being professional and taking things seriously is important, nothing can beat the effects of company-wide midnight round of bowling after it reaches an important milestone, a lunchtime pizza party once per month, or a spontaneous Nerf-dart duel.

5. **Work With Your Employees.** Make sure the employees see you there and working with them. No one likes to work hard for

someone who doesn't work hard themselves. Especially early on, be the first to arrive and the last to leave whenever possible.

6. **Have Your Door Open.** Whether or not you have your own office yet, have your 'door' open. Make sure your employees and managers know that you are approachable at any time about any problem they are having.

7. **Listen.** You have built a great team and are paying top dollar for it. Hold meetings with your management team least every other week, if not more often. Also have informal ad hoc discussions with your partners, managers, and employees often. Get their feedback, discuss the business and its strategy, and inquire every so often if there is anything that you can help with that is frustrating them. A few weeks ago I had a quick spur-of-the-moment meeting with my lead developer for iContact. After inquiring if anything was frustrating him, it came out that he felt he was working in an environment in which he became distracted too often. We quickly devised a solution in which he would work at home four hours per day until we could move into a larger office in which the development team could work in a separate room away from the distraction of the sales and support team. This small change has doubled our developer's productivity.

8. **Build Relationships.** Without understanding at least the basics of what is occurring in an employee's out-of-office life it can be hard to connect with him or her on a professional level. One tactic I've used successfully to get to know each employee personally is to take them and their significant other to dinner the first evening of their employment. It serves as a way to celebrate the occasion as well as learn a little bit about the employee that would not come out in interviews or through reading a resume.

9. **Commend More Than You Criticize.** Too many business owners (and I have been guilty of this as well) will only say something to an employee when he or she has done something wrong or something that has negatively affected the company. While constructive criticism and appropriate guidance has its place, if you seem to only condemn and never praise, your employees will quickly either dislike you or show apathy in their jobs. Continued properly placed praises can be as powerful to getting quality results out of an employee as a large raise. Many people thrive on peer and superior recognition just as much as money. Instituting both an employee of

the month award as well as a quarterly performance review can be extremely valuable to your company.

10. **Consciously Build a Culture.** At iContact, we are truly are a family. We call ourselves the iContact Family. When someone is moving into a new house or needs a ride home from the airport we're there to help. We believe in building people up not tearing people down. We put people first and have respect for the individual. We believe that we should work hard and be innovative, yet maintain a balance in our lives. We believe in not letting balls drop, and that we're all working together toward the same mission. We have a foosball and ping pong table in our office, free sodas, Bagel Monday, and monthly birthday celebrations and Outstanding Performance Award ceremonies. We have a young, dynamic, fun, and innovative culture. It exists because we have consciously built it.

As a manager and business owner, you gain an immense responsibility. You control the activity and purpose that your employees dedicate half of their waking hours to. Make your company's purpose meaningful, communicate your vision, respect and praise your employees, and share your success. If you can succeed in building a team of highly motivated and happy employees that take initiative, have a bias toward action,

> "Make your company's purpose meaningful, communicate your vision, respect and praise your employees, and share your success."

respect you, and truly care for the business, you will have done much of the work in building a strong and quickly growing organization.

Fighting Bureaucracy

While systems are necessary to building a successful company, these systems must be efficient and be built upon processes that can be accomplished throughout the organization without bottlenecks or inefficiency. Proactive empowerment is a management theory I developed out of need and use to help reduce bureaucracy within an organization. It is a methodology through which individuals are empowered to know they are in charge of and perform at their peak while completing certain projects within an organization.

iContact generally has thirty to forty unique projects going on at any one time. Prior to implementing utilizing proactive empowerment, I was generally aware of what the projects were. We did have a weekly directors meetings at which I could get an update and ask questions. I would find myself only asking questions, however, when the topic of discussion triggered the question. I had no systematic way of knowing what projects to follow-up on and ensure projects were moving forward and on track.

One night I sat down and I listed all the projects that were going on in the company and it turned out that there were thirty-six of them. Next to each project I listed who was leading each project as well as the other persons working on. It turned out we had a lot of projects with people working on them, but no one in charge of them.

The problem that we were encountering as an organization was that people who were supposedly leading projects that weren't on the management team did not feel empowered to do whatever they had to do to get the project done. Because they did not know they were leading the project, they did not know they had the authority to figure out how to get the resources needed to achieve their objective.

Since I wasn't doing anything to *block* the projects from happening, I wondered why they weren't getting completed. While at the same time, when the people on the project ran into one roadblock they would assume it was management who was stopping it from progressing, when almost all of the time it was simply a case of people being busy and needing additional reminders from the project leaders.

Over the next week I sat down with the persons involved in each of the thirty-six company projects. I made sure there was a clear leader for each and told them, "I want you to be proactively empowered to work on this and do whatever you need to do within the organization to make things happen and reach this defined goal. Once the project leaders knew that they were in charge and had authority vested in them to navigate through the waters to get to a conclusion, projects were done more effectively and a lot more quickly.

A lot of time the mentality exists outside of management that if there is a road block, "it's not my fault" or "I don't need to anything about it until I hear more about it." A lot of time it's not the team member's fault, but now they knew it was their responsibility to figure out how to get over that hump to get past that road block. The non-management project leads were externalizing the situation by saying if that was an issue that they couldn't do anything about because they are not in management, they would just send a ticket in and wait until they heard back rather than proactively following up and tracking down the cause of inefficiency. With proactive empowerment we had an effective method of getting over that issue

As a very specific example, our Director of Customer Support, Amber Neil, needed a CRM tool to better track the statistics of incoming tickets for customer support for iContact. The tool cost $249. She wasn't in charge of the software budget and she knew she needed it but she didn't say anything about it, she didn't do anything about it for about three weeks until one day she told me, "hey it would be really great to have this thing." I told her that as a Director not only does she not need to fill out purchase orders for items under $300. Although the policy had been in place for a few months, she had not realized she had PO authority and the ability to purchase whatever she needed for her department up to $300 without having to rely on upper management.

That's a very specific case where if I had gone to her in advance and said, "Here's the project I want you to work on, here is the goal, here are the people you are working with, do whatever you need to do to get this done" she would have come to a conclusion much more quickly.

Instead of reactively telling our team members yes you can and having the bottleneck at me or another Director, I now proactively going to them on a project-by-project basis and say, "This is what we are trying to accomplish, you are authorized, and enabled, and empowered to do whatever you need to do to get this done." We are now getting projects done much more efficiently.

Since I have followed this policy of proactive empowerment when a project is starting by writing up a project brief, going to the lead, explaining what we are trying to get done, and empowering them to do whatever they need to do, more projects have been getting done more quickly.

So to summarize, step one of proactive empowerment is to identify what the project is. Step two is to identify the people on the project and the leader. Step three is to provide the brief to the project team and project lead and ensure the lead knows they have the authority to do what is needed to get things done.

35 Lessons I Have Learned

At the end of each year, I post on my blog the most important lessons I learned that year. Here are the major lessons I learned over the past few years.

1. **The People You Surround Yourself With Matters**

Venture Capitalist Steve Nelson shared some advice with me this year that has stuck with me: "Stay involved with only the best. Ask yourself - are these outstanding people? To know, you only need to ask yourself: do they possess great intelligence, keen business insight, outstanding people skills, and unquestioned integrity?"

2. **Life Reveals The Rules Only After You Start Playing**
Life is a game; and a game that doesn't exactly reveal most the rules until it's been played a few times. There are two ways to figure out the rules-- a) talk to smart people who have already done what you're trying to accomplish or b) trial and error. Either way, start playing early.

3. **Judging People is Necessary**
As a child you learn never to judge people. "Judging people" perhaps even has a bad connotation. But in business, you must judge and you must judge often. You must judge based on intelligence, effort, and more importantly results. If you don't judge, you end up with unexamined, unmeasured mediocrity. All humans have equal inherent value, but not all humans' productive efforts are equal.

4. **If Somebody Sues You, Go Talk to Them in Person**
I spent about $35,000 unnecessarily in 2006 by listening to my lawyer and not communicating with a former client that was bringing Virante into arbitration. If I just would have flown out there and spoken with him in person initially instead of 4 months later at the mediation hearing I likely would have saved that $35,000 and a lot of personal stress. The lawyer's advice was correct and proper legally, but the 'legal' solution often costs a lot of money to get to.

5. **Build Consensus with the Core Before You Present Widely**
Build pre-emptive support and communicate your vision individually to your Executive or Director team or in small groups to get feedback and adjust before presenting to everyone. This can be a lot of work, but it's how it is done in companies larger than 20 people.

6. **Life is Too Short to Not Be Passionate About What You Do**
Stand out, make an impact, be compassionate, and help others. Too much injustice occurs in this world to not want to make a positive change at whatever level you can. Torture, human slavery, murder, genocide, starvation. Too many people don't have the opportunities we have, and too many people die needlessly from preventable diseases and starvation to make you not want to do the absolute best

you can in your life. Have fun. Enjoy life. Help others. Reduce
suffering. That is the credo.

7. **"Yes And" Life**

One of the key lessons of improv is to say yes to the scene that your
acting partner is creating. If your partner suggests you're kissing
cousins in a ski lodge, then you are kissing cousins in a ski lodge
AND something else. By saying "yes, and" in response to people
instead of "no, but" you often create better outcomes and build a
much stronger relationship with the person you're interacting with.

8. **There Are Four Must-Attend Conferences for Future Leaders**

In June 2006 I sat next to John McCain and talked about soccer and
energy policy as we watched the semi-final of the world cup for 15
minutes. I had a conversation with Madeleine Albright about security
and aid policy in Africa. I talked about digital camera technology riding
on a bus next to Steve Jurvetson on the way to Michael Eisner's
ranch. I sat next to Glenn Close, Sandra Day O'Conner and Stelios
Ioannou of EasyJet fame in a roundtable discussion on climate
change. How'd I get there? Five years of consistent hard work and
getting invited to attend a conference called Fortune Brainstorm. By
getting invited to and attending a few key conferences you can have
access to pretty much anybody in the world. In my experience so far,
those key conferences are Fortune Brainstorm, The World Economic
Forum, TED, and the Clinton Global Initiative Annual Meeting.

9. **There's A Good Deal of Corruption in the World--It Can Affect
Policy--And Competition Can Reduce It**

In 1995, the telecom companies had the technology to launch DSL.
But they held off for nearly five years. Why? Because the cable
companies didn't yet have the technology ready to launch cable
modems and the telephone monopolies saw hundreds of millions of
dollars of second-line dial-up revenue from their subscriber base.
Instead of providing DSL to Americans and allowing economic-
enhancing broadband access, they (somewhat understandably
perhaps) held back the technology to make more money, in the mean
time using their huge lobbying base to ensure governmental policy
wasn't enacted that would benefit all other businesses, all consumers,
and the entire economy. Finally, in 1999 the technology for cable
modems became ready and marketable and amazingly, DSL
launched. The lesson perhaps is that while business in general and
consumers in general should have the right to lobby and influence, a

single industry should never have the power to lobby at the expense of the wider good.

10. **Compounding Experience & Compounding Resources Allow For Greatness Over Time**

The big wooden flywheel from *Good to Great* has held true in my business experience. It takes a long time to get the flywheel moving at all. It takes a lot of really hard pushes to get it going. Each individual push doesn't move it very much. But if you keep pushing, eventually the wheel starts moving and inertia and momentum start to take hold, causing each subsequent push of equal strength to have a greater and greater impact. In 2003, iContact did $12,000 in sales. In 2004, $296,000. In 2005, $1.3 million. And in 2006, $2.9 million. We worked from October 2002 until December 2003 to generate $12,000 in sales (and $20,000 in expenses!). We worked equally as hard in 2006 as we did in 2003, but instead of $12,000 we generated $2.7 million with the same effort. Intelligent consistent effort compounds as experience, knowledge, and access expands. Sometimes it is difficult to fathom how people like Rockefeller, Carnegie, and Morgan acquired their fortunes and made the impact they did in one lifetime. They started by working their butt off to make $12,000 and forty years later they were working with hundreds of millions. Same way Buffet did it, same way Gates did it. Play life like a long-term game. And always be improving.

11. **Networking Isn't About Handing Out Business Cards**

In every personal development conference you go to you hear that networking is key to business success. And that is in fact true. But most teachers leave out the most important rule of networking. It's not about shaking hands, having a little small talk, and swapping business cards. It's about building real, trusting, mutually giving relationships with quality people.

12. **The World Has a Lot of Problems, But They Are Mostly Fixable**

One of the reasons I want to be a U.S. Senator one day is to be able to influence foreign policy, especially the policy that deals with how our country interacts with other countries from an economic and environmental standpoint. This year, I've been made so consciously aware of the extreme inequities in the world today. Over 2.7 billion people live on under $2 per day[13] and 49,000 people die per day from preventable disease and starvation.[14] Most people don't have the opportunity to be creative through entrepreneurship due to class-divisions and bureaucratic restriction. The developed nations produce an unnecessarily large amount of greenhouse gas causing agricultural famine in non-developed nations. Billions of dollars go to farm subsidies in the U.S. and E.U.[15] creating silos of wasted grain while millions die of starvation due to lack of access to markets in developing nations. I have been deeply affected by these issues and hope to be able to dedicate much of my life the best way I know how doing my best to improve these situations on a global scale through politics, business, and social entrepreneurship.

13. **Community Matters**

And yet, for every thought I have about Malawi, Benin, or Burundi, I think about my home of North Carolina. For every issue in Malawi, Benin, and Burundi, I can see a parallel issue (though at a different scale) here in North Carolina. The Lesson: While you should always educate yourself about the world, what happens in it, and how you can make a global difference, you can most often make the largest difference right at home--and there are always plenty of issues (read: opportunities to improve) right here in our own community.

14. **Be Aware of that Little Voice**

Listen to that little voice in the back of your head. It's usually alerting you to something that might come back to bite you if you don't listen to it.

15. **Communicate**

Don't let non-communication lead to the de-generation of a relationship. Don't be passive aggressive. Attack issues immediately and head-on.

16. **You Eventually Have to Balance the Bias Toward Action**

Full-on bias toward action is great. But only when you have little to lose. Once you have something to lose, you must balance having a bias toward action with analysis, due diligence, and care.

17. **Face the Day**

Don't avoid doing things just because they are hard or may cause conflict.

18. **Find and Eliminate Bottlenecks**

Consistently look for bottlenecks and inefficiencies in communication flows and organizational behavior.

19. **Know What Matters**

Integrity is what matters at the end of the day. There will always eventually be an audit or a lawsuit that has to look into what you're doing right now. So make sure at all times your actions are above board and in good faith.

20. **Business Can Be Harsh**

The business world can be harsh and often times there is someone in your life that you trust that you should not who will eventually try to screw you over.

21. **Avoid Going Around a Manager**

As CEO, if there is a layer of management between you and the person you need to speak to, speak to that person's manager first to make sure it is okay to speak with him or her or just relay the message through that person's manager. Avoid assigning work to people you do not directly manage to avoid priority conflicts. Rather, in all cases except emergencies give the task to that person's manager to assign.

22. **Know the Value of Praise**

Recognition and praise can be just as big of motivating factors for employees as salary and bonuses.

23. **Hiring Takes More Time Than You Think**

Finding the right people when you need them is a significant challenge and can take longer than you would think.

24. **Communicate Openly With Your Customers**

Always communicate openly, fully, and quickly with your customers during any negative events.

25. **QA Is Important**

Quality assurance is a critical part of the software development process. Don't release a new version of your product until it has been thoroughly tested by both an in-house QA team and a subset of your customer base. Bugs that make it into a released version are much more costly both in lost sales and loss of brand goodwill than spending the money needed to fix them up front.

26. **Raising Money Takes Time**

Raising funding for a company will take longer than you expect.

27. **Prepare When Things Are Going Well**

It is better to prepare for the worst when things are going well rather than when they're not.

28. **Sometimes You Have to Set Them Free**

Sometimes you just have to let go. Get the right people, train them, and then trust them. Trust but verify.

29. **Communicate Your Vision Often**

Just because you have a detailed plan in your head doesn't mean other members of your team know it. If you don't consistently communicate your vision and plans, people may think you don't have vision and have failed to plan.

30. **Be Nice to She Who Decides Your Credit Limit**
Be very nice to merchant account processing limit review officers and give them the information they need to review your limit well before you hit it.

31. **Be Accessible to Your Employees & Clients**
Reiterate whenever you can that you are available for any employee to speak with. Have lunch with every member of your team (in cross-departmental groups of 3-4) at least once per year. Publish your email address and phone number for your clients. You can always delegate a client request or problem that comes to you via email or voicemail—but at least you will be aware of it.

32. **Let Your Managers Know When You Go Outside to Learn**
If you're going to talk to someone outside your company about a topic/department you already have some in charge of so that you can learn for yourself, either bring in the manager you have in that are into the discussion or let them know in advance that you will be talking to them. You do not want them to think that you are trying to replace them or make them irrelevant or marginalized.

33. **Don't Undersell Yourself**
The world has a lot of opportunities to grow. If you keep working hard, you will meet people and learn new methods of growing your business and your sales. In the Fall of 2005 I probably undersold the company to potential investors, saying we were the third largest email marketing company trying to become the first and then sell for $25 million to $30 million. I should have said, even if I didn't yet know how we'd accomplish the goal, that our target was to become the leading provider of online communication software and become a public company with an exit of $250 million or more. I didn't even believe in that vision yet then, but I should have.

34. **Randomly Tell People That They Are Doing a Great Job**
As busy entrepreneurs, we don't tell our employees that we appreciate them enough. Tell them they are doing a great job that you appreciate them as at least once per quarter, if not more.

35. **Don't Accelerate In The Snow Without Tread on Your Tires**

Make sure the right underlying processes, systems, and people are in place whenever possible before you attempt to rapidly scale the business.

Chapter 15 — Step 9: Build Strong Systems

> "Achievement comes to someone when he is able to do great things for himself. Success comes when he empowers followers to do great things with him. Significance comes when he develops leaders to do great things for him. But legacy is created only when a person puts his organization into the position to do great things without him."
>
> - John C. Maxwell

Creating Systems & Automating Operations

As your business grows, you will need to build systems and processes and attempt to automate as much as you can. You'll need to build distribution systems, inventory systems, marketing systems, follow-up systems, customer support systems, research and development systems, accounting systems, and hiring systems, among many others. Systems are formalized rules, policies, and procedures that trained individuals are able to repeat time and time again as your company expands. Within iContact have document systems for human resources, accounting, employee training, billing, product development, marketing, sales, management, technical operations, and account management.

> "Systems are formalized rules, policies, and procedures that trained individuals are able to repeat time and time again as your company expands."

From the beginning of your business, as you create each system, write down the details, as well as any general business rules and procedures in an employee handbook. This book will become invaluable as time progresses. The Employee Handbook for iContact is currently 38 pages and contains background information on the company, founders' bios, a listing of officers and the Board of Directors, a company description, a description of our main product, product frequently asked questions, a company timeline, a list of persons to know, an overview of agreements, and office procedures and policies including policies or procedures for:

- Adverse Weather
- Attendance
- Backup
- Change of Information
- Confidentiality
- Commission
- Deliverability
- Disaster Recovery
- Downtime Notification
- Dress Code
- Drug
- Food
- Freelancing
- Holidays
- Job Responsibilities
- Large Sender Acceptance
- Maternity Leave
- Network Usage
- New Employee Training
- Parking
- Paternity Leave
- Payroll
- Performance Evaluations
- Phone Answering
- Phone Usage
- Product Development
- Printing
- Reimbursement
- Server Installation
- Quality Assurance
- Sexual Harassment
- Vacation
- Voice Mail
- Workers' Compensation

As we grow the business and things change, we continuously add to the handbook. A number of forms have also developed at the company, although we try to keep these to a minimum. We use forms for:

- Purchase Orders
- Travel Requests
- New Hire Requests
- Expense Reports
- Creative Briefs
- Client Proposals
- Health Insurance Sign-up
- Dental Insurance Sign-up
- Paid Leave Requests
- Written Reprimands
- Verbal Reprimands
- 401(k) Beneficiary
- Employment Eligibility I9
- Supervisor Reviews
- Employee Reviews
- Letter Stationary
- Envelope Stationary
- Employee Offers
- Confidentiality Contracts
- Non-Disclosure Agreements
- W4 Tax Deductions
- FSA Plan Enrollment
- Vacation Requests
- Job Descriptions
- Direct Deposit Setup
- Workout Room Liability Waiver
- Database Modifications
- Fax Cover Sheets
- Affiliate Thank You Letter
- Collections Letter
- Invoices
- Customer Support Templates

We also utilize a number of spreadsheets in the organization, including:

- Board Package
- Monthly Billing Records
- Purchase Order Records
- CPC ROI Reports
- Operations Plan
- Annual Budget
- Profit & Loss Statement
- Chargeback Record
- Depreciation Schedule
- Development Timeline
- Product Feature Requests
- Personnel Directory
- Balance Sheet
- Accounts Receivable
- Affiliate Check Records
- Revenue Projections
- Sales Compensation Plan
- Large Sender Pricing

We also have a weekly Director Report that provides a wealth of key information including:

Support Metrics

- % Abandoned Calls
- Average Hold Time
- Average Call Duration
- Calls Per Day
- Calls per 10 Minute Interval
- Customer Contact By Type
- Calls Per Week
- Total Time on Phone
- Total Hold Time
- # of Abandoned Calls
- Number of Chats
- Total Time in Chat
- Average Chat Duration
- Number of Email Tickets
- Email Ticket Response Time
- Tickets/Chats/Calls Per Rep

Billing Metrics

- Weekly Sales Figures
- Attempted Transactions
- Successful Transactions
- Declined Transactions
- Check and Wire Sales
- Credit Card Sales
- Amount Credited
- Overdue Accounts
- Amount of A/R
- # of A/R

Marketing Metrics

- Total Visits
- Total Pageviews
- Avg. Pageviews Per Visit
- Avg. Time on Site

- % New Visits
- Bounce Rate
- Total Trials

- Total Full Accounts
- Trial to Full Conversion
- Visitor to Trial Conversion

Product Development Metrics

- Bugs Reported
- Bugs Resolved
- Maint. Tickets Opened
- Maint. Tickets Resolved

- Systems Tickets Opened
- Systems Tickets Resolved
- % of Stories Completed
- Email Sending Speed

Sales Metrics

- Closed Customers by Rep
- Revenue by Rep

- Total Closed
- Total New Revenue

Finally, we have a real-time Management Dashboard that provides real time information on:

- # of Paying Customers
- # of Overdue Customers
- Monthly Paying Customers
- Annual Paying Customers
- Customers by Plan Type
- # of Trial Customers
- # of Affiliates
- Total Sales to Date
- Accounts Receivable Total
- Monthly Reorder Revenue
- Annual Reorder Revenue
- Yearly Revenue
- Monthly Rev. Per Customer
- Avg. Length of a Customer
- Customer Lifetime Value

- Renewed Accounts By Month
- Trial to Full Conversion %
- Annual Revenue By Month
- New Annual Clients By Month
- New Customers By Month
- Net New Customers By Month
- Cancellations By Month
- Retention % By Month
- Revenue Per Customer By Month
- Emails Sent Per Month
- Added Revenue Per Month
- Lost Revenue Per Month
- Net New Revenue Per Month
- New Trial Users By Month
- Monthly Trial to Full Conversion

All of these systems, procedures, policies, metrics, forms, and reports have evolved over the past four years out of necessity to be able to better manage the business. Always remember that investors do not like to invest in systems where the system goes home at night. If you can build proper systems so that your business will operate properly, whether or not you are there to oversee it, your business will grow faster and be much easier to sell. Although it takes longer to set up the system for a task than to do a task yourself, in the long run you can save a lot of your time and effort by setting up the system.

Action Item 6 – What Systems Will You Need in Your Company?

Take a moment and write down any systems or procedures that you will need to develop in your company.

_____

_____

_____

Building your company from a new business into an enduring organization creates some growing pains. Putting in place an Employee Handbook can't help with all of these. You'll also need to do payroll, ensure compliance with HR laws and regulations, create automated reporting mechanisms, and ensure your books are up to higher standards. Specific lessons I've learned related to building systems and procedures include:

1. It's best to outsource your payroll. Figuring out State, Social Security, Medicare, FICA, and Unemployment amounts and making sure exact payments are made on time can be quite a hassle if you choose to do it yourself. We use a company called Paychex to handle cutting checks for our employees and paying all applicable state and federal payroll taxes.

2. Be sure to have a procedure for hiring new employees. All new iContact employees must sign an Employment Agreement, Confidentiality, Non-Disclosure, and Non-Compete Agreement. They also receive a Direct Deposit Enrollment Form, W4, Health Insurance Enrollment Form, and Employee Handbook.

3. Maintain records relating to personnel and performance to protect yourself against lawsuits related to employee termination. Conduct quarterly evaluations of each employee yourself until you are large enough to have a full HR department.

4. Hire a good accounting firm and establish an appropriate accounting procedure. At iContact, we keep all of our financial records and receipts for each month and then mail them to our accounting firm at the beginning of the next month. They input the records into QuickBooks Professional and then mail the files back to us. We get a monthly profit and loss statement and balance sheet. The same firm also handles our yearly taxes.

As you go from being a small start-up to an international player in your industry, you'll have to manage the operations of a number of activities. In all cases, focus on creating efficiency and optimizing every operation. The more you can automate your operations the better. If you can properly navigate the process of creating systems, develop an employee handbook, deal with payroll and HR, establish an accounting process, and focus on efficiency and you'll be well on your way to turning your new business into an enduring company.

Highlight 9: A Case Study on Operational Efficiency

To illustrate how effective systems can lead to operational efficiency and reduced costs, we can take a look at a client of Virante's from 2003 in the nutraceuticals industry. This client sold various products that improve health and reduce pain. When I began working with the client, they were making a few dozen sales per day through their web site.

When a sale would come in, they would have their shipping person type in the customer's information into a label maker, print out postage on stamps.com, type in the address a second time, get a box from the closet, construct the box, find the proper product and put it in the box, find the proper literature and put it in the box, manually enter the address for the third time as well as the product, description, quantity, and cost into QuickBooks and print out an invoice, put the invoice in the box, tape the box up, apply the stamps.com postage, and then go to the post office to mail the package.

When they told me everything they did to ready an order, I was stunned at how inefficient and wasteful their process was. It took over 15 minutes to prepare a single order—whereas the nutraceuticals company I worked with in high school was able to complete a full order in less than 45 seconds on average.

After I consulted with them their system was much more efficient.

Now, instead of typing in the label they download all the new order data from their database all at once and automatically mail-merge all the labels into a Microsoft Word file. The fulfillment person simply had to open Word, start the feed of the labels into the printer, and hit print. They could print ten labels in thirty seconds, instead of spending one minute on each.

Next, I got rid of their need to use stamps.com for postage. I alerted them that instead, they could simply set up an account at their local post office, pay in advance with a check, and take all their packages in through the back door each afternoon. They'd just drop of the packages, tell the attendant which account they were from, and the USPS would handle applying the exact postage.

This knowledge saved another 2 minutes per package, as the fulfillment person no longer had to weigh the package, type in the company and delivery address, and print and apply the proper postage. The next thing we optimized was the packaging. Instead of using a hard to construct box, I told them about padded self-seal mailers. They were not only 1/4th the price of a box, but also required no construction or tape.

Finally, I advised the company that there was no need to include an invoice with the product, as the customer received their invoice via email. This removed the need to re-enter all the data again into QuickBooks, print out the invoice, and put it in the box. This saved a full four minutes per order. They could now automatically import the sales data into QuickBooks in a batch at the end of each week. It would take 30 seconds to import 1000 orders, instead of 30 hours.

By optimizing their shipping operations as such, we saved the company hundreds of dollars each week and increased the maximum capability per day from 45 orders to 450 orders. In your own company, there are likely numerous areas where an efficiency review would be helpful. See what efficiencies you can create and how much money you can save by focusing on automating and optimizing the operations of your business.

Selecting Office Space

Behind every successful business there are systems, processes, and infrastructure. We'll talk about building your systems and processes later. For now, let's focus on infrastructure. By infrastructure I mean everything in your business that must be set up for your business to run. It includes things like internet connections, phone lines, phone systems, computer networks, product liability insurance, and office space. Let's take a minute to review a few tips on how to select good office space.

In my business experience, I have been fortunate to always be able to find good space to conduct my business. When I was a computer consultant between 11 and 4, I worked on location at the client's place of business or residence, and thus did not need and office. As a web site designer when I was 15 and 16 I worked out of my room in my parents' house. It had a hand painted black desk covered with pictures of my friends and places where I had been. It was a great place to get work done and enabled me to save up quite a bit of money.

The first office I ever worked in was that of the nutraceuticals company I worked with in 2001 and 2002. The space was on the second floor of a building, above an air conditioning company, and had a very helpful freight elevator—essential for bringing in the large shipments of product up to our storage closet. The owner received a very good deal on the place as he purchased an extended lease while the place was in disrepair—and then paid a few hundred dollars to have it cleaned, painted, and re-carpeted.

After moving to North Carolina, I did not have an office for a couple months. I worked out of my sixth floor dorm in the Ehringhaus Residence Hall. By October, however, I met Aaron Houghton through the Carolina Entrepreneurship Club and he allowed me to use his 700 square feet downtown Chapel Hill office space at no charge. After we incorporated iContact in July 2003, he continued to allow us to use the space at a discounted rent charge. As I mentioned in Chapter One, it has all of the needed facilities including a T1 line for internet access, a wireless office network, cable TV, a George Foreman grill, a bathroom, a love seat, a coffee maker, a top of the line phone system, a large conference room, and three work rooms.

Now that we have grown to ten employees we have decided to move to a larger office space a few miles away. We'll be moving into this 2,300 sq. foot space this September. In our search we've had to take into account factors such as cost per square foot, upfit costs, property taxes, telecommunication providers, proximity for employees, and the contract length (usually 3 or 5 years). We hired an office space broker to help us and negotiate on our behalf.

Before you begin your own search for office space, you'll have to determine what you will need. Will you need a store front retail location, a large storage warehouse, a high-profile location to impress visiting clients, or simply a room in a shared office building? A commercial real estate broker can help you answer these questions, provide strategic advice, and find you properties that fit your needs. The service of your broker is paid for by a commission from your monthly rent which would be same price regardless, so their services are effectively free.

Once you determine what you'll need, take a look in your local classifieds to see what office space is available in the area. When you locate a potential location, your broker will set up an appointment with the owner or agent. When evaluating potential locations, take into account the number of square feet, the location, parking availability, broadband options, room arrangement, storage space, whether the complex has a receptionist for all the tenants that you can use, amount of security deposit, and average monthly utilities bills.

When you do settle on a place, you'll likely have to get electricity turned on, purchase general business liability insurance, call the DSL or cable company to get a site survey done for internet access availability, and head to the office store to pick up some furniture and supplies. Before you begin furnishing the office, you may wish to take a picture of your empty office. I still have the picture of the empty office I walked into in June 2003 that would become iContact. It's a magical experience to see that empty office, with all your dreams, goals, and plans to build your company into one that will soon fill that room and later something much larger.

Creating Your Accounting System

Before you begin doing much business, it will be of great benefit to get your accounting system in order. Many businesses fail because of improper financial controls and reporting. As proper cash flow management is such a key to building a successful business, it is imperative to always know how much cash you do have on hand, what your expenses are, and what liabilities and assets the company has at any point.

The basis of your accounting system will be your journal entries, income statement, balance sheet, and cash flow statement. Your income statement will keep track of your revenues and expenses, your balance sheet will be able to tell you the value of your assets, liabilities, and owners' equity at any point in time, and your cash flow statement will allow you to monitor the in and outflow of money to and from your business over any set period.

You can use software such as QuickBooks, Quicken Business, or Money Small Business to make managing your financials yourself much easier. Before our company was large enough for a dedicated bookkeeper, I used QuickBooks and all I had to do is import my bank statement once per month for each of my companies and categorize each transaction. The software automatically generated my balance sheet, income statement, and cash flow statement. Today, we outsource our bookkeeping activities to a nearby firm. We simply drop off our bank and credit card statements along with our receipts and paid invoices at the beginning of each month and the firm categorizes them and provides us with updated financial reports as we require them.

When you hire your first employee, you'll have to set up a payroll system. Essentially, this allows you to keep track of what you pay your employees and ensure that you pay the FICA social security tax each quarter to the IRS and State if you are in the U.S.. While it is much easier to have your employees work as independent contractors and send them a 1099 at the end of the year, if someone is working for you full time, you'll have to add them as an employee. For iContact we have decided to outsource this payroll responsibility to a company called Paychex. The simply call us twice per month to get the payment figures and the process the payment, without the proper taxes, and direct-deposit the appropriate amounts in each employee's bank account.

Once you begin to have a few months of transactions in your accounting software, you can use the reporting features to view the ratios of your business. Essentially, these ratios are similar to a report card for your business. They'll quickly tell the experienced business person and investor how your company is doing. The most common ratios are the quick ratio, current ratio, and debt to equity ratio.

<u>Quick Ratio (Acid Test) = Cash + Receivables / Total Current Liabilities</u>

The higher your quick ratio is the better. The more available cash and receivables you have and the less liabilities, the better off you will be. You always want your liquid assets to be greater than your current liabilities. The higher this ratio is, the longer your company will be able to stay afloat if your sales revenue dries up. You want it be at least 1. The quick ratio is also known as the acid test, as it can give a quick look into the health of a company.

Current Ratio = Total Current Assets / Total Current Liabilities

Your current ratio will answer whether your business has enough current assets to meet the payment of its current debts with a safety net for possible losses in current assets, such as inventory reductions or collectable accounts? A ratio of 2 or higher is considered acceptable.

Debt to Equity Ratio = Debt / Equity

To find your debt to equity ratio, simply divide the amount of debt you have by the value of the owners' equity in the company. Try to keep this number close to zero. While debt can be beneficial if used correctly, if your debt to equity goes above one, it may be a sign that you have too many liabilities for the amount of value in your company, creating the potential for bankruptcy.

Focusing on Building Your Business

As a business owner, you'll also want to look at your inventory turnover, gross margin ratio, net margin ratio, accounts receivable turnover, return on assets, return on equity, and return on investment. These ratios will be very helpful in managing your business. And always remember—cash flow is king. If things ever get too complex, that's a good sign—because at that point you're likely making a good amount of money and can afford to hire a CFO.

As soon as you can afford it, hire a good bookkeeper and later on a Chief Financial Officer. You may also want to hire an accountant to help you set up your payroll system and file your tax return each year. Having these persons on your team will allow you to focus on building your business, instead of making journal entries.

Step 10: Scale the Business

> "Make no small plans. They have no magic to stir men's blood and probably themselves will not be realized. Make big plans; aim high in hope and work, remembering that a noble, logical diagram once recorded will never die, but long after we are gone will be a living thing, asserting itself with ever-growing insistency. Remember that our sons and grandsons are going to do things that would stagger us. Let your watchword be order and your beacon beauty. Think big."
>
> -Daniel H Burnham, Great Chicago Architect

There are a few main methods of scaling your business. You can:

- Invest more in online or offline advertising
- Open up offices in other cities and countries
- Create distribution partnerships with firms in other locations
- Franchise your company
- Raise additional debt or equity capital to expand
- Expand your sales team
- Bring on additional management or Board talent
- Sell part or all of your company to a larger company or private equity firm that can help you expand

Regardless of the methods you choose, if you have the right systems in place beforehand your life will be much easier. You never want to accelerate in the snow without tread on your tires. As you build and scale your company, ask yourself this key question, "Will your business be able to make money while you sleep?" All highly successful businesses do.

Doing Business Internationally

By the time I left the nutraceuticals company I worked with in high school, the company's main product was being sold in over thirty countries. We had retailers in many of those countries, however most of the international orders came from individual consumers. It was a wonderful experience to know that the company's marketing message was getting out to persons in Malaysia, Chile, and Uzbekistan. That's what top placement in the search engines and a large network of affiliates can do for you.

Learning how the Customs Systems of individual countries worked was an interesting experience for me. At times it would take over four weeks for shipments to arrive in Canada sent via the U.S. Postal Service. Customs often opened the package and inspected it before sending it on. Strangely, we found that if we shipped via FedEx, packages got through in one week instead of four. Even stranger, packages would arrive in Kuala Lumpur, Malaysia in four days, quicker than most packages to Toronto.

As you begin to open up your sales channel to international markets, you will need to do research on the specific regulations and customs agencies of each country you wish to expand to. There are many strange regulations, tariffs, and taxes that you'll encounter when doing business overseas. Each country seems to have a different policy.

Depending on your type of product, you may need to develop product packaging and labeling in different languages. You may also want to establish distributorships with stores in that country, or hire local sales representatives that know an area to represent your firm and products. You can also look into possibilities such as setting up subsidiaries of your company in each country or establishing official partnerships or joint ventures with existing companies. No matter how you do it, you cannot overlook the international market. If you play it right, your sales outside of your own country will soon grow to exceed those within it.

Creating an Operating Plan for a Growing Company

While the business plan pro forma projections may be all that are required to get a loan or satisfy an angel or seed-round investor, once your business has substantial revenue you will need to provide more detail on your business, convert your accounting to Generally Accepted Accounting Principles format, have your accountant provide accrual based statements, and provide a model that ties together your sales pipeline, customer acquisition rates, marketing spend, and capital expenditures in a more detailed format.

At this point, a full operating plan and model is needed. Within an existing organization, Boards of Directors often talk about "The Plan." They may ask, "Are we at "plan" or above it? Is the "plan" flexible to adjust for a new strategic direction and revenue model?" The plan that is being referred to here is the company's board approved Operating Plan.

The Operating Plan is developed annually with quarterly updates by the Chief Financial Officer with help from the Chief Executive Officer, often needed to raise a second round of funding or a round above $1 million. The operating plan is many cases a massive spreadsheet workbook that contains multiple sheets that tie together the growth assumptions with the revenue projections with the GAAP category expenses, with the R&D, capital expenditure, COGS, and marketing spend with the employee headcount with the budget.

The Operating Plan for iContact includes the components below. Do note that iContact is now a company with over 75 employees and $8 million in annual sales and that you will likely not need as comprehensive of a model initially to effectively run your business. Knowing how this model is created may be helpful, however.

Our operating plan has evolved greatly from the time we hired our very experienced Chief Financial Officer in March 2006. Originally, I simply had a cash basis budget with revenues projected three years and expenses projected one with a upcoming year P&L. Today, our plan is built and managed by our CFO Tim, our accounting manager Lisa, our Director of Financial Operations Robert, and our accounting intern Desmond and has all of the below components:

Revenue Tab

1. Revenue projections for the next 3-5 years, broken down by month, driven by adjustable variables like customer growth per month, customer retention, and average revenue per user (APRU).
2. Historical revenue by month since company inception.
3. Revenue (broken into subcategories revenue by product line, unrecognized revenue, chargebacks, returns, cash basis revenue, and GAAP revenue)
4. Plan revenue vs. actual revenue historical comparison with % variance
5. A sales plan with compensation detail for your sales team (hunters with compensation tied to client acquisition) and account managers (farmers with compensation tied to client retention) that drives your revenue projections.

Expenses Tab

1. Past and projected expenses in GAAP summary format (COGS, Sales & Marketing, R&D, General & Administrative)
2. Past and projected expenses broken down my major expense area category by month (Administration, Labor Cost, Marketing, Travel & Entertainment, Professional Fees, Rent, Communications, Hosting, Depreciation & Interest) with subcategories as needed.
3. Plan expenses vs. actual expenses historical comparison with % variance by category and subcategory.
4. A cost of goods sold calculation information that shows which expenses and headcount feeds into COGS.
5. A benefits detail sheet that lists which employees receive what benefits, what each benefit cost is, and who pays for which benefits.

Headcount Tab

1. Headcount adds and subtractions historically per month.
2. Projected headcount adds for the next 3-5 years by department by month, with projected compensations, tying directly in labor costs on expense and P&L tabs.
3. Analysis of average company revenue per employee and average salary per headcount.
4. Breakout of existing headcount by department with name, title, and salary.

Statement of Operations (P&L) Tab

1. Projected revenue summary by month
2. Projected operating expenses broken down my major expense area category by month
3. Operating income by month
4. Any non-operating expenses such as depreciation and interest expenses.
5. Net income by month, historical and projected
6. EBITDA by month, historical and projected
7. Historical revenue, expenses by category, and net income for each year company has existed

8. Forwarding looking P&L for upcoming 1 to 2 years based on projected revenues and projected expenses.

Balance Tab

1. Expenditures by category for capital items budget (servers, computers, phones, hosting, software, furniture) feeding directly into the capital expenditure line on the P&L and depreciation schedule.
2. Depreciation schedule with listing of all physical and technical assets, their purchase value, and the length over which you've chosen to amortize their value.

Cashflow Tab

1. This section combines the GAAP income or loss from the Statement of Operations, with the changes in working capital, capital expenditures, long term debt and equity from the Balance Sheet to arrive at the net cashflow for the company each month.
2. If the difference in negative then you are burning cash and it is important to know your average cash burn over the most recent months divided into your checkbook balance (cash position) for the company. The result gives you the number of months you have remaining before you need to have additional money coming into the company.

Together, these sheets make up "The Plan." Essentially, the goal of the plan is to model your business in spreadsheet format that makes the job of a financial manager, operations manager, or an investor doing due diligence easier.

Being "at plan" simply means that you've hit your revenue, cash flow, and net profit projections. Being "above plan" means you've exceeded your revenue, cash flow, and net profit projections. Being "below plan" means you've underperformed based on your revenue, cash flow, and net profit projections.

Are Your Projections Too High, Too Low, or Just Right?

The CEO and CFO often have multiple factors influencing the plan that they submit for Board and sometimes investor approval. They do not want the revenue projections to be too high, or else they will look like they underperformed as leaders and if too far off not have enough money in the bank to sustain operations. They also don't want the plan to appear to be too low for then they will a) not motivate their team with an easy plan to hit and be perceived as leaving growth on the table and b) receive a lower valuation from investors in any financing rounds who are basing part of the valuation off of the plan. Submitting a revenue projections plan that is known to be low so as to improve performance perception is called sandbagging.

Overall, the incentives tend to balance where CEOs and CFOs are submitting "expected case scenarios" that they expect to be able to hit with 50% confidence, with some risks on the downside and opportunities on the upside identified.

In reality, most venture-backed companies are below plan most of the time, though they all of course shoot to be above it. This occurrence is likely due to the short-term incentive to publish higher revenue projections in a venture-backed company to get a higher pre-money valuation in a funding round due to perceived higher future revenues and profits.

In truth, some less than forthright venture firms tend to encourage this practice, wanting the CEO to publish unreachable revenue targets so that they can have an argument for obtaining additional control within an organization or in extreme situations, forcing a down-round of capital to be raised in which the funds are raised at a valuation that is lower than the prior round (doing all kinds of nasty things to existing common shareholders).

In an ideal situation, as a venture-backed CEO you will neither have to sandbag or overshoot. If you can show 100% annual growth, knowing you'll actually hit it and perhaps exceed it, few people will accuse you of sandbagging and two to three years of sustained history exceeding plan will do wonders for your pre-money valuation and ability to control the terms of the deal.

Review of the 100 Most Important Steps

I am a believer in the value of step-by-step guides as well as reviews of the most pertinent material. In this section, I'll review the one hundred most important steps in building a company to one million dollars in sales. Do note that the following steps may not be in the exact order and may not apply to every type of business. The general order remains approximately correct and the majority of steps will likely apply to your business.

1. Come up with a business idea.
2. Use the MAR opportunity evaluation model to evaluate that idea and determine if it is a true business opportunity.
3. Research suppliers of your product.
4. Determine if what you can charge for the product will cover the cost of producing it plus an ample markup.
5. Talk to potential customers and evaluate whether you will be able to sell your product.
6. Determine name for your company.
7. Write a business plan.
8. Complete your pro forma income statement.
9. Determine how much you'll need to raise to get your business to cash flow positive—the point where you are making more than you are spending.
10. Get feedback on and improve your business plan. Go to your local chapter of the Service Corps of Retired Executives and review your plan with them.
11. Determine your financing strategy. Determine where you will raise any needed funds.
12. Determine who will own what percent of the company.
13. File your articles or certificate of incorporation with your Secretary of State. Incorporate as an LLC, S, or C corporation if in the United States. You can incorporate yourself, through an online service, or through your law firm.
14. Obtain an Employer Identification Number (EIN) from the Internal Revenue Service so you can open a bank account and hire employees.
15. File form 2553 with the Internal Revenue Service if you intend to be an S corporation.
16. Select a corporate law firm in your area accustomed to working with entrepreneurial companies like yours.
17. Have your law firm create non-disclosure, non-compete, and confidentiality agreements and have all involved with your company sign them.
18. Hold your initial board meeting and sign the Organizational Consent document.

19. Decide if you want to have a stock options plan and create an options pool.

20. Discuss if you wish to use vesting (granting equity to initial founders over time based on how long they stay with the company and what they do). If you decide to do vesting, have your law firm write a stock restriction agreement, have all involved in your company sign a copy, and then have each person consider filing an 83(b) election if in the United States.

21. Issue your stock certificates.

22. Have your law firm draft consulting agreements for any independent contractors and employment agreements for any employees. Sign these agreements.

23. Open and fund a bank account, put in any initial contributed capital, and order checks.

24. If you decide you'll need to raise money, look into the different sources of money, including debt capital from family, friends, or the bank or equity capital from accredited private investors or venture capital firms. If you think you can start out small, bootstrap, and grow organically from revenues, evaluate whether you wish to grow your company in this manner.

25. If you decide you'll need to raise the money from private investors, have your law firm work with you to refine your business plan and connect you with potential investors. You may need to figure out how to develop your product and start making at least some revenue before investors will take you seriously.

26. Raise the money you will need.

27. Apply for a credit line at your bank as well and a couple of company credit cards.

28. Purchase small business accounting software such as QuickBooks and keep track of all expenses and revenue, or hire an accounting firm to take care of this for you. You also may wish to outsource your payroll.

29. Come up with the name for your product(s).

30. Trademark the names of all your product(s).

31. Trademark the name of your company.

32. Develop your product(s), if you will be selling a product. Ask for quotes from different suppliers.

33. Have a logo created.

34. Either purchase or lease office space.

35. Furnish your office with desks, chairs, couches, filing cabinets, and light fixtures.
36. Purchase any needed office supplies.
37. Purchase any software you will need.
38. Call your phone company and have them install a phone line or purchase a VOIP system.
39. Purchase phones.
40. Obtain broadband Internet access and a wireless router and set up a wireless office network.
41. Decide what roles you need additional help in and can afford to pay someone to fill, then hire those persons.
42. Obtain general liability insurance and any other types of insurance you may need.
43. Have business cards made.
44. Have letterhead made.
45. Have a brochure and any needed sales collateral designed.
46. Design the packaging and labeling for your products.
47. Have your labeling reviewed by your lawyer.
48. Print enough labels and packaging for your initial production run.
49. Obtain a Universal Product Code (UPC) bar code if you will be selling your product in stores or to retailers.
50. Order an initial inventory of products.
51. Have professional pictures of your product(s) completed.
52. Register the domain name for your company site and product site(s)
53. Obtain hosting for your web sites.
54. Design your company web site.
55. Make sure you have traffic analysis software such as Google Analytics installed on your site and check your visitor count and traffic details often.
56. Add sales copy to your web site that is written to first attract attention, generate interest, establish credibility, create desire, and provoke action.
57. Install a shopping cart on your web site.
58. Apply for a merchant account so you can accept credit cards on your web site and in your business or sign up with a service such as PayPal or ClickBank. If you are a service based company, and will be paid via checks, there will be no need to apply for a merchant account. Start doing business right away, making sure to always

leave extra business cards with clients in order to leverage word of mouth. You may also want to purchase an ad in the local phone book.

59. Sign up to an email list management service such as iContact and add a newsletter sign up form to your web site.

60. Sign up for an autoresponder service and add an eight day informational ecourse in order to generate leads, build trust with customers, and recommend your product.

61. Add content to your web site. Ask others for permission to syndicate their content and write a few articles yourself to start to portray yourself as an expert in your industry.

62. Optimize your web site for the search engines.

63. Build a related links to your web site.

64. Add a discussion forum and blog to your site.

65. Once the merchant account is approved, obtain a gateway such as VeriSign or Authorize.net and connect it to your shopping cart or point of sale terminal.

66. Install an autobill/continuity program and integrate it with your merchant account, shopping cart, and affiliate program. Decide on what type of incentive you will give to those who sign up for the autobill program.

67. Decide what your money back guarantee will be.

68. Decide what you will charge for shipping if applicable.

69. Create a mission statement and corporate values statement for your company. Consciously build the culture of your company from the beginning

70. Hire any needed employees before you start selling.

71. **Start selling!**

72. Sign up for a live person chat so customers on your site can chat with your customer support team.

73. Install a CRM system to manage your customer interactions and sales funnel.

74. Consider starting a contest/sweepstakes for your product in order to obtain additional prospect data and leads.

75. Utilize your blog and other forms of social media like videos and podcasts to gain more exposure for your product or service and start a conversation with your customers.

76. Investigate regulatory issues in other countries and determine which countries you can export your product to.

77. If you are selling a product, hire someone to fulfill orders or use a fulfillment house.
78. Establish relations with local media.
79. Write and mail out a press release to local newspaper, radio, and television media or hire a public relations firm to handle this for you.
80. Start an affiliate program. Install your affiliate program software and decide what commissions you will pay on referred sales. Go through the search engines and trade journals to find potential affiliates. Contact the potential affiliates in person or via phone, mail, or email.
81. Build a few hundred affiliates that promote your product(s) for a percentage of each sale. Mail the commission checks to your affiliates each month.
82. Start sending out your monthly email newsletter to those who signed up on your web site and to your customers.
83. Follow-up with your customers once per month to ask how they are doing with your product. Ask for and add testimonials to your web site and marketing materials.
84. Look into upcoming trade shows and attend them. Consider creating a booth and exhibiting at and/or sponsoring any especially important shows for your industry.
85. Once you have some data on your visitor to sale conversion rate and the amount affiliates are paid per visitor sent to your site, work on building strategic alliances with larger partners.
86. Consider establishing a wholesale price for your product and looking for distributors of it.
87. If you decide to offer your product via stores, design and create point of sale items such as a display case and print collateral.
88. Take a look at the operations of your company and see what areas you can make more automated or more efficient.
89. Bring on a bookkeeper to handle your accounting work for you if you have not already.
90. You may wish to create an employee benefits program if you have not already, to ensure you retain your most valuable workers.
91. Write a company handbook and wiki and begin to establish formal systems and processes. Make things efficient and try not to overload workers with forms and red tape.
92. Once you become cash flow positive, look into paying for CPC, CPM newsletter co-registration, print, radio, or television advertising or

advertising via direct mail. Keep a close watch on return on investment at all times.

93. If your product(s) fit the proper criteria, look into creating an infomercial to promote them. Look into sponsoring athletes or related events or providing your product to high profile persons free of charge.

94. Allocate some funding for research and development and attempt to develop additional products.

95. If appropriate for what you are selling, develop a sales compensation plan and build out a sales force for your product.

96. Create an operations plan that ties together your revenue projections with your expenses, headcount, and capital expenditures.

97. Hold a retreat at least once a year at which you and your managers discuss any issues and brainstorm on how to grow the business.

98. Build out the first layer of management within your company and hire a Director of Human Resources and Executive Assistant when you are able.

99. Now that you have revenue, go to the bank and expand the size of your credit line.

100. Consider raising investment capital more seriously now that you have some revenue.

Congratulations! You now have a business doing over $1 million in annual sales. Depending on the revenue multiple your company is valued at (usually between 1x and 6x) and the amount of ownership you've retained, you may personally be a millionaire on paper now. There is a long way between being a paper millionaire and an actual millionaire, however. Keep focused on building a great product or providing a world-class service, creating good jobs, giving back to your community, scaling ad spend with a positive return, creating needed systems and processes to ensure efficiency, and hiring great people and you will make it.

While building a company to $1 million in sales is a worthy goal, the end goal for many is either a sustainable cashflowing organization that can provide ongoing dividends to shareholders or an exit event which may take quite a few years longer to reach. It is important to keep in mind that a company can exit in just four ways:

1. Get bought by the general public by having an initial public offering
2. Get bought by or merge with another company

3. Have an orderly shutdown in which all creditors & employees are paid
4. Go bankrupt

Beyond the One Million Dollar Level

If you've been able to create a successful company with paying customers, an in-demand product, an experienced team, and solid systems you'll be well on the road to reaching the $1 million mark in sales. Once you reach the $1 million dollar level in sales, your business will begin to take on a much different character than the one it had when you began. Your systems will begin to go into full stride and, depending on your profit margins, you may be able do things such as hire a large sales force, a team of MBAs, and experienced industry executives, spend on research and development, and execute national print and media advertising campaigns.

You'll have much easier access to credit you may need for further expansion and be able to gain the respect of larger companies, enabling you to create more and more profitable joint ventures. You'll be able to join the Entrepreneurs' Organization if you are under 40, and put money into spinning off other ventures. You'll be able to start thinking about selling your company or putting the plans and people in place to shoot at a public offering in another three to four years—or continue to enjoy a good income from profits each year if you prefer to keep the company as a lifestyle business. Congratulations, you have made it!

(Okay if you haven't actually made it yet and have just been reading this whole time, at least you can visualize it. Step one to achieving a goal is being able to visualize it).

Part Four: Choosing to Be Successful

Chapter 17 Steps for Success

"It is not the critic who counts, not the man who points out how the strong man stumbled, or where the doer of deeds could have done them better. The credit belongs to the man who is actually in the arena; whose face is marred by dust and sweat and blood; who strives valiantly; who errs and comes short again and again; who knows the great enthusiasms, the great devotions, and spends himself in a worthy cause; who, at the best, knows in the end the triumph of high achievement; and who, at the worst, if he fails, at least fails while daring greatly, so that his place shall never be with those cold and timid souls who know neither victory nor defeat."

– Theodore Roosevelt, 1910

Having a Bias toward Action

In my experience, prior to being able to become a successful entrepreneur, there are some important concepts to study. These include having a bias toward action, knowing how to frame failure, building relationships, and having a positive attitude. Let's get things started by discussing one of the more important principles—having a bias toward action.

Too many times, someone will have a goal, yet never get going on the path toward reaching it. Many aspiring entrepreneurs have a business idea, yet spend months and months writing the business plan in a state of analysis paralysis—never taking action. If you are going to be a successful entrepreneur however, you must have a bias toward action.

When I am speaking, I illustrate this principle with an anecdote. Imagine yourself at your house, wanting to go to your friend's house four miles away. You do not want to leave until all the traffic lights on the way are green. Of course, it is clear that you will never leave. This paralysis happens to many in everyday life. If you want to get there, however, you must get going now. Yes, there will be stop signs and red lights along the way, but you'll get through them—and you'll make it to your friend's house much sooner than if you waited for all the lights to be green along the way.

You can drive from Los Angeles to New York, driving only at night and only seeing two hundred feet ahead of you at any one time. Yet you can make it, only seeing part of the journey at a time. Just because you cannot see the path toward reaching a goal yet, don't not make that goal. To be successful, you must first define what success means to you. You have to start with a goal in mind, perhaps even a big hairy audacious goal (BHAG). Once you've defined your goal, you can get started on it. Have a bias toward action and get going. You may not know all the steps or the problems and challenges you'll run into just yet, but that is okay.

As you progress toward your goal, you will continue faster and faster up the learning curve. You'll build inertia and as you move forward you'll gain new knowledge and just as important, build new relationships which will be very important in helping you reach your goal. As the inertia turns into exponential snowballing, your new knowledge and new contacts will create new possibilities and opportunities, allowing you, with continued persistence, to reach your goal.

To take advantage of this principle of inertia and snowballing, however, you must have a bias toward action. To initiate the momentum, you must get started. Once those initial small accomplishments begin falling into place, inertia will take effect as these new possibilities snowball you up the learning curve closer and closer to your goal. Every important goal you will reach will be preceded by thousands of actions without which you would not have had the opportunity, contacts, or knowledge to accomplish the final important achievement.

On Failure & Learning from Mistakes

Most people are afraid to fail. They worry constantly about not living up to expectations, making a mistake, or trying something new. Because of this, many never get started on the path toward reaching their goals—and thus assure themselves of the very thing they are afraid of—failure. In order to become a successful entrepreneur you will likely have to 'pay your dues.' You will likely fail a few times, learn from your lessons, and only then be able to come through a winner. While you don't have to take wild chances, you do have to take calculated and educated risks.

In the world of academics, mistakes are perceived as bad and to be avoided. For the first twenty-two years of your life, you are taught that mistakes are bad and embarrassing—when in fact mistakes are simply opportunities to learn something new. The more mistakes a person makes, the more they will have learned and the greater chance they will have of succeeding on their next try. The key, however, is to learn from your mistakes and avoid making the same mistake twice.

Thomas Edison would have never invented the light bulb if he did not take this principle to heart. Edison "failed" 6,634 times before he found a filament that would create light for a sustained period of time. He did not view these as failures, however. On the 6,635th try to find a proper filament for the light bulb, Edison did not see himself has having failed 6,634 times. He reframed the situation so that to him he had successfully eliminated 6,634 possibilities, refining and narrowing his search as he proceeded, drawing him closer and closer to his goal.

Two other failures you may have heard of are Levi Strauss and Christopher Columbus. Strauss headed for the gold mines of California in hopes of gold and glory. But he found none. Instead, this failure gave him new knowledge of a gap in the marketplace. He began selling pants out of canvas for the miners that were succeeding. Today, we've all heard of Levi Strauss jeans. Columbus failed miserably on his goal to find a route to India. However, in failing he ran into a new opportunity—that of the new world. By taking action and learning from your mistakes and failures, you'll gain new knowledge and become aware of many new opportunities. When you come to the edge of what you know, it's time to make some mistakes.

> "When you come to the edge of what you know, it's time to make some mistakes."

Building Quality Relationships

In business and in life, it is what you know, who you know, _and_ how well you know them that will determine the opportunities you have and whether you can reach your goals. You must make an exerted effort to get out there and build relationships. Every single person you meet might just become your next business partner or largest client. Every single person you meet knows hundreds of other persons to whom they can refer you, if you can just take the time to establish a relationship. In my teaching a group of high school students in the Summer of 2003 Boston and Chicago I told my students to think of every student at their school as a valuable person that could help them in many unforeseen ways ten, twenty, or seventy years down the road. You must view everyone you meet in the same manner.

In ever business I have ever had, time and time again our best advertising has been word of mouth and referrals from past customers. Humans are social creatures and will put much more credence in a referral than an advertisement. You'll be amazed at the amount of business you can generate just by doing things like asking those you know who else they may know that could use your products or services, joining your local Chamber of Commerce, and volunteering in your community. Here are a few more tips for networking:

> Never burn your bridges.
> Send thank you cards.
> Have plenty of business cards on hand.
> Follow-up when asked to do a favor with those you may need a favor from down the line.
> Strategically volunteer with organizations that have members or directors you'd like to network with.
> Ask to shadow persons whom you would like to get to know and whose job positions interest you.
> Connect those in your network whom you think may be able to help each other.
> Invite those who have experience in business or your industry to serve on an informal Advisory Board for your company.

Action Item 7 – Finding Mentors Through Lunch Dates

Step 1: Take a moment and write down the names of any persons that have already done what you want to accomplish. If you don't know any specific individuals, write down the names of people who may be able to connect you to persons who have already done what you wish to accomplish.

_____

_____

_____

Step 2: Commit to yourself that you will figure out how to contact these people and ask them to have lunch with you so that you can ask them a few questions about how to get started or improve your business.

I _____ commit to asking each person on the above list to at least have lunch with me in the next six weeks.

.
Signed

X_____ Date: _____

You will be surprised how many people that you thought were unreachable or unavailable will be willing to meet you, if you ask authentically for help and can have a flexible calendar.

Step 3: Have lunch with the individuals who respond favorably and learn as much as you can. If you hit it off with any individual ask them if they'd be willing to be an informal mentor to you and meet with you every few months. Each individual you meet will likely be able to connect you to another individual who can help you. Send a thank you card in return and let them know you very much appreciated their time and that you'd be happy to help them in any way you can.

Building a large and valuable network is not something that can be done in a few weeks. It takes years. I place great importance on my network—both my local network and my worldwide network. Since age 17, when I realized the importance of building a network, I have carefully kept track of all those whom I come in contact with.

I use what I call a 'top of the funnel' strategy and add every person I meet to my contact database. I keep notes on the last time I spoke to them, what organization they are with, and any other pertinent items. I then keep in touch with each person and send them email updates every so often on what I am up to and send them my monthly 'Entrepreneurs' Chronicle' newsletter, also via email.

I segment my network by groups so I can send targeted information and leverage each segment when they are needed. I have segments for a personal Advisory Board, friends and family, college entrepreneurs, book updates, press contacts, international entrepreneurs, people I can stay with when I go on my book tour, and the newsletters I send out each month—The Entrepreneurship Chronicle and Email Marketing Monthly. It is truly is amazing how much more value I get out my network by simply staying in touch.

As part of your networking effort, always be on the lookout for potential mentors. You'll find that a commonality across every successful entrepreneur out there is that—at one point or another they had a mentor that they can point to as being essential in getting from one level to another in business.

If there is someone you respect or someone who is in a position you'd like to be in one day, ask them out to lunch one day. The worst that could happen is they say no. If they say yes, ask them how they did it, what challenges they've faced, and any advice that they may have for you. Then, if things work out and you've established good rapport, ask them to be a formal mentor to you and eat lunch with you once per month.

In general, most people are willing to help you. You must ask, however, and you must be genuine. You must be willing to take a chance, take a risk, and ask someone. You must have confidence. You must not come with a sales pitch, but rather with a few questions seeking advice.

If you can find a common link between yourself and another person— such as the same Alma Mater or the same industry—most likely they'll at least give you ten minutes of their time by phone or exchange a few emails with you. At the end of your meeting, always ask for referrals. One can achieve nearly any positive goal by asking for help and asking for referrals. I call this "referraling yourself to the top."

The Carolina Entrepreneurship Club at UNC runs two programs that are designed to help business owners build relationships. The first is called MentorMatch. Through this program we match successful entrepreneurs from the Raleigh, North Carolina chapter of the Entrepreneurs' Organization with undergraduate student members of the club for a lunch. If the entrepreneur and student agree, they can establish a formal mentoring relationship after the first lunch, although neither is under any obligation.

Another program that has met with great success is our monthly Business Roundtables. At the roundtables we invite all the members of the club who either own a business or are thinking about starting one. At each meeting, we talk about the progress we've made with our companies in the mean time and any issues we are facing. The group has been a wonderful source of learning for the newer members, and very helpful source of peer advice for the more experienced members. Classic personal development writer Napoleon Hill called such a thing a "Mastermind Group" and has emphasized the value of such a group numerous times throughout his works. See if you can find similar MentorMatch programs or roundtables in your area.

No matter how you define success, no one can build a million dollar business, climb Mt. Everest, or win an election without the help of many people. Start building your network now and you'll reach your goals much faster.

Highlight 10: A Note from the Author for Teenage Entrepreneurs

In case there is anyone reading this book that is considering starting their own company in place of going to college, let me say this. Be very careful. For most people I would say that both a college degree and the college experience would be extremely beneficial. College can be a great time to refine a business plan and build the contacts needed to make it a reality, so choose carefully. The value of friendships, alma mater connections, and the additional experience with "learning how to learn" is undeniably valuable.

If you can work on your business while you are in college, you can create a tremendous foundation for your success after you graduate. My rule of thumb is this: If you can get a business started before or while in college that is making more than $5,000 in sales per month, feel free to take time off to focus on the business. Until the business gets to that point, stay in school and work toward finishing.

If you do choose to start a business while you are in college or instead of college make sure you have a mentor and a support team to help you along the way. The two young adults I know who have been able to create successful companies without going to college had mentors that helped them with their businesses, developed a support team of lawyers, CPAs, and a board of directors, and hired top quality talent to help manage and grow their businesses. Further, you need a good idea that can scale beyond being a local business. No matter how hard you work if you cannot provide a service or product that the market demands you will not succeed.

College is not a prerequisite for success in business by any means, but it can be a path. There are plenty of ways to network, develop as a person, and to learn what you want to learn without being in a structured educational environment. However, if you have other goals such as becoming a teacher, scientist, engineer, politician, or working in a large corporation, a degree will usually be necessary.

On a final note, I have seen many motivated people not go to college and instead of building a support network and successful businesses have fallen into the hands of idleness. Do not let this happen to you. Either way, you will reach your dreams. Just keep at it and work hard.

The Power of Direction & Focus

Many people go through life without having any guiding direction. They never set goals for themselves, or if they do, never take any steps toward accomplishing those goals. If you are to become a successful entrepreneur, you must learn how to set goals and plan—for both the short, mid, and long term.

While I surely have a bias toward action, one cannot know what action to take without a bit of planning. I have a certain method by which I set my goals and plan the steps that I'll need to take to achieve them. I call it the Outer-Dissection Method. The reason this overall strategy is called the Outer-Dissection method is that you first start with your goals and then work backwards to break everything down into smaller and smaller pieces and sub goals.

Take your big goal and from that create certain strategies that you will use to accomplish those goals. Strategies, for example, may take one or thirty years to accomplish. A corporate planning sheet using this method might look like the one below. A personal chart would look similar, but would simply leave out the ownership category and you will be the owner of each step.

Diagram 5 – Tracking Goals, Strategies, Tactics, Deadlines, and Accountability

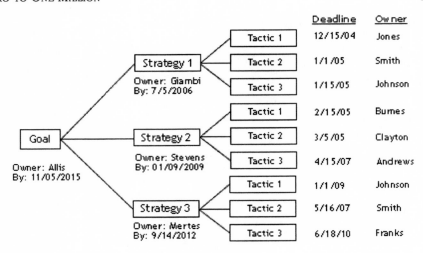

Within each strategy, you create a series of tactics that as a whole will allow you to accomplish the strategies. Each tactic may take as long as six months or as short as a few weeks. Finally, you'll break these tactics into individual tasks. Within each tactic, there may be a handful or hundreds of individual tasks that must be accomplished. It is important that there be deadlines for each task, tactic, strategy, and goal.

As an example, your goal may be to win the Nobel Prize in Economics. One strategy needed to accomplish this goal is to go to a top school to get your Ph.D. One tactic needed to accomplish this strategy would be to obtain good grades during your undergraduate education. One task to accomplish this tactic may be to do your homework tonight.

Essentially we are taking large goals and breaking them down into smaller and smaller subsections—and then working diligently on accomplishing each step. There is tremendous power in focusing on what you need to achieve in the short-term (for me, finishing this chapter) and mid-term (for me, building iContact) while being well aware of how these efforts work into your long term plan (for me, working to improve the world on a global scale through entrepreneurship, social entrepreneurship, investing, politics, public policy, and philanthropy).

Becoming Driven & Passionate

"A goal is a dream with a deadline."

– Napoleon Hill

The common denominator among every single highly driven and successful person I have ever met, regardless of field, is that they have committed their goals to writing and created for themselves a purpose driven life. It is my belief that every passionate individual can benefit tremendously from creating a Personal Goals List, Chief Definite Purpose (I call this a BHALG), and Personal Mission Statement written and posted where they sleep.

Below I share the three step process that I have developed (partially organically and partially with the guidance of *Think and Grow Rich, Good to Great, The Seven Habits of Highly Effective People, How to Win Friends and Influence People,* and *The Secret*) to help me become a driven, passionate individual that wakes up every day motivated to work toward my short-term, mid-term, and long-term goals.

Action Item 8 – Create Your Personal Goals List

Step 1: Take a moment in a quiet place and take some time to think about where your life is now and your goals and plans for the future. List your short-term (0-6 months), mid-term (6-24 months), long-term (2-10 years), then lifetime goals are in the following table.

Short Term Goals (0 to 6 Months)	
Mid-Term Goals (6 to 24 Months)	
Long-Term Goals (2-10 Years)	

Lifetime Goals (10+ Years)	

Step 2: Share your goals with those close to you that you trust and get feedback on how you may go about accomplishing it. Speak with people who will build you up and support you in your efforts, not tell you that you will never accomplish this dream. Type up this list and print out your Personal Goals List, post it in your bedroom, then review it at least annually.

The next step is to create at least one Big Hairy Audacious Lifetime Goal (BHALG). This can be your chief definite aim and part of your core purpose of being. You may or may not already have a BHALG. Regardless, thinking about it and committing it writing will give you a better chance of reaching it and going through whatever adversity you will have to go through in your quest.

Action Item 9 – Write Your BHALG

Step 1: Take a moment and write down a Big Hairy Audacious Lifetime Goal (BHALG). If you do not already have a clear BHALG that comes to mind, make this goal something you believe is next to impossible, something that up until *right now*, you never thought you could or would actually have the ability to accomplish. This may take a few days or a few months to come up with, or it may flow naturally. Think big and think global.

_____

_____

_____

Step 2: Share your BHALG with those close to you that you trust and get feedback on how you may go about accomplishing it. Speak with people who will build you up and support you in your efforts, not tell you that you will never accomplish this dream. Type up your BHALG, print it out, and tape it to the wall of your bedroom.

Step 3: Dissect the strategies, tactics, and tasks that you will need to accomplish this goal, and go for it. Play life like a long term game and create five year game plans that build upon one another that allow you reach this goal within 30 years. While ensuring your own happiness, never forget your BHALG. If you know without a doubt you will accomplish this goal, you will. If you don't think you will, you will not. Make it a driving chief definite purpose, while understanding what investments you need to make along the way to make it possible.

Don't be afraid to set your goals high, as often you'll learn new things and meet new people along the way that will allow you to accomplish things you may think impossible today. Further, if you shoot for the stars, you'll land on the tree tops—but if you shoot for the tree tops you'll land in a mud pit. Once you've detailed each of your goals, write a short, one paragraph mission statement that summarizes your most important goals. My personal mission statement at age 18 was:

To be a founder or co-founder of a company with greater than $2 million in sales by age 21, to be financially free, to take a company public, to write a best-selling book, to be happy, to marry and have kids, and to set up a foundation to encourage education, reduce poverty, improve health, better economic conditions, encourage entrepreneurship, and prevent corruption in developing nations.

My personal mission statement today at 23 is:

To be one of the leaders of a generational movement to improve the United States and the world through entrepreneurship, social entrepreneurship, investing, politics, public policy, and philanthropy; thereby increasing access to

> opportunity and creating stronger global societies, while being financially free, taking multiple companies public, creating thousands of quality jobs, driving innovation, writing a best-selling book, being happy, marrying and having children, and setting up a foundation to work on reducing poverty, ensuring environmental sustainability, and investing in human understanding, education, healthcare, and microfinance.

Now, write your own Personal Mission Statement.

Action Item 10 – Write Your Personal Mission Statement

Take a moment and write a draft of your personal mission statement, including the major goals you have for your life.

_____

_____

_____

_____

_____

Step 2: Type up your Personal Mission Statement, print it out, and tape it to the wall of your bedroom.

Now that you have a Personal Goals List, a BHALG, and a Personal Mission Statement and can see things on the macro scale, you can begin the planning process that will allow you to execute in the short term. To do this part of the process, I do certain things weekly, monthly, and annually.

Every Sunday night I spend approximately three hours catching up on my emails from the past week and planning out my next week. I send myself emails for any open tasks that I need to complete. About twice per week I write in a journal in which I review the day, who I met, what I accomplished, any mistakes I made, and what is coming up. Finally, at least once per week

I'll read both my Personal Prayer and the Entrepreneurs' Creed, which I have framed at home and in my office. Reading these seem to inspire me and give me the motivation needed to push through adversity and execute.

Personal Prayer: God, thank you for my life. Thank you for all the blessings you have bestowed upon me and the gifts you have endowed me with. I pray this moment for those who are not as fortunate as I, those in need, and those under duress. I hope to have the wisdom and strength to dedicate my life as an entrepreneur, writer, investor, and politician to improving standards of living, removing corruption, bettering lives, and reducing hurt in my country and across our world. God let me be strong and grant me wisdom to proceed on this venture. Grant me the ability to live my life to the fullest. Grant me the control to think accurately and master my mind, the will to be consistently unique, the ability to be a master of relations, the motivation to excel, and the energy, health, and enthusiasm to never waste a moment of your precious gift. God, thank you for my life.

The Entrepreneurs' Creed: I pray this day to the Entrepreneurial Gods. I set myself before you and this world as an entrepreneur. I analyze the markets and take educated risks through planned ventures and investments. I accept the basic law of the entrepreneur - that of supply and demand. If I am right, I will be rewarded with capital and stature. If I am not, I will bankrupt my accounts, yet gain in wisdom so as to improve chances on my next try. While keeping in mind externalities, I create what us as humans demand, and in turn make the world an improved place for all. Through my work I help create dynamic economies in which the standard of living is always increasing through innovation and technological progress. Through my work I encourage competition, and provide lower prices on and a higher quality and a better selection of goods and services. Towards this end I shall always be persistent, continually learn, be a master of relations, and be forever motivated to excel. I am an entrepreneur. Grant me strength,

> vision, persistence, motivation, and energy.

The second part of this process is the monthly review. On the last day of each month, I review everything that I have accomplished each month, the new relationships I developed, the mistakes I made, and how I have progressed toward my goals. I re-analyze how I want to set my priorities going forward, and refocus on my goals. Here is a review of the planning processes I go through:

- **Weekly:** Write in your journal at least twice per week covering who you met, what was accomplished, the mistakes made, and what is coming up. Read your personal prayer at least weekly. Catch up on your correspondence and plan out your week each Sunday night.
- **Monthly:** On the last day of each month, write a review of what you accomplished in the previous month along with how you are progressing toward your short and mid-term goals.
- **Annually:** During the last week of every year, read over all the monthly reviews and create a plan for the next year highlighting what you will be focusing on and what new strategies and tactics you should pursue. Set your annual goals and review your progress on last year's goals. Also read over your Personal Mission Statement and update it if need be.
- **Every Five Years:** Write a 20-25 page personal plan describing what you wish to accomplish over the upcoming four years. Sign this document and get feedback on it from close associates.

In my experience, there are six core steps in accomplishing any goal, including that of building a business. These are:

1. Write Down Goals
2. Create Vision & Strategy
3. Implement Actions
4. Measure Results & Obtain Feedback
5. Find What Works & Make Mid-Course Correction
6. Repeat the Process, Building Upon Your Successes and Learning From Your Mistakes

Diagram 6 – The Cycle of Setting and Achieving Larger and Larger Goals

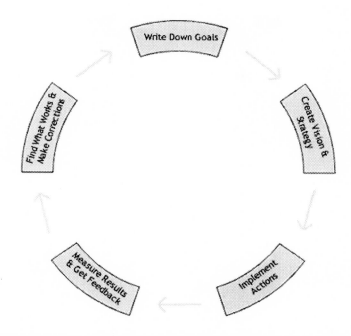

This process, repeated continuously, will guide you toward accomplishing any goal. While using it will not guarantee success, as this is based on the strength of the strategy and numerous other exogenous variables, this model can be of great help in structuring your progress and refining your plan. As Napoleon Hill says, "If you can conceive it and you can believe it you can achieve whatever you set your sights on."

It is absolutely amazing what life can bring and what the universe can provide if you simply go through the process of identifying what you truly want out of life and then focusing on making that desire a reality.

Becoming Great

In this world, each of us have the opportunity to either be great or mediocre. Presuming you've determined that you want to become great yourself, it helps to see what other traits great people have in common. Here are some of these characteristics which enable great people to come up with and develop world changing ideas:

1. Ability to Communicate

2. Ability to Judge

3. Ability to Motivate
4. Adaptability
5. Courage
6. Curiosity
7. Devotion to Goals
8. Drive
9. Dynamic Energy
10. Enterprise
11. Enthusiasm
12. Honesty
13. Idealism
14. Imagination

15. Individualism
16. Knowledge
17. Optimism
18. Outgoingness
19. Patience
20. Perception
21. Persuasion
22. Salesmanship
23. Sense of Humor
24. Versatility
25. Willingness to Take Risks

Giving Back

I did an exercise when I was 20 years old that changed my life forever. I wrote down how I wanted to use my life to make a difference in the world—to help build stronger communities and societies here at home, and also work to end poverty and hunger globally. When I learned from reading an annual world health report from the World Health Organization that over 18,000,000 people die every year (49,365 per day) from preventable diseases and starvation the gravity of some of the most important issues of our day hit me.

When I learned from a World Bank report that as of 2001, 2.7 billion people lived on under $2 per day (42% of the humans in the world), the realization made me want to spend my life working entrepreneurially to address these issues. When I read *The End of Poverty*, by Columbia Economist Jeffrey Sachs in 2006, I further committed to being a leader of my generation to address the problems and ensuring that by the end of my life at least 95% of the wealth I create goes back to creating societies with greater access to opportunity and sustainably assisting people who have not had the opportunity I have been so fortunate to have.

As I added to my knowledge through travel, reading, and speaking with people who live in developing nations, I updated my mission statement and began to write what I call a Purpose Statement. Along the way, the added depth of purpose has given what I strive to do every day deep personal meaning. For me, entrepreneurship is not about making lots of money and living an extravagant life, it's about being able to make a positive impact in the lives of thousands, and hopefully someday, billions. If you can find how starting and building a successful business can help you have a larger meaning in your life and allow you to give back to your community, you will be able to more easily find your core motivation and align what you do, with what you love.

Finding a deeper meaning and core motivation for doing what you do is a critically important part of getting through the difficult times along the way to becoming a successful businessperson. I have found this meaning for myself. As I wrote in the introduction to this book my Purpose Statement is:

> **I wish to spend my life working through entrepreneurship, social entrepreneurship, investing, philanthropy, public policy, and politics to end poverty in developing nations and at home, ensure environmental sustainability, help people understand that we are one humanity and that our commonalities are much greater than our differences, and help expand access to opportunity, healthcare, and education across the world for every human of every nation.**

Right now, please take a moment to write down how you hope to use your talents, resources, and time on this planet to make a positive difference in the world. This can be a powerful exercise, so please take a couple minutes to complete it.

Action Item 11 – Finding Deeper Purpose in Your Life

Take a moment and write how you hope to use your business, time, energy, and resources to make a positive difference in the world.

I wish to spend my life…

_____

_____

_____

_____

_____

_____

_____

_____

_____

_____

_____

    Many extremely successful industrialists and entrepreneurs over the past 150 years have chosen to give back. Andrew Carnegie funded libraries all over the United States and created his foundation to 'promote the advancement and diffusion of knowledge and understanding.' Rockefeller created the Rockefeller foundation to 'promote the well-being of mankind throughout the world.' Ford created the Ford Foundation to 'promote democracy, reduce poverty, promote international understanding, and advance human achievement.' Bill Gates has created the Bill and Melinda Gates Foundation to 'enhance global healthcare and reduce global poverty and expand access to educational opportunity and technology.' Gates has said many times that he will give 95% of his wealth back to society before he dies. He considers himself a steward of wealth, as should any successful entrepreneur.

    As an entrepreneur, score is kept by who can create the most value. Money comes to you directly in proportion to how much value you create by rearranging the resources of land, labor, capital, and entrepreneurial ability into the outputs that society desires. If we are successful, we can create millions, perhaps billions of dollars of value to society and in turn become wealth through stock appreciation, going public, or selling the company.

    I hope you will give back as well what you can, along the way as you build your company—and especially after you have become wealthy. It is our job as enlightened entrepreneurs to give back to the society and world that has enabled us to succeed, to work to create fuller access to opportunity. Giving back can make our lives full of meaning and purpose, and make us more driven entrepreneurs at the same time.

    I know if you set your mind to it you will become an extremely wealthy individual and make millions of dollars in your life. You may not see the way now, but if you commit to the goal and believe it, you will achieve it in time. It may take ten or twenty years, but if you choose to be, you will become a multi-millionaire. Knowing that you will become a multi-millionaire someday if you make the choice to be, I ask right now that you commit to contributing at least 90% of any wealth you make by the end of your life into a foundation or endowment of a charitable organization that can work to make our world a better place.

Action Item 12 – The Enlightened Entrepreneur's Commitment

I, _____ _____ commit to contributing at least ninety percent of any wealth I earn during my lifetime into a personal foundation or endowments of charitable organizations that will work to address the major issues of our world such as poverty, hunger, education, healthcare, environmental sustainability and any other area that I believe will make the world, my nation, my state, and my community a better place.

X _____ Date: _____

In Closing

I would like to leave you with a few points that I have found especially helpful to keep in mind on my journey. Know that you will encounter adversity on the path toward building your company. You must have persistence and keep at it. It may or may not be a good time in your life to go after an entrepreneurial opportunity, and you may or may not have that great idea just yet. You must take the long run approach. Don't let your age, whether you are young or old, restrict you in any way. Build relationships for the long term, do whatever you must, including interning or working for others for a period of time to gain experience and excess capital, and keep at it with dedication and tenacity.

While the health company I worked with in high school did get to one million dollars in sales after fourteen months of when I began working there, it was not by any means a fourteen month process. It was actually a five year process, as the owner first became aware of the product and began investigating it in 1997.

When I arrived, the company had a complete product with packaging, brochures, logos, labels, business cards, and letterhead already created. The initial market research and product tests were done, and the office space, bank account, and incorporation was already taken care of. At iContact, it took us three years to reach the million dollar in sales milestone.

If you are coming into this as a first time entrepreneur, I would give yourself at least five years to reach this one million dollar mark. It may take three years of personal development, networking, and experience to even get to the point where you are ready—both financially and otherwise—to start your company. You may first need to find a business model or idea that you can run with and establish your network and knowledge in a field. Once, and only once, you begin to do this will opportunity begin to hit you in the face.

On the other hand, if you are an experienced business executive with many industry contacts, a great idea for a new product or business model that you know will dominate the marketplace, and $200,000 saved up in your bank accounts, you may be able to build a million dollar company in less than a year. Of course, you've spent the last twenty building your network, knowledge, and financial resources—constantly thinking about and analyzing new opportunities, waiting for the perfect time to go out on your own.

Being an entrepreneur is certainly not for everybody. The strain and additional risk it may put on you and your family may not be worth the potential reward. If what you get out of this book is that entrepreneurship is not right for you, you will have saved lots of heartache. But if you do find entrepreneurship is for you, and you can make and learn from enough mistakes and gain enough experience to finally succeed, it can be extremely rewarding.

As you continue to develop and evaluate your business ideas, find partners, and develop as a businessperson, I hope you will take a proactive role in planning, goal setting, and personal evaluation. Your success will depend on your work ethic, your initiative, and how strong your network is. At the end of the day, it is up to you. I will leave you with these ten tips.

1. Becoming a successful entrepreneur is not easy. You must have persistence, dedication, tenacity, and the ability to deal with adversity.
2. Being an entrepreneur is not for everybody. But if you find it is for you, and you can find a way to succeed, it can be extremely rewarding.
3. You may not be able to do everything at once. Take a long run approach. Play life like a long term game.
4. If you presently do not have the financial resources, the experience, or a good business idea, intern at or get a job at a company in an

industry you are interested in and start building your network and gaining experience.

5. Always focus on building quality relationships with good people.
6. Regardless of what you are doing make sure you are constantly learning.
7. Take a proactive role in planning, goal setting, and personal evaluation.
8. Don't be afraid to ask for help. People are often very willing to help you if you ask genuinely.
9. Get experience however you can, build your network, have confidence, and be in it to win. It is up to you. Get out there and do it. Take the initiative and have a bias toward action.
10. If and when you succeed, give back. There are so many fellow brothers and sisters in our world who are not as fortunate as you and I have been.

Good luck. Do let me know if I can be of assistance to you in your journey (my email address is ryan@icontact.com). Know that how you go about your journey is just as important as what you do once you've reached your destination. If I can inspire just one person who ends up making a positive difference in the world and helps others do the same, my job will be done. I hope that person will be you.

Appendices

Financial Vocabulary

Building one's financial intelligence is a key step along the path toward becoming a successful entrepreneur. Below is a listing of financial vocabulary with easy to understand definitions. This list includes common accounting, investing, and business terms.

Financial Vocabulary Glossary

Accounts Payable – money you owe for products and services already received

Accounts Receivable – money owed to you for products/services already delivered

Angel Investor – a private high net worth individual who will invest money in medium or high potential ventures in exchange for percentage ownership in a company

Appreciating Asset – something you own that is going up in value

Appreciation – increase in value over time

Asset – something you own that has value

Balance Sheet Formula – assets minus liabilities equal owners' equity. (A – L = OE)

Balance Sheet – a financial statement that keeps track of assets, liabilities, and owners' equity.

Bond – debt instrument through which companies and governments can raise money

Cash Flow – the in and out of money to/from your business

Cash Flow Statement – a financial statement that keeps track of all the money that goes in and out of your business.

COGS – the cost of goods sold. What you pay for what you sell.

Depreciating Asset – something you own that is going down in value

Depreciation – reduction in value over time

EBITDA – earnings before interest, taxes, depreciation, and amortization

Equity – ownership in a company

Expenses – what you spend

Gross Income – Total revenue minus COGS

Gross Margin – same as gross income

Income Statement – a financial statement that keeps track of revenue, expenses, and profit.

Income Statement Formula – Revenue minus expenses equals net income. (R – E = NI)

IPO – initial public offering, selling part of your company on the stock market in exchange for investment capital in your business

Liability – something you owe, or something that is taking money out of your pocket each month with no positive cash return

Net Income – same as net profit

Net Profit – Total revenue minus total expenses

Option pool – a percentage ownership in your company set aside at founding for those who may come aboard later.

Owners' Equity – The value of what the shareholders/owners have put into a company

Revenue – what you earn

Venture Capital – investment money raised from firms that invest in high potential ventures in exchange for percentage ownership in a company

Vesting – earning equity over time instead of all at once

Recommended Books

The following books were used in the creation of *Zero to One Million* and are recommended for further reading.

Globalization & Economics

1. *The Lexus and the Olive Tree* by Thomas L. Friedman
2. *The World is Flat* by Thomas L. Friedman
3. *The Commanding Heights* by Daniel Yergin and Joseph Stanislaw
4. *Political Ideologies and the Democratic Ideal* by Ball and Dagger
5. *The Worldly Philosophers* by Robert L Heilbroner
6. *Reinventing the Bazaar: A Natural History of Markets* by John McMillan
7. *Globalization and Its Discontents* by Joseph Stiglitz
8. *The Mystery of Capital* by Hernando de Soto
9. *The Secret History of the American Empire* by John Perkins
10. *The End of Poverty* by Jeffrey Sachs

Entrepreneurship

1. *Rich Dad Poor Dad* by Robert Kiyosaki
2. *Rich Dad's Guide to Investing* by Robert Kiyosaki
3. *Losing My Virginity* by Richard Branson
4. *Zero to One Million* by Ryan P. M. Allis
5. *The Young Entrepreneur's Guide to Starting and Running a Business* by Steve Mariotti
6. *The Young Entrepreneurs' Edge* by Jennifer Kushell
7. *New Venture Creation* by Jeffrey Timmons
8. *Multiple Streams of Income* by Robert G. Allen
9. *Entrepreneurship.com* by Tim Burns

Marketing

1. *The Anatomy of Buzz* by Emanuel Rosen
2. *The Tipping Point* by Malcolm Gladwell
3. *Blink* by Malcolm Gladwell
4. *The Purple Cow* by Seth Godin
5. *The Idea Virus* by Seth Godin
6. *Permission Marketing* by Seth Godin
7. *Guerilla Marketing* by Jay Conrad Levinson

Management

1. *Built to Last* by Jim Collins
2. *Good to Great* by Jim Collins
3. *Execution* by Larry Bossidy
4. *Winning* by Jack Welch
5. *One Bullet Away* by Nathaniel Fick

Personal Development

1. *Think and Grow Rich* by Napoleon Hill
2. *The Seven Habits of Highly Effective People* by Steven R. Covey
3. *Succeed and Grow Rich Through Persuasion* by Napoleon Hill
4. *How to Win Friends and Influence People* by Dale Carnegie
5. *The Secret* by Rhonda Byrne
6. *The Student Success Manifesto* by Michael Simmons
7. *The Law of Success in Sixteen Lessons* by Napoleon Hill
8. *Secrets of the Young & Successful* Jennifer Kushell
9. *Unlimited Power* by Anthony Robbins
10. *The Millionaire Mind* by Thomas J. Stanley, Ph.D

Resources for Entrepreneurs

Here is a listing of a few resources and organizations that may be of help to you along your entrepreneurial journey.

- **Allbusiness Small Business Resource** - www.allbusiness.com
  Top resource for small to mid-size business owners and entrepreneurs
- **Collegiate Entrepreneurs Organization** – www.c-e-o.org
  Organization for undergraduate students interested in entrepreneurship
- **Entrepreneur Magazine Online** - www.entrepreneur.com
  Magazine content, resources and community for entrepreneurs and business owners
- **Entrepreneurship Resource Center** – www.zeromillion.com
  Companion site to this book, containing over 3000 articles on entrepreneurship, business, economics, personal development, marketing, and web marketing, interviews with entrepreneurs, and a discussion forum
- **Entrepreneurs' Organization** – www.eonetwork.org
  Worldwide under-40 organization for entrepreneurs with businesses with revenues US $1 million+ yearly
- **EntreWorld** - www.entreworld.com
  Articles and content for entrepreneurs
- **Ewing Marion Kauffman Foundation** - www.emkf.org
  Foundation encouraging and supporting entrepreneurship
- **Inc. Magazine Online** - www.inc.com
  Magazine content, resources and community for entrepreneurs and business owners
- **Junior Achievement** – www.ja.org
  Organization that promotes the free enterprise system through volunteers and classroom-based interactive learning

- **Let's Talk Business Network** - www.ltbn.com
  Syndicated radio show on business and entrepreneurship
- **National Commission on Entrepreneurship** - www.ncoe.org
  Active entrepreneurship policy group on Capital Hill sponsored by the Kauffman Foundation
- **Service Corps of Retired Executives** - www.score.org
  Have your questions answered by experienced business professionals
- **Start-Up Nation** – www.startupnation.com
  Great start-up resource from the acclaimed Sloan Brothers
- **Students in Free Enterprise** – www.sife.org
  Organizes University competition for completing projects related to free enterprise
- **The Lowe Foundation** - www.lowe.org
  Foundation supporting the entrepreneurial spirit
- **Young and Successful** - www.youngandscucessful.com
  Content for entrepreneurs and database of thousands of entrepreneurs worldwide
- **YoungEntrepreneur.com** - www.youngentreprenuer.com
  Articles and information for entrepreneurs aged 0-40 and small business owners

Appendix 4   Entrepreneur Interviews

The Distinguished Entrepreneur Interview Series was conducted during April and May 2003 while I was a research assistant at the University of North Carolina at Chapel Hill's Center for Entrepreneurship. To be selected for the interview, entrepreneurs had to be the CEO or founder, either currently or in the past, of a company with more than $5 million in annual sales.

Below, I have selected six of these interviews for publication. I would encourage you to read through these in depth. There is some very good information and advice on the changes in businesses, education, the keys to entrepreneurial success, and much more.

Christy L. Shaffer, Ph.D., CEO, Inspire Pharmaceuticals, Inc.

Dr. Shaffer joined Inspire from Burroughs Wellcome, Clinical Research Division, in June 1995 as the first full-time employee. She has held a variety of positions at Inspire including VP of Development, and Chief Operating Officer. She was appointed to President and Chief Executive Officer, and became a board member in December 1998 and currently serves as CEO.

What attributes make a successful entrepreneur?

Ability to lead and motivate others; ability to concisely communicate the idea; ability to execute a plan beyond the idea concept; ability to build the right team.

What do you believe are the necessary elements for a business venture to succeed?

Obviously you have to have technology that works. However, the ability to execute the plan is key. Therefore, having the right team in place and building a 'can do' culture within the organization is also very helpful.

How essential do you see an undergraduate degree or MBA being for an entrepreneur?

Not essential at all, although helpful.

What role has academic education played in your own life versus the role of experiential learning and what has been the relative importance of each?

Very helpful in getting the basic training necessary in the field of science. However, the 'hands-on, real life' growth experiences are also key to the process.

What are the three most important lessons you have learned about business and entrepreneurship in your lifetime?

Knowing when and how to hire the right people that complement my own skill set (never be afraid to hire someone who knows more than you do in a particular field).

What have been the keys to your success?

All points I raised in above questions. Also, having excellent communication skills and maintaining a positive attitude.

What advice would you give to an aspiring young entrepreneur?

Don't give up; if you believe you can achieve.

What books would you recommend to aspiring entrepreneurs? Which books have influenced you the most?

Good to Great

Describe some of the biggest challenges or obstacles you've have encountered as an entrepreneur? How were these overcome?

Not having initial experience in raising venture capital. I simply had to learn by doing!

What memorable mistakes, if any, have you made in business? What did you learn from them and how can they be avoided?

Nothing truly memorable to date but no doubt I will at some point.

What trends and changes do you see occurring in business today? What new technologies and industries will everyone be talking about in twenty years?

More virtual activities; more focus on doing business globally.   Enhanced methods of rapid communication.

What are the best and worst things about being an entrepreneur?

Best – you are constantly challenged and have fun
Worst – you are constantly busy and stressed out; less time for family

Would you rank the following attributes in order of greatest to least importance for an entrepreneur?

> Persistence - 7
> A College Degree - 15
> Knowledge of Accounting and Finance - 14
> Knowledge of Marketing 13
> Confidence - 6
> Leadership and the Ability to Inspire - 1
> Ability to Communicate Effectively - 4
> Integrity - 5
> Having the Right Advisors - 12
> Good Networking Skills - 11
> Motivation and Ambition – 9
> Having a Good Idea or Plan - 2
> Being Able to Build a Solid Team – 3
> Being Able to Execute – 8
> Having a Bias towards Action – 10

Colin Wahl, Founder, InvestorForce

Colin is Vice-Chairman, Founder and Board member of Investorforce. He wrote the business plan for InvestorForce and launched this firm in 1999. The company raised funding from strategic investors including CalPERS (California Public Employees Retirement System), Merrill Lynch, Mellon Bank, Thomas Weisel Partners and Internet Capital Group. Investorforce provides investment firms a technology-based platform to help raise assets from institutional investors. Investorforce won the 2002 "World-class Performance" award from Electronic Commerce World for bringing web-based operations to the institutional investor and Hedge Fund markets.

What attributes make a successful entrepreneur?

1. Persistence – the ability to bounce back from frequent disappointment
2. Passion – an ability to get excited and motivated by a higher purpose than money
3. Leadership – an ability to inspire others

What do you believe are the necessary elements for a business venture to succeed?

1. A Strong Management Team -- that "really" works well together, sets the vision & strategy
2. An ability to execute – put ideas into action
3. Intellectual honesty – don't fool yourself about what is/is not working
4. Market-driven approach – build the business by listening to customers
5. Continuous improvement – always strive to improve and get better

How essential do you see an undergraduate degree or MBA being for an entrepreneur?

Not essential, but I think having an undergraduate/MBA truly enhances your probability of business success by helping you "ask the right questions" and reduce the number of mistakes you will inevitably make as an entrepreneur.

What role has academic education played in your own life versus the role of experiential learning and what has been the relative importance of each?

Academic learning has exposed me to business building & management concepts/ideas and experiential learning has allowed me to put these concepts/ideas into practice…I truly believe you need both equally – like taking lessons before playing golf/tennis or a chalk talk before a big game.

What are the most important lessons you have learned about business and entrepreneurship in your lifetime?

1. Be persistent and never give up, pause think and keep going
2. The team is the brains of a business…it has to work like a well-oiled machine
3. Execute with excellence, many great ideas never happen or fail due to poor execution
4. Just get out there and do something…"let opportunity hit you"

What have been the keys to your success?

1. Finding great people to work with as part of a team
2. Being passionate about my ideas and getting others excited about them.

What advice would you give to an aspiring young entrepreneur?

Go for it, it's an incredible chance of a lifetime – as the saying goes, better to have tried and lost than never to have tried at all! The riskiest thing to do is not to try…then the chance of success is zero. The downside: even if things don't work out you will gain amazing experience that will help you even if you end up having to go back to working for someone else.

What books would you recommend to aspiring entrepreneurs? Which books have influenced you the most?
- <u>Control Your Own Destiny or Someone Else Will</u>, Noel Tichy and Stratford Sherman
- <u>Enthusiasm Makes The Difference</u>, Norman Vincent Peal
- <u>Think and Grow Rich</u>, Napoleon Hill

□   <u>How to Win Friends and Influence People</u>, Dale Carnegie

Describe some of the biggest challenges or obstacles you've have encountered as an entrepreneur? How were these overcome?

Being turned down repeatedly for funding – persistence, keep coming back in smarter ways (for example, building working prototypes, bringing potential customers to due diligence meetings)

Building a strong management team – great individual players did not work well as a team. Made hard decisions to prune the team and bring in new managers that played well together.

What memorable mistakes, if any, have you made in business? What did you learn from them and how can they be avoided?

Brought outstanding individuals onto the management team, but they did not work well as a team. Learning: just as the tallest basketball players do not necessarily make the best basketball team, the best individual managers do not necessarily make the best management team. How to avoid? – don't just look for the best people...make sure the chemistry works
Grew the company too fast. Learning: lose focus and spread resources too thin. How to Avoid: pick a niche, focus your resources/energy, get successful and then expand.

What trends and changes do you see occurring in business today? What new technologies and industries will everyone be talking about in twenty years?

Trends/changes – more people will opt for the entrepreneurial route for lifestyle reasons and financial independence vs. relying on a large corporation where job security is increasingly deteriorating and lifestyle choices are difficult to control. I also see the merging of technologies such as the Internet and TV and phone, fax, and PDAs. Finally, in regards to global expansion, 3rd world countries will continue to grow, creating huge business opportunities for U.S. companies.

What are the best and worst things about being an entrepreneur?

<u>Worst</u>

Loneliness – you are on your own, nobody supports you because it's hard for them to see what you see and feel the excitement that you feel in the early stages.

<u>Best</u>

Freedom – much more control of your own destiny and your entire life!

Would you rank the following attributes in order of greatest to least importance for an entrepreneur, and comment briefly on the importance (or unimportance) or each.

1. Persistence – need to get through tough times, you will never get to the good times without getting through the difficult times.
2. Motivation and Ambition – "you" have to be the business catalyst
3. Leadership and the Ability to Inspire – need to "work through others"
4. Confidence – get through the tough times
5. Being Able to Build a Solid Team – build brains of the company
6. Having a Bias towards Action – ideas mean nothing if not executed
7. Ability to Communicate Effectively – inspire people, focus them in tough times
8. Integrity – be ethical and fair always…this is the heart of your business
9. Being Able to Execute – business is about "making things happen"
10. A College Degree – helps build critical thinking skills
11. Having a Good Idea or Plan – need this to focus resources and people
12. Having the Right Advisors – get an outside perspective and prevents "tunnel vision"
13. Knowledge of Marketing – need this skill/insight to grow revenue
14. Knowledge of Accounting and Finance – know where $ is going, how and why.
15. Good Networking Skills – helps in hiring, raising money and business development

Dave Rizzo, Director, MCNC

What attributes make a successful entrepreneur?

There may in fact be different attributes for different people. For me, I felt the need to do something on my own outside of an established culture. So, first, I would say a healthy independence. Second, a high degree of confidence. A sense that even if I fail things will be fine. Third, a willingness to get your hands dirty, answer the phones if necessary. Fourth, an inherent ability to sell yourself and your company. There are probably many more!

What do you believe are the necessary elements for a business venture to succeed?

1) You have to provide something that people actually want. You have to know the answer to this, not just assume they want what you provide.
2) You must have an unwavering respect for your customers. Treat them like royalty.
3) You must be able to attract people that complement your own personal skill sets.
4) You must be willing to let people do their jobs, you have to let go.
5) Cash is king, watch it like a hawk.
6) Make sure you're adequately capitalized. I'd rather own 10% of a large enterprise than 100% of a bankrupt one.

How essential do you see an undergraduate degree or MBA being for an entrepreneur?

In today's economy, where low value add jobs get shipped offshore, I think an advanced degree is critical. I don't believe it necessarily means that it has to be an MBA. High value add companies are going to have to focus on innovation as a constant process. I think it would be highly desirable to have some form of technology or science in one's background coupled with an MBA.

What role has academic education played in your own life versus the

role of experiential learning and what has been the relative importance of each?

I majored in Economics and that discipline is excellent in that it really teaches the concept of trade-offs and scarcity. At the time I went through college and into the working world an MBA or advanced degree was not as important as it is today. Had I to do it over I would have pursued both my MA in Economics and an MBA. I did have the opportunity to pursue significant professional development at the Wharton School and the Brookings Institute.

What are the three most important lessons you have learned about business and entrepreneurship in your lifetime?

1) I would rather be 80% right and make a decision today, than 100% right and make one six months from now. 2) Hire a CFO a year before you think you need one. 3) Fire people six months before you think you should....their peers are watching while you wait.

What have been the keys to your success?

1) Hiring good people. 2) Market timing. 3) Ability to attract capital.

What advice would you give to an aspiring young entrepreneur?

Don't go it alone, it's lonely. If you can't find an experienced entrepreneur, find some friends to start with you. Ask for help when you need it. Everyone wants young companies to be successful. Form a good Board. Dot your I's and cross your T's on all the legal stuff so it does not come back to bite you later.

What books would you recommend to aspiring entrepreneurs? Which books have influenced you the most?

Crossing the Chasm by Geoffrey Moore

Describe some of the biggest challenges or obstacles you've have encountered as an entrepreneur? How were these overcome?

The downturn in the economy was huge. It required the shedding of non-essential business lines and a refocusing on core activities. It also fundamentally changed the capital markets, requiring more focus on M&A activities.

What memorable mistakes, if any, have you made in business? What did you learn from them and how can they be avoided?

Remember an IPO is nothing more than a financing event. Don't get swept up in investment banker hype. NEVER, spend sales and marketing dollars solely to influence Wall Street. Keep your sales and marketing dollars focused on near term customer acquisition.

What trends and changes do you see occurring in business today? What new technologies and industries will everyone be talking about in twenty years?

Businesses are much more willing to source labor offshore. As a result, it's critical that you focus on value add propositions that are unique to the customers business environment. I don't think we will see revolutions in technology. Rather, I think we will see continuing evolutions but at an increased pace.

What are the best and worst things about being an entrepreneur?

Other than the stress of initial startup there are no bad things about being an entrepreneur. You have control over your destiny, your calendar, and the vision is yours. What's not to like?

Would you comment briefly on the importance of each of the following commonly listed attributes of entrepreneurs:

Persistence - Very important, if you have a tendency to give up when things get tough…don't jump in the water.

A College Degree - More important now than in the past but creativity and intelligence can come in all forms. Not necessarily required.

Knowledge of Accounting and Finance - Not that important at least initially, you can buy this help

Knowledge of Marketing - Knowledge of your markets is critical. Knowledge of marketing less so, again, you can buy this.

Confidence - Critical, not only for your personal well being, but your customers will place a lot of value on your own level of confidence.

Leadership and the Ability to Inspire - Essential, if you can't convince others, you're going nowhere.

Ability to Communicate Effectively - You either have to have this or you have to have a partner that is outstanding at this. You must be able to articulate the value proposition.

Integrity - What could be more important? If you don't have this, you won't last six months.

Having the Right Advisors - Critical, you have to know what you don't know and complement it. Good Advisors can also open doors.

Good Networking Skills - Pretty important but sometimes overrated.

Motivation and Ambition - If you don't have this, what's the point of starting your own business?

Having a Good Idea or Plan - This is important but it's also important to have flexibility in the plan. The one thing you know about a plan after you write it is that its wrong.

Being Able to Build a Solid Team - Unless you're a one person show, this is perhaps the most important skill you will need.

Being Able to Execute - Again Critical

Having a Bias towards Action - Critical but not like a cowboy. Thoughtful action is appropriate.

Randy Myer, Founder, Best Friends Pet Care

Randy Myer is an adjunct business professor at UNC's Kenan-Flagler Business School. He is the former CEO and founder of Best Friends Pet Care, now the nation's largest pet services company. As the COO of Lindblad Expeditions, he managed all operating departments for this $60 million family business. He also is a former vice president and partner with Booz Allen Hamilton, where he worked for 13 years. He has been a visiting lecturer at Kenan-Flagler since 1998. He holds an MBA from Harvard and a BA from The University of North Carolina at Chapel Hill.

What attributes make a successful entrepreneur?

Sales and marketing skills are a must whether it is convincing outsiders to invest or customers to buy. The successful entrepreneur must be an astute and gifted sales person and have a flair and creativity to market a product with very little money, resources and time.

What do you believe are the necessary elements for a business venture to succeed?

First class management team and a WOW idea. Much has been said about the quality of the team and all of it is true. But finding the right product, the right market niche and the customer acceptance and excitement for your product is still critical. Previously successful entrepreneurs may find raising money easier but those of us who have done it know that earlier successes do not mean that your latest idea will. Take Dean Kamen – there is a long road ahead to make the Segway a successful product and not just a fad.

How essential do you see an undergraduate degree or MBA being for an entrepreneur?

Hard to measure but the discipline of learning probably means that one would likely be better at pre-screening potential new business ideas and writing a convincing plan that would get investors interested. The value of experiential learning by being exposed to a variety of academic and real world individuals can only help if the student uses that experience to build a business and business model that works. Why would Bill Gates, Jud Bowman and others have succeeded without that educational experience – probably because of a superior product and the ability to surround themselves with talented people but whether they would have made fewer mistakes along the way and whether their counterparts fail at a higher rate is subject of speculation.

What role has academic education played in your own life versus the role of experiential learning and what has been the relative importance of each?

It is hard to say that academic education per se contributed nearly as much as the experience factor since my entrepreneurial career began 20 years after my last class

What are the three most important lessons you have learned about business and entrepreneurship in your lifetime?

1. Spend more on quality people upfront – budget and cash limitations are bad reasons to lose your best people
2. Start planning your exit strategy earlier than you think – the relationships you develop with strategic partners or buyers take longer to develop than you think
3. Do what you believe is right for the customer first and the investors second. It may get you fired but the business will succeed with satisfied customers and unhappy investors longer than the reverse

What have been the keys to your success?

Picking the right people to be part of your team and having a good marketing and sales instinct

What advice would you give to an aspiring young entrepreneur?

Make sure you have the marketing and sales experience in your industry under your belt – or get a partner who does. Pick your partner based on their experience, values and complementary skills – not based on friendship or money.

What books would you recommend to aspiring entrepreneurs? Which books have influenced you the most?

Inside The Tornado by Geoffrey Moore

Describe some of the biggest challenges or obstacles you've have encountered as an entrepreneur? How were these overcome?

Moving the ship at twice the present speed but with half the money. I always had more good ideas than the time or money to make them happen. It forced me to prioritize and reprioritize frequently.

What memorable mistakes, if any, have you made in business? What did you learn from them and how can they be avoided?

Hiring mistakes - and then trying to make them work longer than I should have. Do not compromise your standards because of time or money constraints. And remember training is for big companies with lots of resources.

What trends and changes do you see occurring in business today? What new technologies and industries will everyone be talking about in twenty years?

China – and how its markets look like those of the U.S. 50 years ago.

What are the best and worst things about being an entrepreneur?

The best part is the rewards—financial and psychological. The worst is the impact on your health and your family. If you have young kids and a spouse that needs you, take a different road. It takes five years minimum of living and breathing the company to succeed.

Would you rank the following attributes in order of greatest to least importance for an entrepreneur, and comment briefly on the importance (or unimportance) or each.

7. Persistence
14. A College Degree
10. Knowledge of Accounting and Finance
9. Knowledge of Marketing
12. Confidence
3. Leadership and the Ability to Inspire
5. Ability to Communicate Effectively

> Integrity – Given
> 11. Having the Right Advisor
> 13. Good Networking Skill
> 4. Motivation and Ambition
> 2. Having a Good Idea or Plan
> 1. Being Able to Build a Solid Team
> 8. Being Able to Execute
> 6. Having a Bias towards Action

Are there any other thoughts, insights, or advice for aspiring entrepreneurs that you'd like to add?

Pick an idea that others who know the industry say "WOW, why didn't I think of that". Along with the financial viability, that is the one measure of a great business idea.

Todd Ballenger, CEO, KendallTodd, Inc.

Todd Ballenger is the CEO of KendallTodd, Inc. He has over 14 years experience in the financial services industry as a licensed securities, insurance, real estate, and mortgage lending professional. Todd founded three companies; Capital Savings Co, Inc., Advantage Capital Mortgage, USA, and PlanMax Financial. These three companies closed over $2 billion dollars in residential and commercial loans before being rolled into a NASDAQ IPO in 1999.

What attributes make a successful entrepreneur?

Ability to flow with changes, focus on what the market wants or what we can reasonably project from both hard data and intuition that the market will want, hard work, focus on task, willingness to listen to outside influences, etc.

What do you believe are the necessary elements for a business venture to succeed?

A focused business plan where the team allows the business direction to change as one body, and does not become fractured by changes that result in a business getting on a horse every day and trying to ride in more than one direction. Experience helps, but is attained if one has the desire to stay the course and see the business through to its eventual success or failure. Money helps, but the type of business will impact how much of that is ultimately needed, and too much money often does more harm than good as the company moves too fast when they are just learning to ride their bike, making injuries all the more palpable.

How essential do you see an undergraduate degree or MBA being for an entrepreneur?

You learn what you have to learn to stay in business, or you perish. Not having an MBA, I can't reflect on how it hindered me. Many friends who have MBAs say the connections they made had more of an impact on their success than what they learned in the MBA program long term. If I were to do it again, I'd get a JD with an MBA which I think is the most powerful combination.

What role has academic education played in your own life versus the role of experiential learning and what has been the relative importance of each?

Academic education was required up until the point that I graduated from college. True experiential learning happens whether you want it to or not, but it is more prized after you gain control to direct it to areas that most impact your personal interests, desires and goals, and therefore I think it has more long term depth than academic education, but both play important roles, as without academic learning the nature of the experiential learning would be different.

What are the three most important lessons you have learned about business and entrepreneurship in your lifetime?

1) the business is a business, and the death of a business does not equate to the death of the founder – going through a really 'bad movie' makes you appreciate the good ones and I would have never expected to learn so much from the challenges of a failed IPO

2) that good advice is priceless, and the money that I thought I saved on good legal, accounting, etc. in the early phases of my business cost me far more than I saved

3) that my employees don't need to know anything more than what they need to know to be effective in their very clear and defined job descriptions – the idea of being a visionary is an initial draw to many, but once they start working for you it becomes a threat, and is best kept under a dark cloak until specifically unveiled with clear details on how the 'change' to the old vision affects them – because that is all they really care about.

What have been the keys to your success?

Ability to flow with changes, focus on what the market wants or what we can reasonably project from both hard data and intuition that the market will want, hard work, focus on task, willingness to listen to outside influences, etc.

What advice would you give to an aspiring young entrepreneur?

Get a great coach that has experience in your industry, then get a great coach that has no experience in your industry, and listen to them both.

What books would you recommend to aspiring entrepreneurs? Which books have influenced you the most?

Good To Great
Corporate Lifecycles
How to Win Friends and Influence People
Anything on Negotiation – Herb Cohen is my favorite
Anything on Selling – Zig Ziglar and Tom Hopkins stand out

Describe some of the biggest challenges or obstacles you've have encountered as an entrepreneur? How were these overcome?

Cash flow competency – and effectively having a plan that incorporates that into the business – we bootstrapped so we learned to work on the cash flow from three months prior, In other words, spikes in cash do not make a trend until you have sustained them for three months, so if it is January, spend the cash you had available in October and you are less likely to spend your way into trouble.

What memorable mistakes, if any, have you made in business? What did you learn from them and how can they be avoided?

Trying to merge with another company and not realizing the impact on the two different cultures. I'd spend a great deal more time focusing on compatibility and not just the numbers.

What trends and changes do you see occurring in business today? What new technologies and industries will everyone be talking about in twenty years?

Wireless bandwidth and connectivity have my attention now. The use of those tools with the ability to integrate data to make life flow with less friction will still be a subject of discuss in 20 years. I believe a much larger percentage of the work force will be working from their home offices and telecommuting in the next five to ten years. I run my new business from my home and value the freedom and flexibility.

What are the best and worst things about being an entrepreneur?

Worst - The fact that you often work 80 hours a week as an entrepreneur to avoid working 40 hours a week as an employee.

Best – The possible returns for your efforts monetarily, personally, professionally.

Would you rank the following attributes in order of greatest to least importance for an entrepreneur?

> 2-Persistence
> 13-A College Degree
> 11-Knowledge of Accounting and Finance
> 10-Knowledge of Marketing
> 7-Confidence
> 4-Leadership and the Ability to Inspire

5-Ability to Communicate Effectively
1-Integrity
9-Good Networking Skills
6-Motivation and Ambition
14-Having a Good Idea or Plan
3-Being Able to Build a Solid Team
8-Being Able to Execute
12-Having a Bias towards Action

Alston Gardner, CEO, OnTarget, Inc.

Alston Gardner is a founder and principal in Fulcrum Ventures, LLC a venture development firm focused on early stage information technology, biotechnology and health care companies in the southeast US. Mr. Gardner was the founder and CEO of OnTarget, Inc. prior to its acquisition by Siebel Systems (NASDAQ) in late 1999. Under his leadership, OnTarget grew from start-up to the industry leader in sales force development with $75 million in revenue and 100+ professionals in fifteen countries.

What attributes make a successful entrepreneur?

The successful entrepreneur must have the **vision** to identify a problem no one else is solving, or a market niche no one else is serving, or a strategy no one else is pursuing. They must have **passion** for solving that problem with riches as the byproduct not the end. The must have the ability to **focus** all of their time and energy to the exclusion of everything else in their life. They must be willing to **risk everything** to succeed.

What do you believe are the necessary elements for a business venture to succeed?

A successful business venture starts there and ends with the CUSTOMER. Great ideas, committed people, and capital are important because the ideas will attract the customers, the people will make sure they buy and keep them there, and the capital will allow the entrepreneur to take advantage of the opportunity.

How essential do you see an undergraduate degree or MBA being for an entrepreneur?

Not at all. My degree is in History. Most of my business education came in Exec. Ed classes or reading.

What role has academic education played in your own life versus the role of experiential learning and what has been the relative importance of each?

My academic education provided me analytical/logical frameworks, the capacity to make an argument, and the ability to persuade. My "street" education taught me far more about human behavior, passion, and perseverance. Both are critical for success.

What are the three most important lessons you have learned about business and entrepreneurship in your lifetime?

1. Imagination, passion and hard work trump formal business education every time.
2. Relationships (customers, partners, and employees) are the most important asset and they are not on the Balance Sheet.
3. Leadership is less about the exercise of power and more about serving others – customers, shareholders, and subordinates.

What have been the keys to your success?

1. A lot of great people who believed in my ideas and leadership and were willing to do amazing things to fulfill our mission.
2. Luck

What advice would you give to an aspiring young entrepreneur?

1. Focus on solving a problem for your customer rather than making money. Your customers, vendors, and employees can tell the difference between commitment to others and greed.

2. Always know how you're going to make money. Test your business model with disinterested third parties.

3. Surround yourself with smart, committed people. Write out your beliefs and principles and make sure everyone in the organization knows and follows them.

What books would you recommend to aspiring entrepreneurs? Which books have influenced you the most?

In no particular order:

1. <u>Built to Last</u> by Collins will help an aspiring entrepreneur understand what makes a great enterprise.

2. <u>True Professionalism</u> by David Maister will teach you how to act like a professional.

3. <u>The Marketing Imagination</u> by Ted Levitt will teach you about the "whole product".

4. <u>Selling the Invisible</u> by Harry Beckwith will teach you about customers.

5. <u>SPIN Selling</u> by Neil Rackham will teach you how to handle yourself in sales situations which is the most critical skill in a new enterprise.

6. <u>Please Understand Me</u> by David Keirsey and Marilyn Bates will teach you how Jungian psychology can be applied to day to day life so that you can work with anyone.

7. <u>The Elements of Style</u> by William Strunk and E.B. You will be judged on your writing. You don't have to be Shakespeare, but you have to get it right.

8. <u>The Bible</u> – especially Ecclesiastes & Solomon from the Old Testament, the New Testament will teach you about leadership.

Describe some of the biggest challenges or obstacles you've have encountered as an entrepreneur? How were these overcome?

The biggest challenge I had was changing my role and my leadership style as the company grew. Early on I was obsessed with knowing everything in the business. We didn't have extra people so I had to know everyone's job. We couldn't afford to lose a customer so I knew all of the customers. We were short on cash so I knew every detail of the accounts payable and the accounts receivable. This incredible intensity served us very well early on and could have been an impediment to growth. Over time, I had to recruit a leadership team, define a new organization structure every 18 months, and delegate most of my responsibilities. The skills and abilities needed to succeed in these two environments are almost mutually exclusive. Very few entrepreneurs can do both and most are unwilling to set their egos aside to even try.

I had a great advisory board and an incredible team who grew along with me. *Corporate Lifecycles* by Ichak Adizes also really helped me understand what changes I need to make to meet the challenges of each stage of our growth.

What memorable mistakes, if any, have you made in business? What did you learn from them and how can they be avoided?

The mistakes I made usually came from compromising our business principles. Every time I varied, we got burned. It is really important you know what you stand for and what you are unwilling to do. You don't need a long list or you'll become inflexible. Six or seven key principles are enough.

What trends and changes do you see occurring in business today? What new technologies and industries will everyone be talking about in twenty years?

1. **Information is available to everyone** – Customers, vendors, competitors, and employees have access to all of the same information you do. Competitive advantage will be who you are, what you stand for, and how you do business. These are the most difficult things to emulate.
2. **Global and local focus.** Every business will be pushed to become global in some respect. Your customers will drive it. Your suppliers will drive it. Your competitors will drive it. While you must know what's going on around the world, you must deliver a local experience for the customer. For example, bank customers want very expensive

technology allowing them to access their accounts from anywhere in the world and they want a personal relationship at the local branch.

Would you rank the following attributes in order of greatest to least importance for an entrepreneur, and comment briefly on the importance (or unimportance) of each.

1 = Most Important   5 = Not Important

1	Persistence
5	A College Degree
4	Knowledge of Accounting and Finance
2	Knowledge of Marketing
1	Confidence
2	Leadership and the Ability to Inspire
2	Ability to Communicate Effectively
3	Integrity
3	Having the Right Advisors
3	Good Networking Skills
1	Motivation and Ambition
2	Having a Good Idea or Plan
1	Being Able to Build a Solid Team
1	Being Able to Execute
1	Having a Bias towards Action

Appendix 5 The Mission of the Anti-Poverty Campaign

Throughout this book, I have mentioned the non-profit organization that I have founded and the goals that I have for it. Here is a bit of additional information on our mission and purpose.

The Anti-Poverty Campaign was founded in November 2005. It is based in Chapel Hill, North Carolina. Our mission is to increase standards of living, reduce poverty, and encourage sustainable economic development in the developing countries of Africa, Asia, and Latin/South America.

Our strategy for accomplishing this goal is to make entrepreneurship and business development possible for every person in every country, fight corrupt government and business, work with governmental and non-governmental organizations to enhance the business and social infrastructure, establish proper legal and property ownership systems, promote free trade and remove tariffs and subsidies, improve entrepreneurship and business education at the grassroots level in every country, and connect entrepreneurs, investors, and governments at every level so as to encourage the exchange of contacts, ideas, methods, and investment capital.

We believe that competitive market economies, free from collusion and corruption, are essential to creating an incentive to produce and thus are essential to a high standard of living. We believe that the ability to be an entrepreneur should be made available to every human from every country. To this end, we will promote not pure capitalism, but rather efficient competitive market economies that take into account those at both ends of the socioeconomic ladder.

We believe in promoting the principles of liberalism. We believe in a republic and democratic system of government, religious freedom, and the promotion of individual initiative. We believe there is a distinct and important role, though limited, for government, especially in the early stages of a country's development.

We want to give the over two billion persons who live on under $1 per day the chance and ability to make something of themselves, create a life free of poverty, and provide value to society. Presently, breaking out of poverty, becoming an entrepreneur, or significantly improving one's status is not possible for the majority of persons in the world. In the way is corruption in government and deficiencies in business and social infrastructure, proper legal frameworks, entrepreneurship education for those at the lower socioeconomic ends of society, and communication among aspiring entrepreneurs.

To reach this goal we will follow the tactics given in our strategy stated above. We will

1. Encourage and teach entrepreneurship at every level;
2. Fight political and business corruption;
3. Help build the business and social infrastructure;
4. Lobby for free trade in goods;
5. Help establish proper legal and property ownership systems; and
6. Connect entrepreneurs at all levels with investors and governments.

First, we will encourage entrepreneurship at every level. The skills of always improving processes, focusing on efficiency, and properly managing people will be important to all members of society. While not everyone will want to be an entrepreneur, we believe that it is a right of mankind to be able to start a business, create value, and if a business succeeds profit from working hard and intelligently.

We must democratize entrepreneurship and streamline governmental systems so as to create a society in which it is not just those with money and connections who are able to start a business. We believe that entrepreneurship creates competition in the marketplace, creates an efficient use of resources and distribution of goods and services for society's needs, and over time ensures that the price of goods and services goes down while the quality goes up—thus increasing standards of living.

We must teach entrepreneurship in the villages, towns, and cities, and in the schools and homes. Often this will not be the type of entrepreneurship you'll learn in an American business school. There will often be no venture capital, no down rounds, no initial public offerings, no option pools, and no seasoned executives to attract. Rather, we'll just as often be teaching how to register a business in a country, the difference between a balance sheet and an income statement, or the difference between revenue and profit. We hope to be at all levels, from working with governments and NGO's such as the World Trade Organization and World Bank to arranging methods of international distribution and trade for local artisans and farmers to helping write the curriculum at a new graduate business school in Nairobi to assisting with the creation of the first formal stock market in a country.

Crucial to our ability to reach our objectives will be the extent to which we are able to reduce political and business corruption in our world. While the majority of this has been routed out in developed countries over the past century, much still remains in developing nations. We must promote democratic elections, checks and balances in government, and the development of organizations that play roles similar to the Securities and Exchange Commission of the United States. We must fight despotism, nepotism, favoritism, fraud, tax evasion, and financial manipulation.

The third part of our strategy is to assist in the development of the business and social infrastructure. There are very few entrepreneurial support organizations, effective Chambers of Commerce, or universities completing top-tier research in developing countries. We must work to encourage the growth and assist in creating the structure for such organizations.

We must help to launch research labs, entrepreneurship clubs, and tech transfer offices at universities, encourage an active Chamber of Commerce in every sizable town, and bring entrepreneurial networking organizations such as the Entrepreneurs' Organization (EO), World Entrepreneurs' Organization (WEO), Service Corps of Retired Executives (SCORE), Collegiate Entrepreneurs' Organization (CEO), and The Indus Entrepreneurs (TiE) to the developing world. Finally, we will work to establish efficient tax systems and with part of this revenue, along with revenue from international aid create a social safety net that gives a hand out for a limited time and forever a hand up.

One of the major problems in our world today is that countries continue to have tariffs on foreign goods and subsidies for their domestic producers, hurting the people of other countries as well as their own countries. Through the General Agreement on Tariffs and Trade (GATT) and now the World Trade Organization (WTO), much progress has been made on this front since World War II.

One of the most egregious free trade violations today, however, is being made not by the developing countries, but rather by the industrialized countries, namely those in the European Union as well as the United States. This is the problem of farming subsidies. The rich nations of the world pay over $320 billion each year as subsidies to their farmers while they pay just $50 billion in aid to developing countries. These subsidies create artificially high prices and keep producers in developing countries out of the marketplace, essentially relegating the farmers of the developing world to poverty and enriching the large agribusiness companies of the developed nations, while consumers everywhere suffer from higher prices. While a case can be made that *some* of these subsidies are necessary to maintain enough domestic food production for national security, many must go. The WTO talks in Cancun in September 2003 were the first step toward removing them. The Anti-Poverty Campaign will join this fight.

As Peruvian economist Hernando de Soto notes in *The Other Path* and *The Mystery of Capital*, a significant problem in the developing world is the lack of formal property laws. Without official title to their land, even if it is only a ten foot by ten foot slum, the poor have little incentive to improve their house and surroundings and just as important are unable to leverage this asset to obtain a microloan from the bank that they could use to start a small business or turn their wood panel or hardened mud walls into concrete or brick. We must establish formal property laws throughout developing nations and we must do this immediately. Further, we must establish legal systems that do not unduly benefit any party or caste, are fair to all members of a country, and take atrocities such as corruption and torture very seriously.

It will take many decades to build The Anti-Poverty Campaign into the foundation we hope it will become. There are many people who have dedicated their lives to increasing standards of living, solving the global problem of poverty, and encouraging economic development in the third world. We are with you and we hope you will be with us. For more information on our mission and organization, you can visit http://www.antipovertycampaign.org. If you may be interested in helping us achieve our goals, I encourage you to contact us.

Appendix 6 Join the Community at Zeromillion.com

In July of 2002, I decided to start an online entrepreneurship resource through which I could begin to develop a community. I registered the domain name www.zeromillion.com and began work on the site. I found a few friends to help me and by the end of August, we had published over 150 articles on the topics of business, marketing, web marketing, ebusiness entrepreneurship, social entrepreneurship, personal development, and economics.

Today, the site contains over three thousand pages and features a lively discussion forum, dozens of interviews with CEOs and entrepreneurs, free ebooks on web marketing, an online journal of my adventures as a young entrepreneur, and the monthly Entrepreneurship Chronicle. I would encourage you to visit the site and join our community.

Whether you have questions on search engine optimization, want to discuss the latest about Web 2.0 or the UN's actions, or are looking to get feedback on your business idea, the discussion forums and content-rich sections of the site are a tremendous resource. You can join the community now at www.zeromillion.com/talk/.

I hope you will follow my journey as I work to build iContact. You can follow along through my blog at www.ryanallis.com/blog/. I thank you for reading *Zero to One Million* and hope you will recommend it to all your friends and colleagues.

Yours entrepreneurially,
Ryan P. Allis
Chapel Hill, NC
ryan@icontact.com

Notes

_____

_____

_____

_____

_____

_____

_____

_____

_____

_____

_____

_____

_____

_____

_____

_____

_____

_____

_____

_____

_____

Action Items:

[1] Davies, Glyn. <u>A History of money from ancient times to the present day</u>, 3rd. ed. Cardiff: University of Wales Press, 2002. 720p.

[2] Mortimer, Chambers; Hanawalt, Barbara, et al. <u>The Western Experience</u>, 8th ed. New York: McGraw-Hill, 2003. pp 474.

[3] Heilbroner, Robert L. <u>The Worldly Philosophers</u>. Page 25-31. New York: Touchstone. 1999.

[4] Hill, Charles W. <u>International Business</u>. pp. 317. New York: McGraw Hill 2001.

[5] <u>Financial Market News</u>. Yahoo Financial. BYNDQ.PK. October 16, 2003. <http://biz.yahoo.com/e/030306/byndq.pk8-k.html >

[6] <u>Excerpt from Tim Draper Speech</u>. Draper Fisher Jurvetson , May 6, 1999 <http://www.drapervc.com/about/a_philosophy_frset.html>

[7] <u>Financial Market Data</u>. Yahoo Financial. October 22, 2002. <http://finance.yahoo.com>

[8] Friedman, Thomas L. <u>The Lexus and The Olive Tree</u>. New York: Anchor Books, 2000.

[9] Ibid, Page XI

[10] <u>Leading First Day Gainers of 1998</u>. CNN Money. July 16, 2002 <http://money.cnn.com/1998/12/21/markets/ipo/>

[11] <u>The Challenge of Central Banking in a Democratic Society</u>. Federalreserve.gov. December, 5, 1995. <http://www.federalreserve.gov/boarddocs/speeches/1996/19961205.htm>

[12] <u>Small Business Administration Web Site</u>. Small Business FAQ Card. December 2000. <http://www.sba.gov/advo/an_crd98.txt>

"It is not the critic who counts, not the man who points out how the strong man stumbled, or where the doer of deeds could have done better. The credit belongs to the man who is actually in the arena; whose face is marred by the dust and sweat and blood; who strives valiantly; who errs and comes short again and again; who knows the great enthusiasms, the great devotions and spends himself in a worthy cause; who at the best, knows in the end the triumph of high achievement, and who, at worst, if he fails, at least fails while daring greatly; so that his place shall never be with those cold and timid souls who know neither victory or defeat."

— Theodore Roosevelt

This book is dedicated to the 18,000,000 humans that will die in 2008 due to preventable disease and starvation and the 2.7 billion humans living on less than $2 per day in income.

We have the entrepreneurial talent and resources to end extreme poverty and ensure access to education, healthcare, and clean water, while making our world and country stronger and safer as a result.

We have unprecedented wealth and opportunity in this time and age. As you succeed, please give back as an enlightened entrepreneur.

It will take the effort of a generation. Please join us. Support the Millennium Development Goals. Post the goals in your office or home.

You can download a template at
http://www.icontact.com/files/millenniumgoals.doc.

Printed in the United States
200327BV00004B/94-723/A

9 787774 570175